Postcard History Series

Around Highland

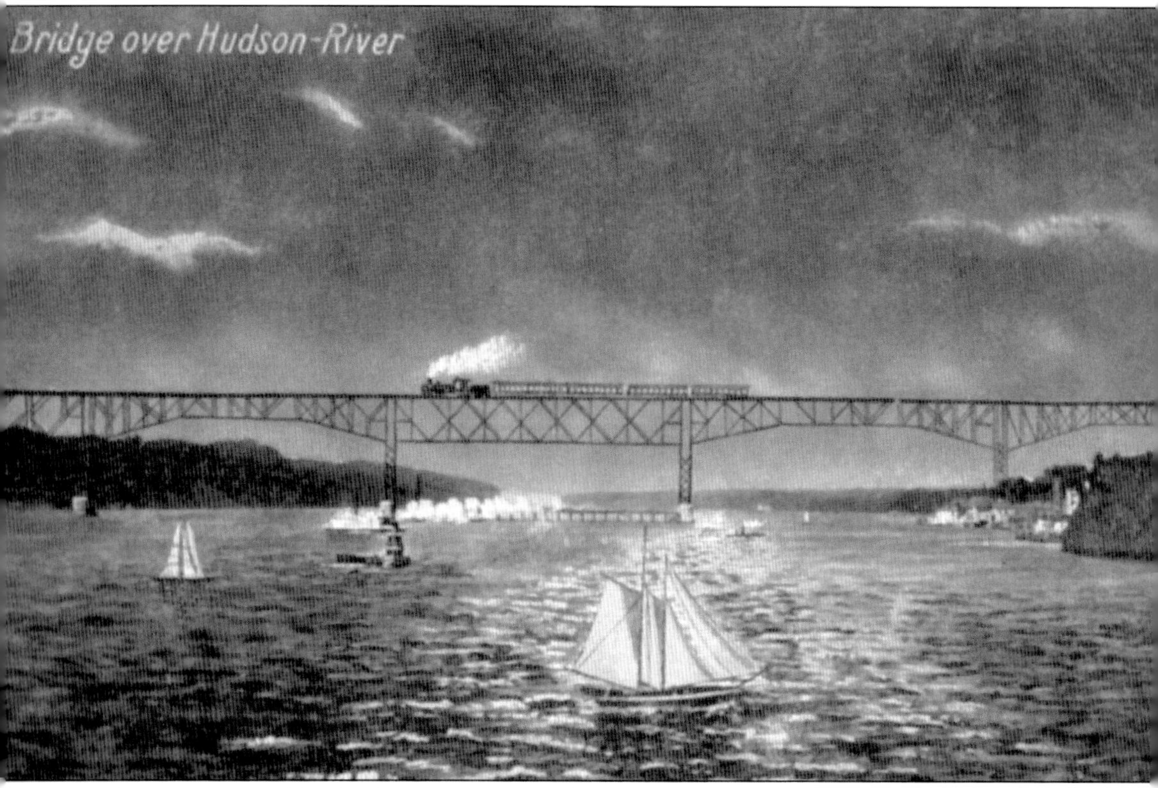

The 1888 railroad bridge between Highland and Poughkeepsie was hailed as an engineering marvel during the 19th century. The first scheduled train crossed the span on January 1, 1889, and trains continued to use it until a fire burned the bridge's railroad ties on May 8, 1974. For the next 35 years of its life, the bridge sat idle in hazardous condition. Then, after a change in leadership, a combination of private and public funding was obtained to make the historic structure into what is today—the world's longest pedestrian bridge. (Vivian Wadlin collection.)

On the Front Cover: In this c. 1895 postcard, we see a daytime version of the same postcard shown above. The 1888 railroad bridge between Highland and Poughkeepsie is now one of New York State's major tourist attractions. Operated by the state since 2009 as the Walkway Over the Hudson State Historic Park, it is second only to Niagara Falls in the number of annual visitors at any New York state park. The bridge may be entered from both the Highland and the Poughkeepsie sides. One of Highland's best-kept secrets is that when getting on the walkway in Highland, one is right over the Hudson River in minutes, while from the Poughkeepsie entrance, almost half of the walkway is over the city's streets. Also, while parking fees are charged in Poughkeepsie, there is free parking on the Highland side. (Vivian Wadlin collection.)

On the Back Cover: This c. 1905 postcard shows two prominent buildings near the corner of Main and Church Streets. The building in the foreground, now the Highland Public Library, was the home of Dr. Casper H. Ganse. This landmark was threatened with demolition, since the overcrowded library had drawn up plans for tearing it down and constructing a modern building on the site. To the right of the Ganse House is a home built for the Elting family in 1897, now the Michael Torsone Memorial Funeral Home. (Courtesy of Town of Lloyd Historian's Office.)

POSTCARD HISTORY SERIES

Around Highland

Ethan P. Jackman and Vivian Yess Wadlin

ARCADIA PUBLISHING

ISBN 978-1-4671-2163-7

Published by Arcadia Publishing
Charleston, South Carolina

Printed in the United States of America

Library of Congress Control Number: 2013951305

For all general information contact Arcadia Publishing at:
Telephone 843-853-2070
Fax 843-853-0044
E-mail sales@arcadiapublishing.com
For customer service and orders:
Toll-Free 1-888-313-2665

Visit us on the Internet at www.arcadiapublishing.com

Contents

Acknowledgments

Around Highland is a sequel to Ethan P. Jackman's 2009 book, *Highland and the Town of Lloyd.* A book in Arcadia's postcard series was a logical follow-up. Fortunately, the owner of the largest collection of Highland-area postcards is Vivian Yess Wadlin. Jackman and Wadlin have collaborated on many projects in the past, ranging from the effort to save the Aaron Rhodes House to historical displays at Vintage Village (which operated at the former George W. Pratt & Son lumberyard from 2003 to 2009) and the present effort to preserve the Ganse House (pictured on the back cover).

Unless otherwise noted, the postcards in this book are from Vivian Wadlin's collection. Other cards reproduced here are from the collections of Gail Russell and Shirley Anson and from the Town of Lloyd historian's collection. Town historian Elizabeth A. Alfonso was also very helpful in answering questions on Lloyd history. Also helping were Robi Josephson, Carol Johnson, and Dorothy Gruner.

Introduction

This is the second book about the history of Highland, Ulster County, New York, to be published in recent years. In it, we look at that history from a unique perspective—through pictures that were originally used on postcards. During the early part of the 20th century, Highland was known as the "Gateway to Ulster County," with visitors arriving by riverboat, railroad, and a trolley line. Many came as tourists, staying for weeks or even months at local hotels, inns, and boardinghouses. The business of publishing picture postcards flourished during that era, and there was a demand for postcards as souvenirs and to send to those back home.

Today, in the 21st century, when we are bombarded with images from every direction, it may be hard to contemplate a time when looking at a picture was a novelty and a treat. The invention of photography even raised a moral dilemma for some, as scholarly religious writers propounded that photographs violated the Biblical prohibition against "graven images," a belief still held by some Amish sects today.

In our age of point-and-shoot cameras, it is also hard for us to contemplate how difficult it was to take a picture in the early days of photography. Before the invention of negative film, photographers had to capture their images on pieces of glass that needed to be coated with wet chemicals in a dark room or tent right before each shot. The process got a bit easier when pre-coated dry glass plates became available, but positioning the camera on a firm mounting, focusing the image in the camera, loading a cassette containing the glass plate, exposing the plate (sometimes for several minutes), and carefully storing the exposed plate could still take upwards of half an hour for each photograph. When the photographer was finished taking his pictures, he would then need to develop the plates in chemical baths and print them on light-sensitive paper.

The processes were complicated, but the demand for photographs was there, and photography emerged as a new profession. Even some doctors gave up their medical practices to become photographers. Most early photographers worked only in their studios, supplying a lucrative demand for portraits. At first, it would take a very hardy photographer to venture out into the towns or the wilderness to capture scenic images.

Collectors often find old books that resemble scrapbooks or photo albums but are filled with postcards. They may be relegated to the back of an antique shop now, but at one time they were among a family's most prized possessions. Souvenir postcards would bring remembrances of places that had been visited, and postcards received from others would show pictures of places that otherwise might never be seen.

The US Congress first authorized the mailing of postcards in 1861 with an act that primarily concerned postal routes but had a provision buried in it that deemed cards to be mailable matter as well as other things, such as packages of seeds. The minimum cost of mailing a card was set at 1¢. In 1872, Congress decided to create a semi-monopoly for the post office by authorizing it to issue blank postcards with 1¢ of postage printed on them. Private postcards could still be mailed, but if they had messages written on them, they would be charged the 2¢ letter rate—twice the cost of the government's postcards. If there was only an advertisement or a photograph printed on a postcard, it could still be mailed for a penny.

It was not until 1898 that the government reduced the postage rate to 1¢ for all postcards, but there were still some restrictions. Nothing but the address was allowed to be written on the back of the postcard. That is why we find many early picture postcards with words on the fronts, squeezed around the margins of the pictures. The law was changed again in 1907, and postcard backs were allowed to be divided into two spaces, with one for the address and one for a message. That type of postcard is still mailable today, although the postage is no longer 1¢.

After the law changed in 1907 and picture postcards with messages could be mailed for a penny, a postcard "boom" began. During its fiscal year ending June 30, 1908, the US Post Office reported that 677,777,798 postcards were mailed. The entire population of the United States was only about 88.5 million at that time. Millions more postcards were kept as souvenirs and never got mailed. Sometimes, the message space on a postcard would be used to arrange a meeting or to thank someone for a courtesy received. Some people just sent them with random comments that seem as unimportant as many of today's messages on Twitter or Facebook.

A whole new industry of postcard publishing sprang up to supply these hundreds of millions of postcards, but there were no dominant nationwide companies. A small printing house and a good local photographer with some marketing skill could succeed at postcard publishing. In Highland, druggist Charles E. Browne photographed and published his own series of postcards showing local views. Highland's largest retail business, the Wilcox Store, also got into postcard publishing. A New York City publisher, Moore & Gibson Company, ventured upstate and published views of Highland and other areas in and around Ulster County.

Moore & Gibson had its postcards printed in Germany, as did many other publishers in the early 20th century. The skills of German printers at that time exceeded those of American printers. Their specialty was to have artists create colored lithographs based upon black-and-white photographs. That is how the first color picture postcards were produced. Sometimes we find postcards showing the same scene, but the colors are different because the printer used different inks for each printing. The scene shown on the cover of this book was published in color, and it has both a "day" and a "night" version. The "night" version is the first picture inside of this book. Both of these postcards are lithographs, not photographs, and a close examination of them shows that the artist did not copy everything exactly the same way in each version.

Germany's printing plants were largely destroyed during the First World War, and American printers tried to fill the void. However, labor union rules at most large printing plants resulted in much higher costs for a product that was generally of lower quality. Other factors also contributed to a rapid decline in the popularity of postcards. While the postcard had been the only quick and inexpensive way to send messages, the telephone was being used more and more for that purpose. The thrill of getting a picture postcard in the mail was not as exciting as going to see the new moving pictures, nicknamed the "movies." By 1920, the postcard boom years were over.

Although the illustrations in this book are limited to postcards, through them we can see that the postcard era was also one of Highland's finest eras.

One

"Downtown" Highland

Highland is the largest community in the Town of Lloyd, and until the advent of shopping malls in the 1960s, the central business district, often called downtown Highland, was also the main area of commercial activity. Originally, the Town of Lloyd was part of the Town of New Paltz, but with the approval of the state legislature, Lloyd seceded from New Paltz in 1845. The earliest settlement in Lloyd was at the riverfront in 1754, but further inland, other settlers started farms in the late 1700s. Around 1830, one of the farmers, Philip Elting, decided to start his own village where the route between Newburgh and Kingston intersected with the road to the river, and he built several stores there. Even after the secession of Lloyd from New Paltz, mail coming to the eastern part of Lloyd had to be addressed to a post office named New Paltz Landing and often wound up in the village of New Paltz by mistake. In 1865, a meeting was held to address that issue and the fact that Elting's village never had an official name. The name of Highland was chosen, probably because the new village was on the high land above the river. The riverfront village became Highland Landing.

On March 17, 1891, a fire wiped out the central part of the business district on the east side of Vineyard Avenue, which was then called Main Street. Although no picture postcards of Highland exist from before the fire, there are several photographs of Highland and the Town of Lloyd that show how the early village looked. Many of the merchants who lost their buildings in the fire were quick to rebuild, and by the fall of 1891, the business district had come back to life. A row of modern brick buildings had replaced the old wooden shops. The centerpiece of the new buildings was the massive Wilcox Store, which advertised itself as "The Store." It stood on the present-day site of the Ossie Building, but it was destroyed by another fire in 1948. Some of the other buildings from 1891 that are shown in the postcards are still in use today.

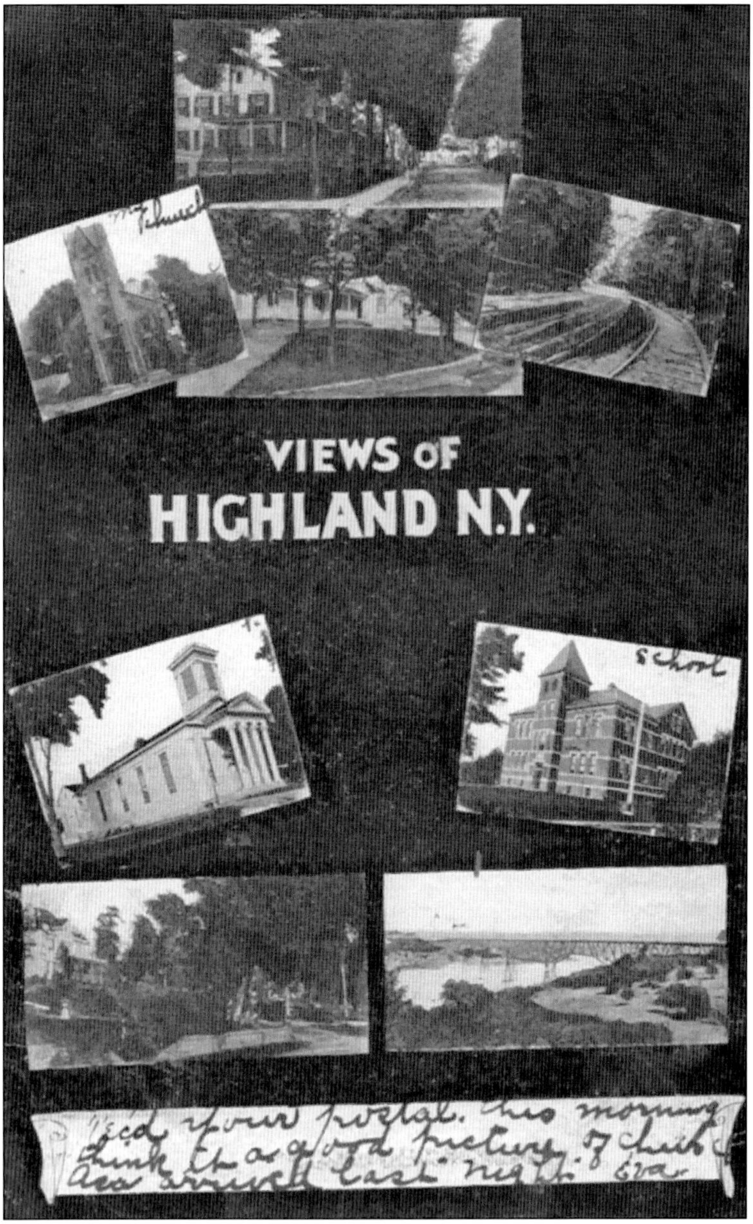

Greetings from Highland! This c. 1905 composite postcard of Highland scenes was one that tourists would mail back to the folks at home. In the upper left is the Methodist Episcopal church, now the United Methodist church, which was erected in 1869. Opposite the Methodist church on the right is a section of the New Paltz Turnpike, now River Road; although tracks for trolley cars are visible, it was still a dirt road full of ruts from wagons and carriages. Between these two views are some street scenes in Highland. In the lower half of the card on the left, one can see the Presbyterian church that was erected in 1844. Opposite it is the original Highland High School, built in 1903. Below these two pictures are the Elting property on the left (see page 33) and the railroad bridge to Poughkeepsie on the right. Note that a handwritten message was squeezed in at the bottom of the card because postal regulations allowed nothing but the address to be written on the other side.

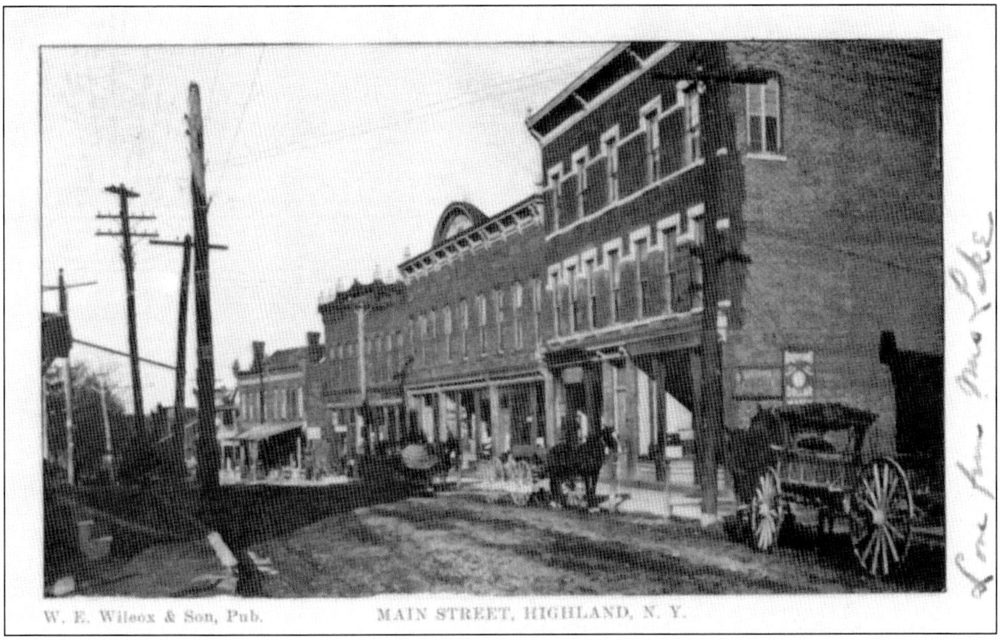

These two views of downtown Highland were made between 1891 and 1900. Although an early automobile may be seen, wagons, carriages, and horses were the primary means of transportation. The upper postcard was published by the Wilcox Store, whose store building is in the center of the photograph, capped by a semicircular crown that bore the name "Wilcox" and "1891." The building to the right of Wilcox's had the office of the *Highland Post* newspaper on its right side and Charles E. Browne's drugstore on the left. Note that the streets are not paved. The poles were for telegraph and, later, telephone lines. Because there was no electricity in Highland yet, the modern brick buildings were lit by gaslights, while older stores and most homes still used kerosene lamps for lighting.

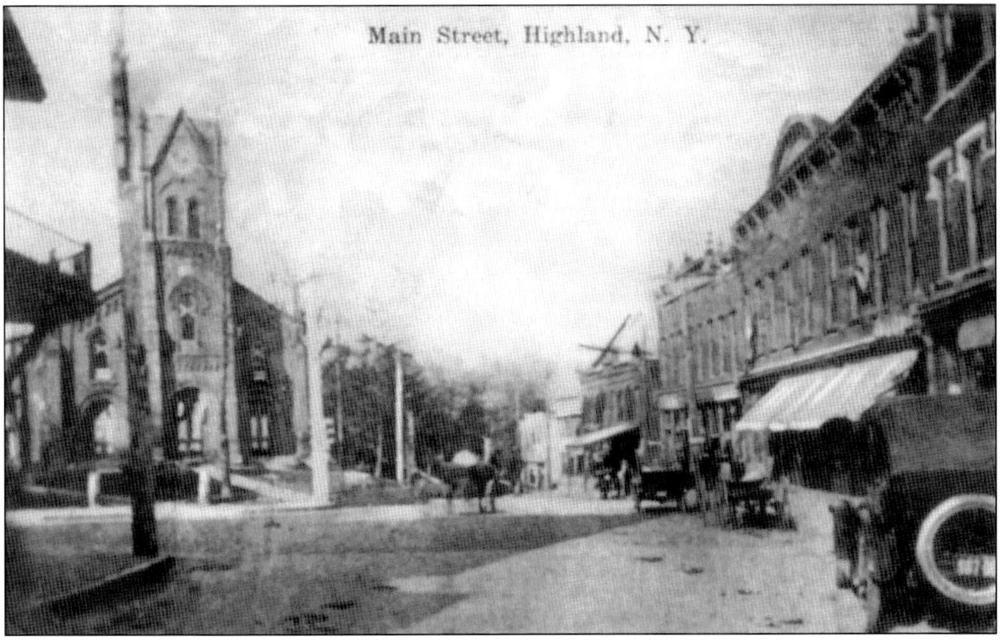

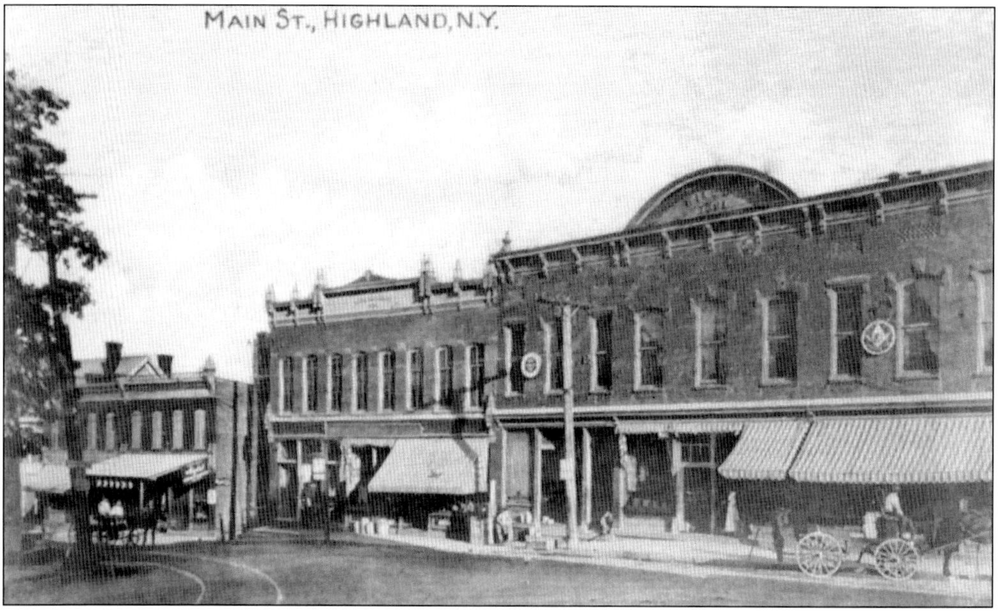

The Wilcox Building, pictured on the right, consisted of three storefronts. Wilcox had a harness shop on the left side, a dry goods store in the middle, and a grocery on the right. Meeting rooms upstairs were rented by various organizations. The Rose Building, to the left of the Wilcox Building, housed J.W. Feeter's hardware store and Rose's Hall on the second floor. Another grocery was in the next building (now Three Guys Pizza).

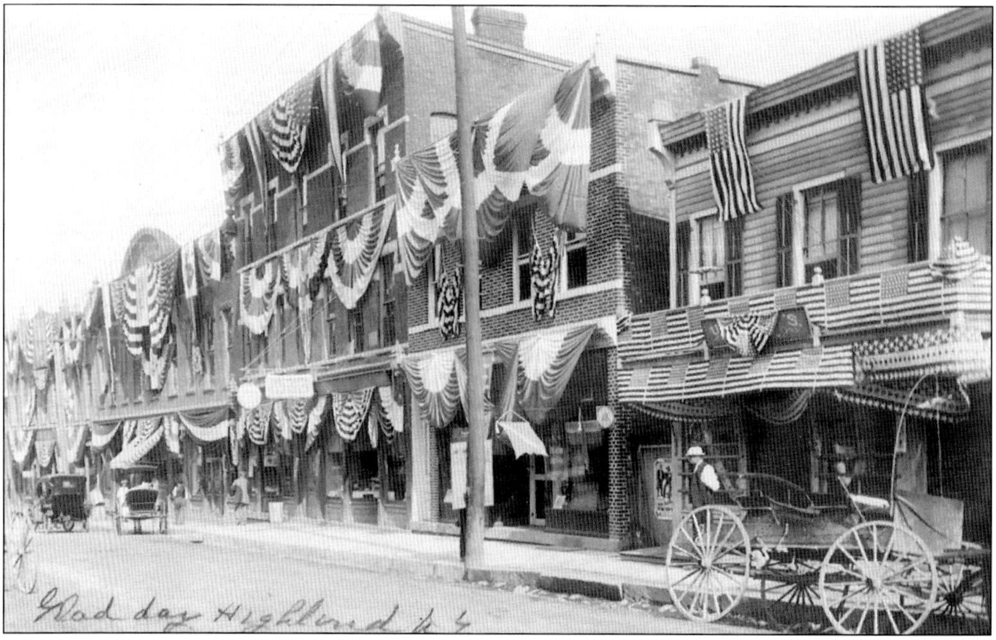

Downtown Highland has been the scene of many patriotic celebrations. On this occasion, August 24, 1915, the whole town is decked out for a celebration that was called Glad Day. It marked the opening of a new paved state road to Highland from the riverfront along the route of the New Paltz Turnpike (now River Road). According to newspapers, there were about 5,000 attendees, making this Highland's largest celebration ever.

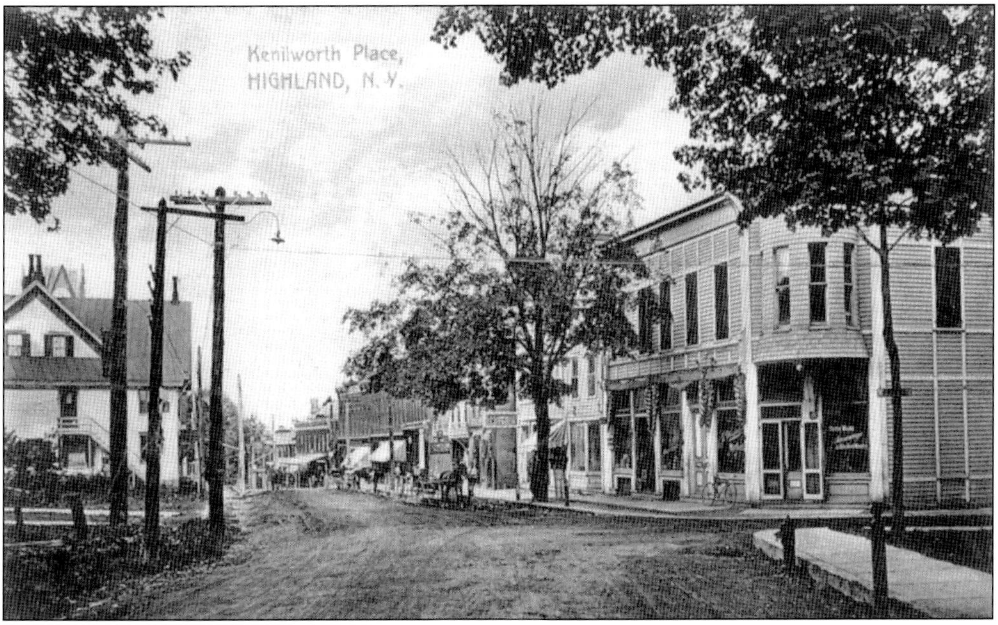

Located on the corner of Milton Avenue, the Kenilworth Building anchored the other end of Highland's main business street. When this photograph was taken around 1905, Erichsen's Meat Market, famous for its homemade sausage, was located there. This building is still standing today, and for decades it has housed a succession of pizza shops. Originally, it had a tower on the corner, obscured by a tree in this view.

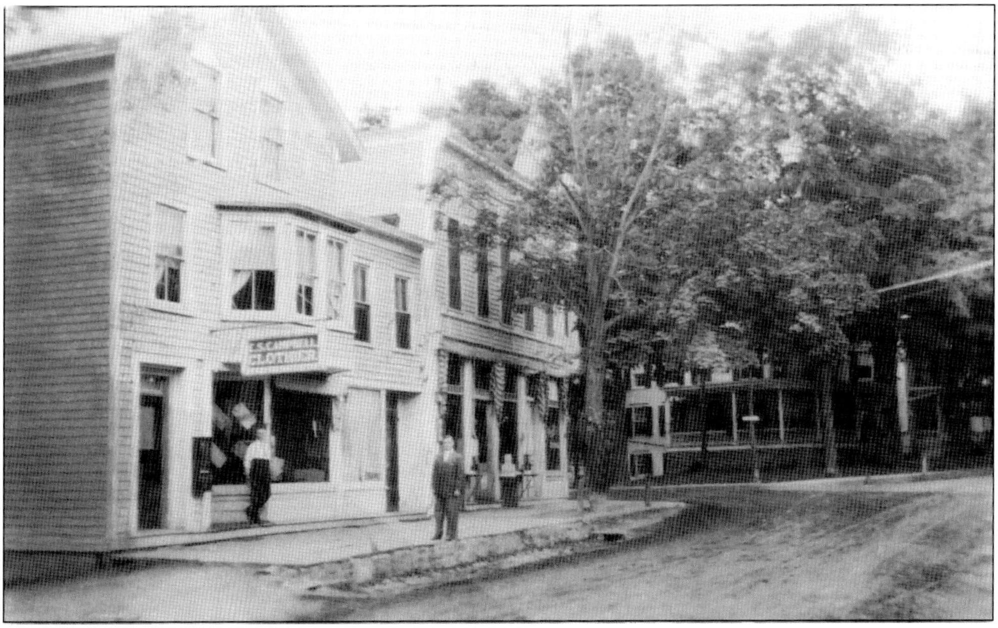

This is another view of the Kenilworth corner, from the opposite direction, looking toward Milton Avenue. The store on the left was the tailor shop of S.C. Campbell. In the 1930s, the Park Filling Station dispensed gasoline on the other corner. It was operated by Livingston Rhodes, son of Civil War veteran Aaron Rhodes. It also sold snacks, such as hot dogs and Highland brand ice cream. (Courtesy of Town of Lloyd Historian's Office.)

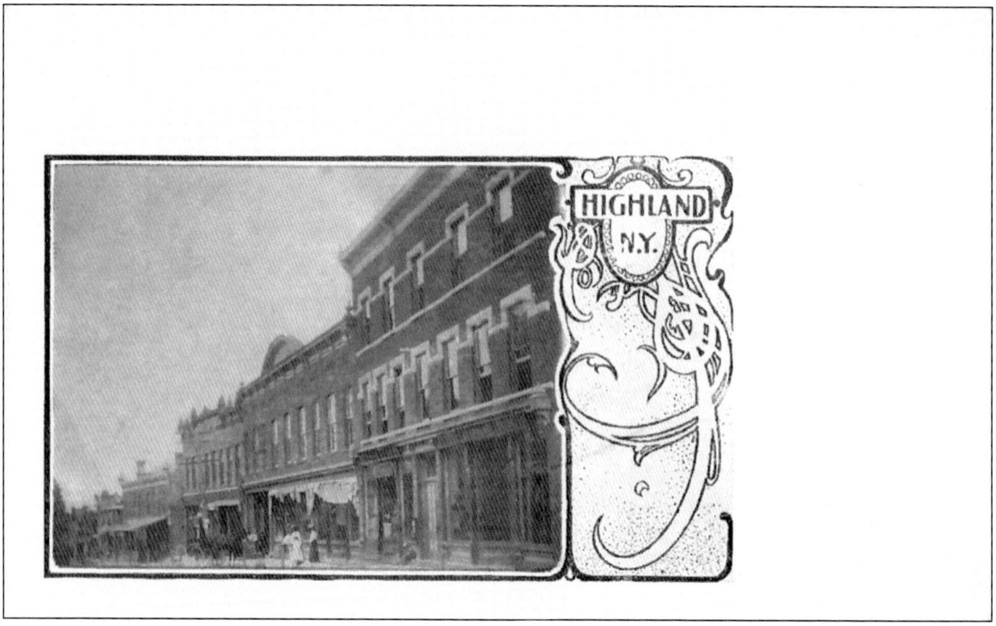

The two postcards on this page are representative of a souvenir style that was popular from about 1895 to 1905. The reduced size of the image area allowed more space for handwritten messages on the front of the postcard. Until Congress changed the law in 1907, the back of a postcard could contain nothing but an address. The bottom card shows a large hay wagon in front of the corner where the First National Bank of Highland later built its impressive limestone building. The large building shown in this photograph was called Deyo's Hall and, later, the DeGraff Building. It had retail businesses on the ground floor, and the second floor was the quarters of the Sunshine Lodge of the International Order of Odd Fellows. This building was demolished to make way for the bank in 1922.

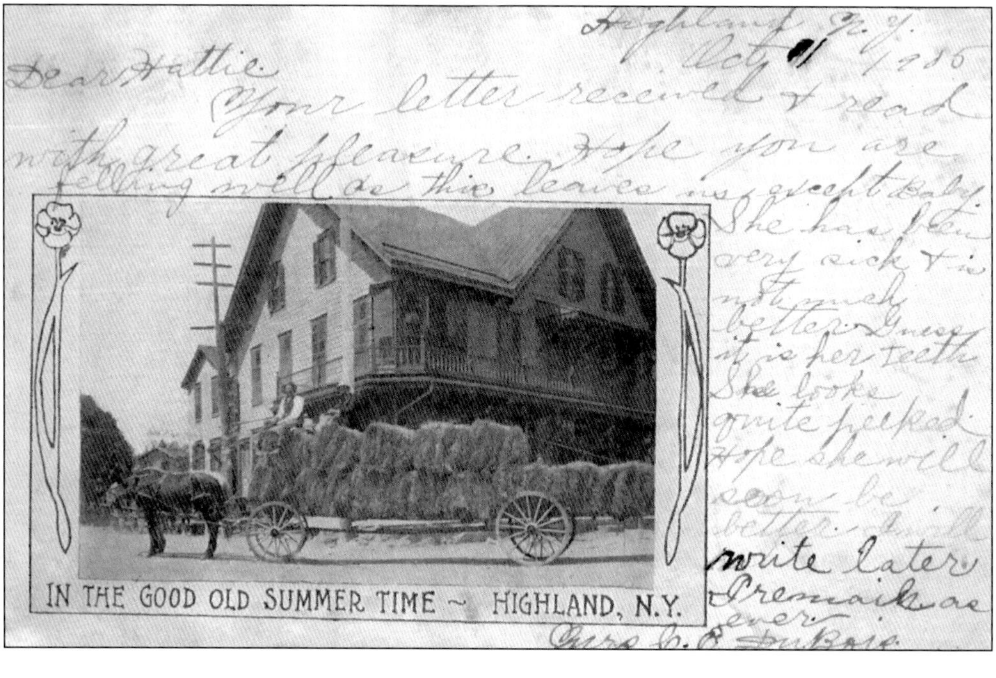

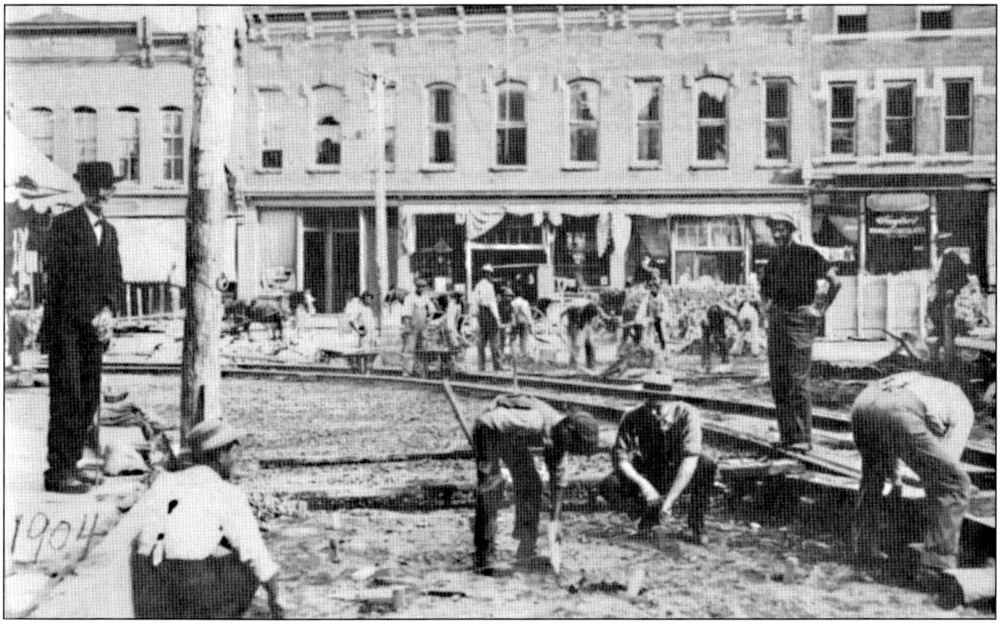

A paved road was a rarity at the beginning of the 20th century, but the state legislature passed a statute for the improvement of public highways in Chapter 115 of the Laws of 1898. Kingston construction company McNamee & Rice was awarded a contract to pave 7.08 miles of the post road in the Town of Lloyd, mostly with macadam, but where the road went through Highland, bricks were used in the center of the village. The paving operation drew many curious onlookers, and two photographs of it were published as postcards. Some references gave the year of the paving as 1903 or 1904, but a recent check of documents in the state archives confirmed that it was actually done in 1907 at a cost of $60,560.15. The trolley tracks laid in 1897 are pictured here. (Both, courtesy of Town of Lloyd Historian's Office.)

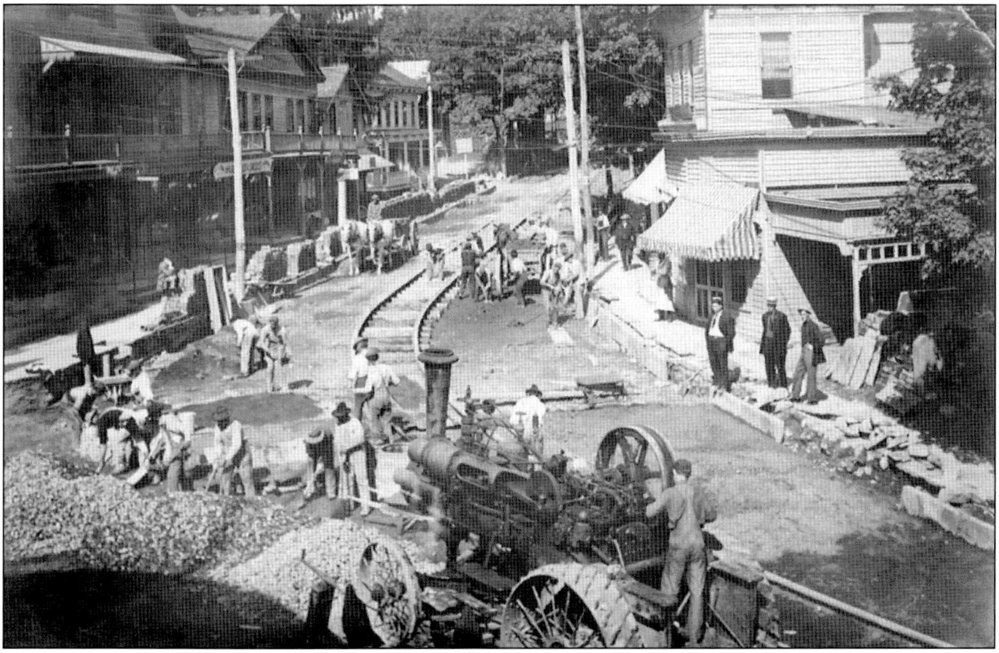

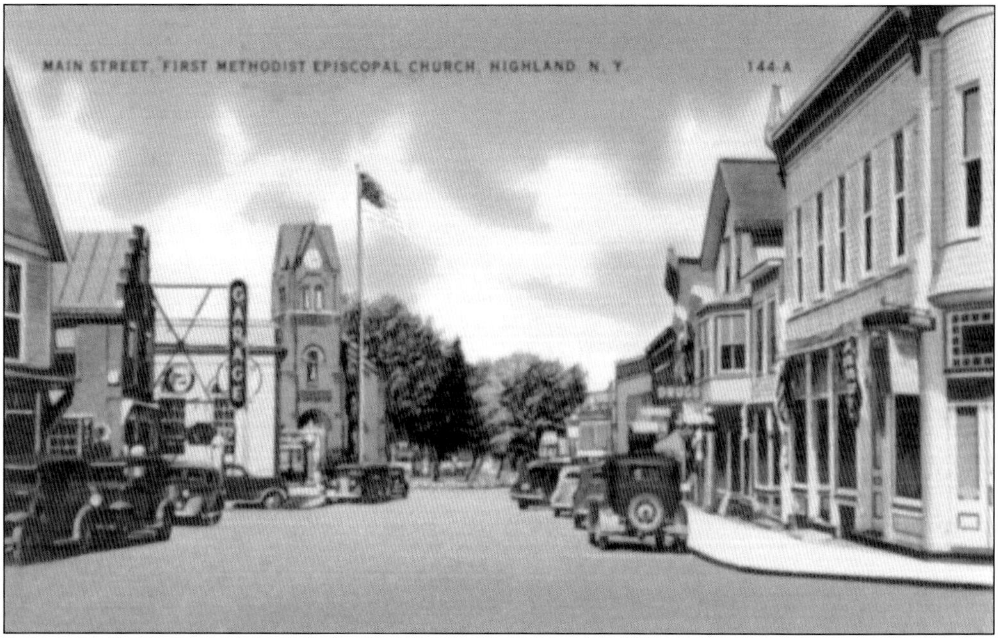

Automobiles and paved streets are the main differences from earlier times, as evidenced in these two views of downtown Highland during the 1930s. A notable addition is the tall flagpole in front of the Methodist church at the end of the street. It was dedicated in 1926 as a memorial to the soldiers who served during World War I and was donated by Congressman Harcourt J. Pratt, the son of Highland businessman George W. Pratt. The large "GARAGE" sign on the left side of the street marked Louis Smith's Garage. After this automobile dealership moved to Route 9W, the Highland post office was located there from 1942 to 1952. On the opposite side, the Kenilworth Building housed Lorin S. Callahan's grocery store. Later elected the town clerk of Lloyd, Callahan was the longest-serving town clerk in the state's history when he retired.

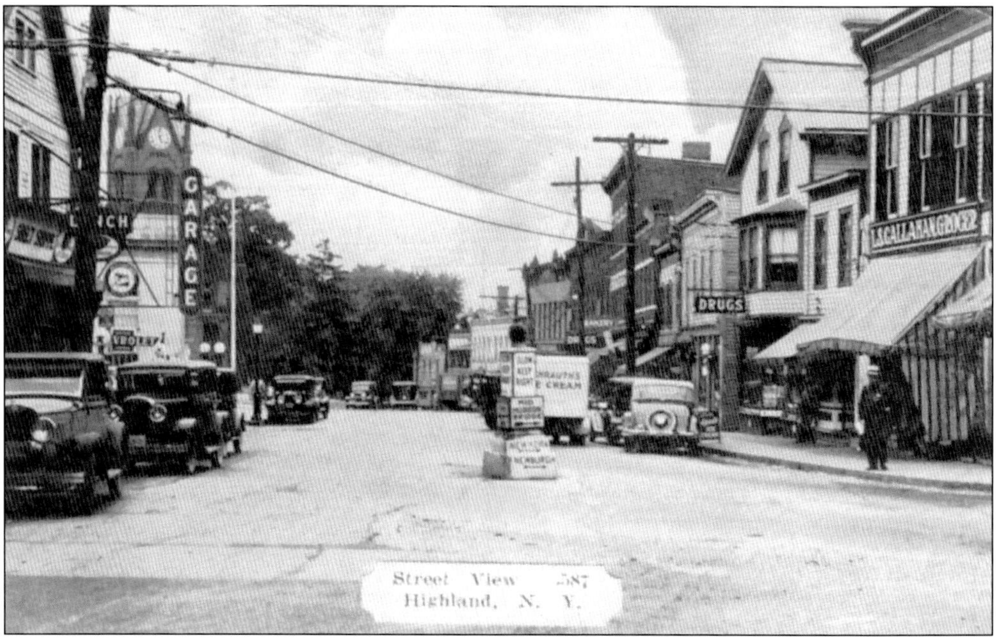

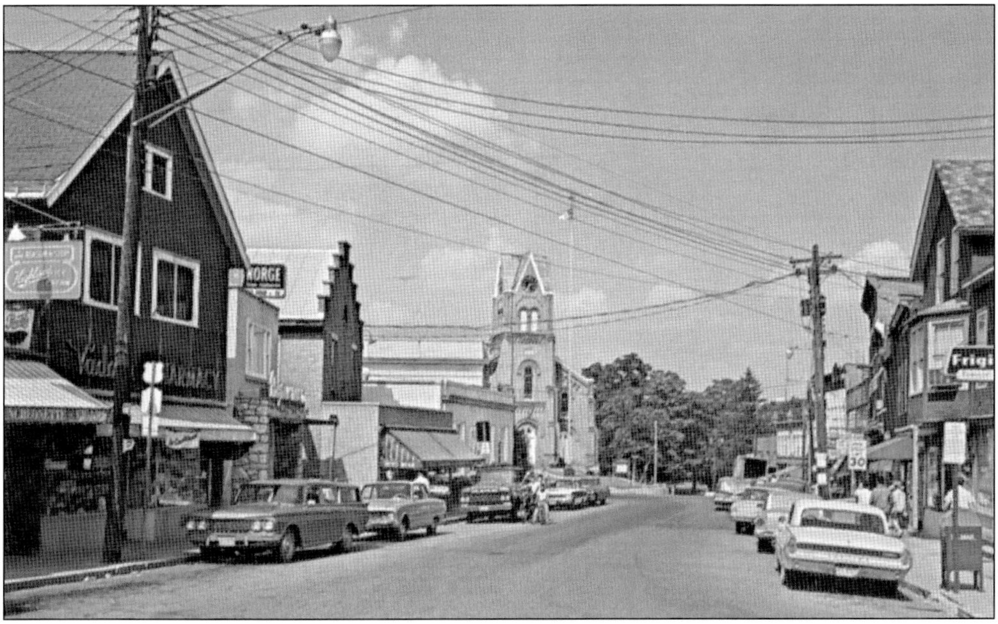

Downtown Highland was still the subject of postcard publishers around 1960, when M-M Photo of Newburgh published these full-color glossy cards. In the top view, looking from Milton Avenue toward the Methodist church, the building on the left housed Vadala's Pharmacy until that pharmacy moved into the former hardware store space in the Rose Building during the 1990s. Harry Fogle had a Rexall drugstore in Highland on the opposite side of the street, shown on the left in the bottom view. The 1891 Wilcox Building had been destroyed by fire in 1948, and Fogle's store was located in a modern two-story building that housed various businesses, including the Savings and Loan Association of Kingston. The classical 1923 bank on the opposite corner was Highland's most prominent commercial edifice.

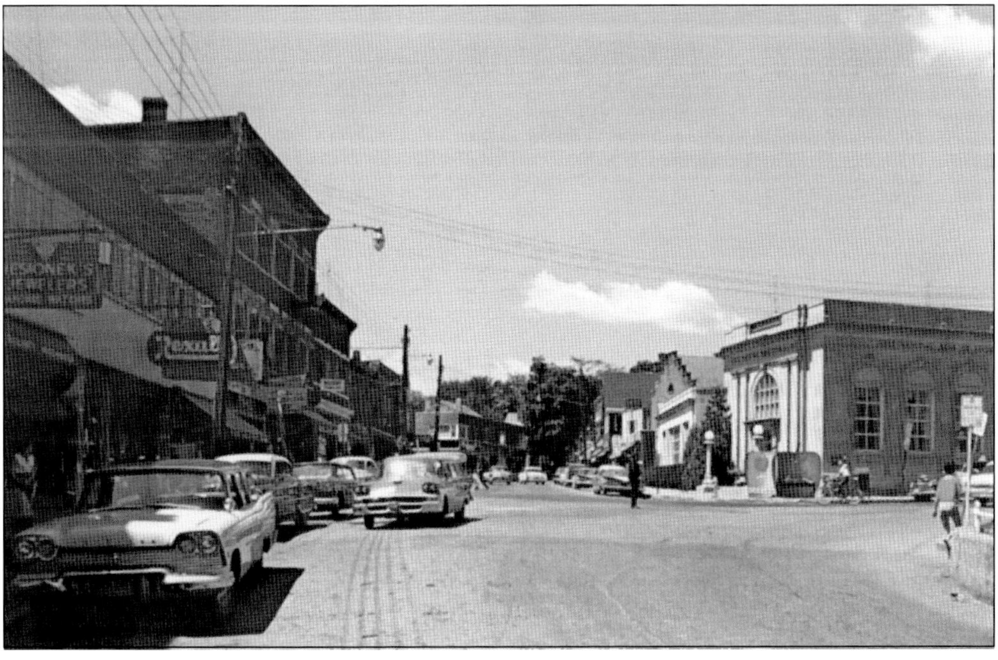

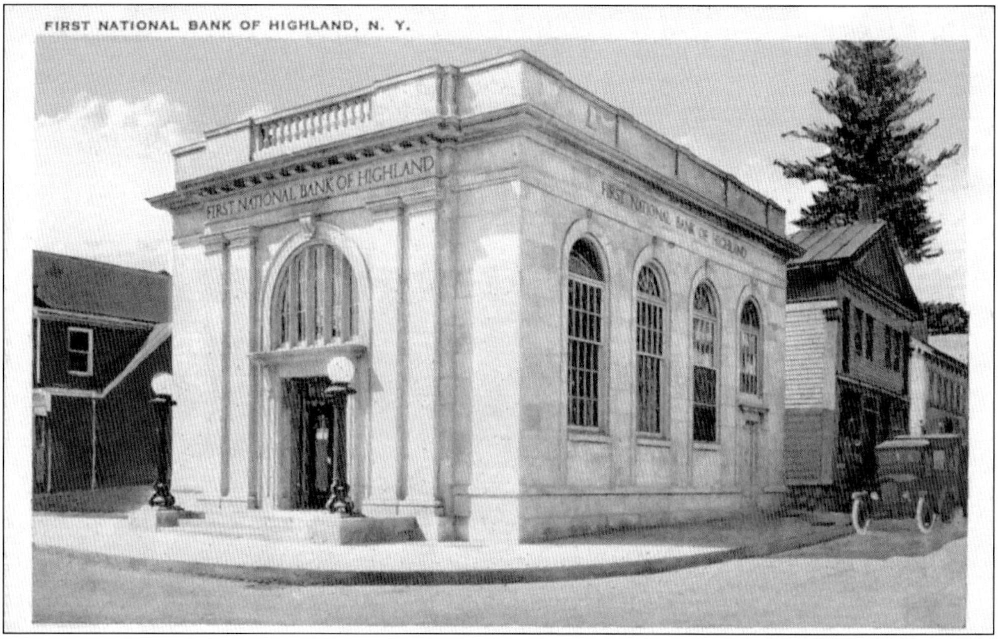

The First National Bank of Highland was chartered in 1900, and its first office was in rented space down the street from the Wilcox Building. By 1920, it had grown to the extent that a new bank building was commissioned. Kingston architect Gerald W. Betz designed a classic limestone structure, which was erected in 1923 on Highland's most prominent corner. This building replaced Deyo's Hall (see bottom of page 14).

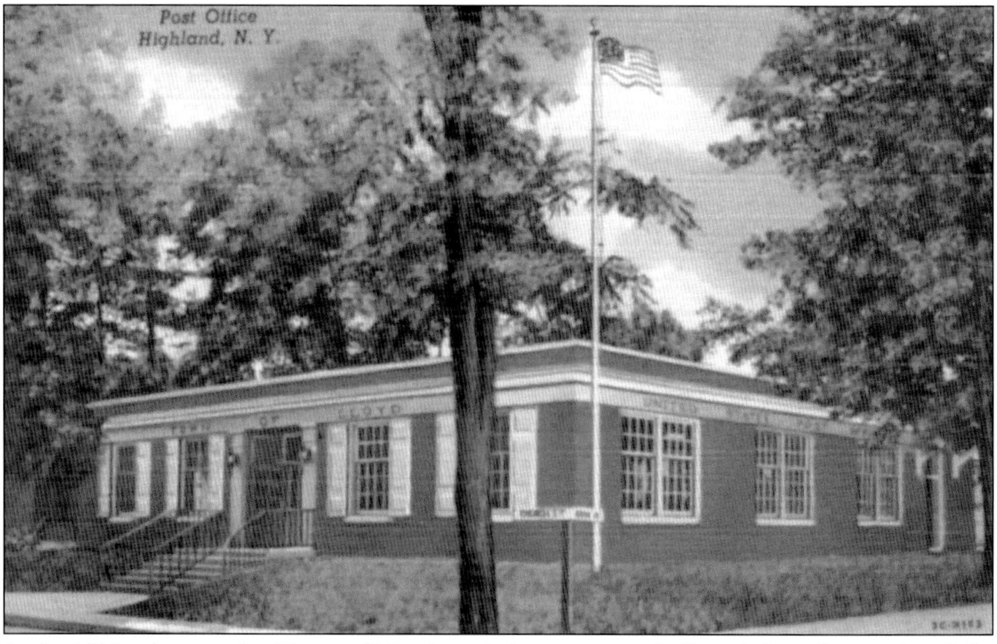

In the 1950s, the growing Town of Lloyd needed a new town hall, and the volume of mail for Highland required a larger post office. The present town hall on Church Street was originally only one story high when it was completed in 1952. However, the town offices only required half of the one floor, so in a unique partnership, the other half was leased to the post office.

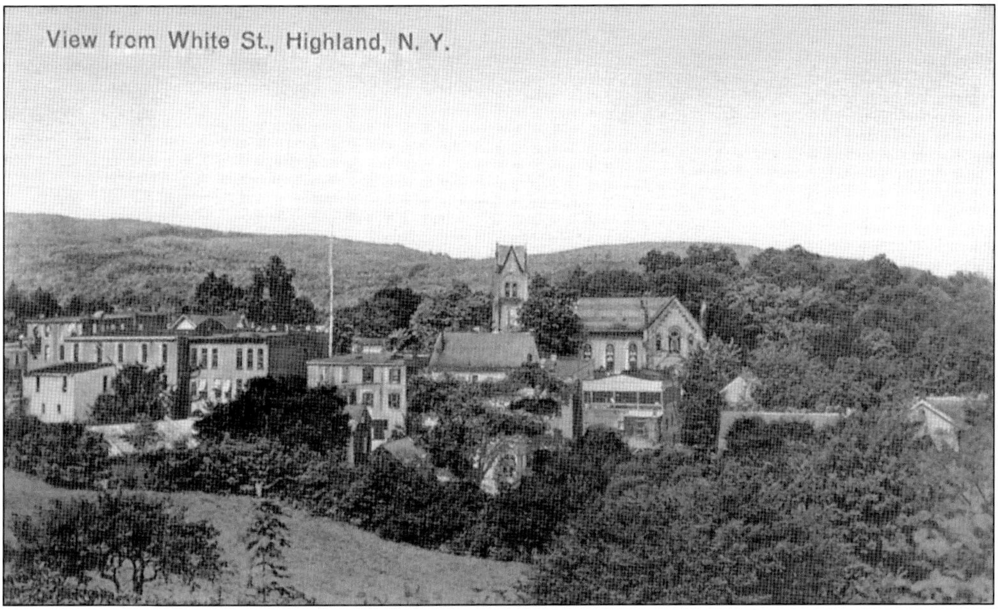

From White Street, Highland is seen nestled among the mountains in this German lithograph postcard. The most noticeable structures are the Methodist church and the backs of the brick buildings in the business district. Although not visible in this view, the Twaalfskill Creek runs at the rear of these buildings. The nearer buildings were on the other side of the Twaalfskill, including a water-powered mill. (Courtesy of Gail Russell.)

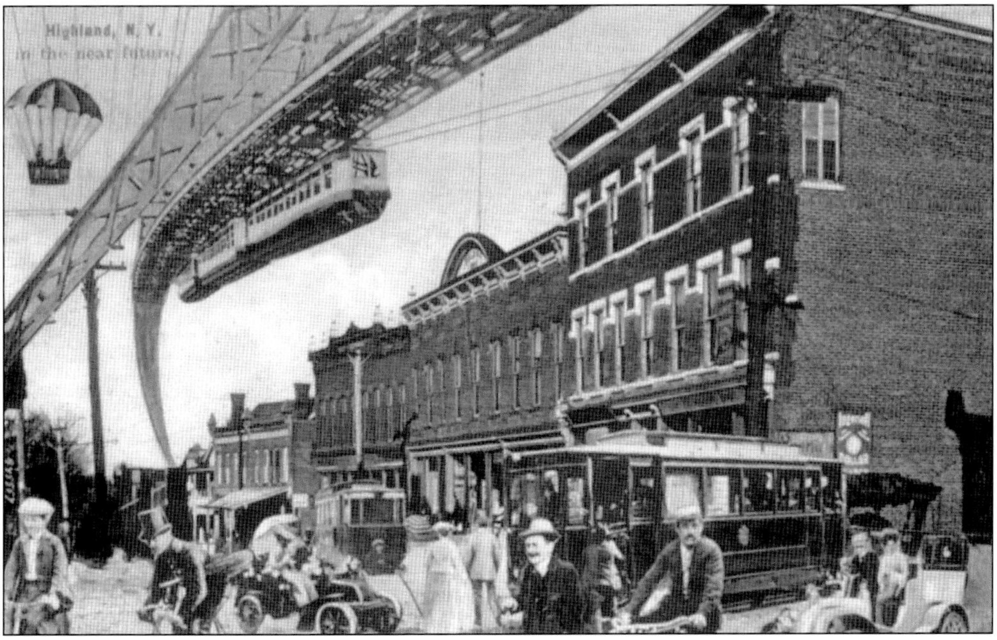

This view of downtown Highland is subtitled "in the near future." Streetcars and automobiles were added to the same photograph shown on page 11 (top), creating a traffic jam. The most futuristic idea, the aerial tramway, may yet become a reality, as one is now being proposed to go between the park at Highland Landing and the 1888 railroad bridge, now the Walkway Over the Hudson State Park.

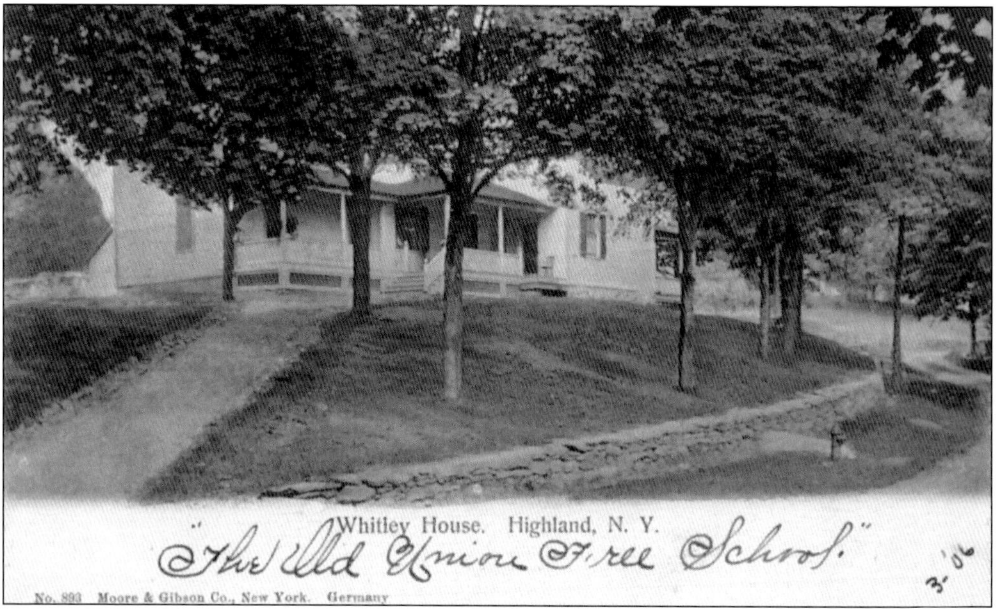

The Union Free School of Lloyd School District No. 2 was one of 11 schools set up in the town after the state legislature passed the Education Act of 1812. Each town was required to create school districts and levy school taxes. Still in effect today, the system of school taxes has not fundamentally changed since 1812. The original building, located on Grand Street across from Thorn's Lane, had one story. It was enlarged into the structure seen in these two postcards. After a new high school was constructed in 1903 (see next page), the school district sold this property, and it became a tourist home, the Whitley House. This building no longer exists, and a new private home has recently been erected on the site. The stone wall and steps leading up from the road are still visible today.

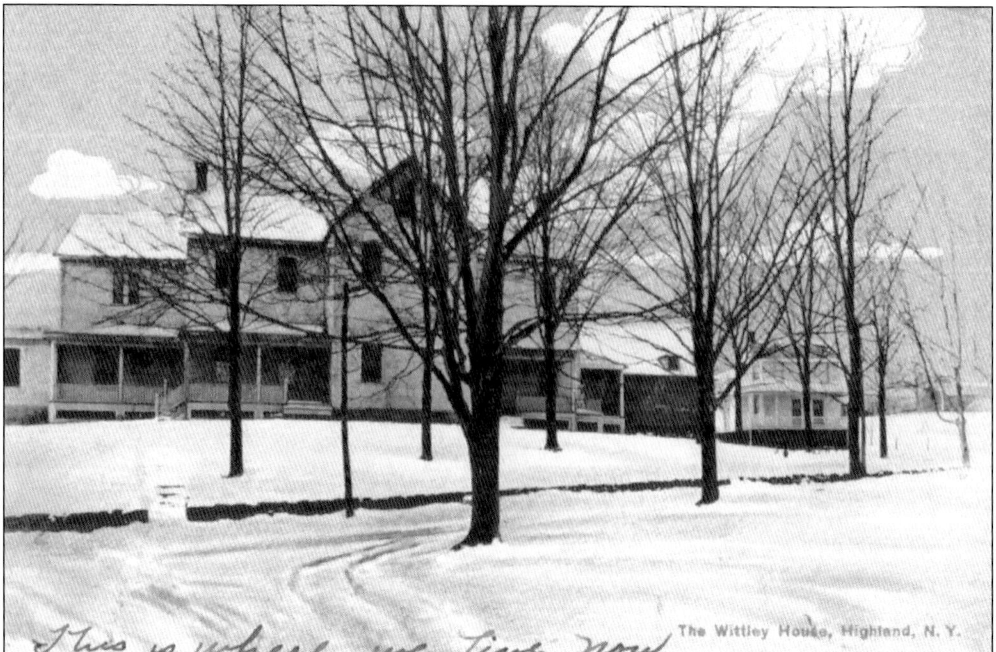

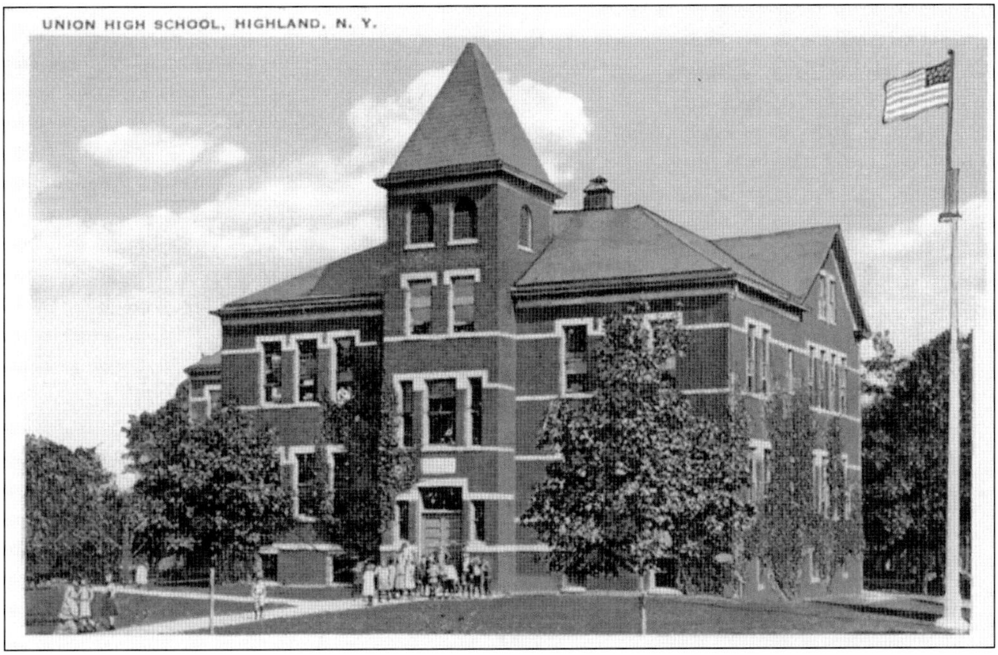

The new Union Free School of 1903 stood on Main Street, in front of the present Highland Middle School. An addition was put on the left side of the building around 1912 and one on the right side around 1924. Abandoned and partly damaged by fire, the school board demolished this building in the 1970s, to the chagrin of local preservationists who had suggested other uses for it.

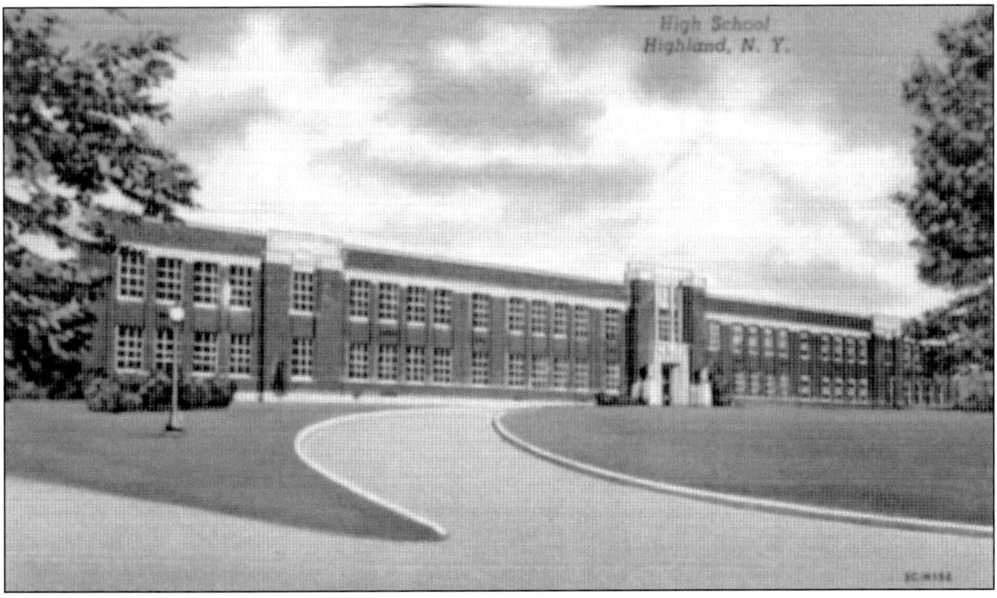

This was Highland's next high school building. Opened in 1939, it was designed by architect Donald P. Emley and built by Highland contractor Eugene Ossie. It was located directly behind the 1903 school, which then became an elementary school. The high school building shown in this postcard also served as an elementary school after 1962, when a junior-senior high school opened on Pancake Hollow Road. Today, the above building is a middle school.

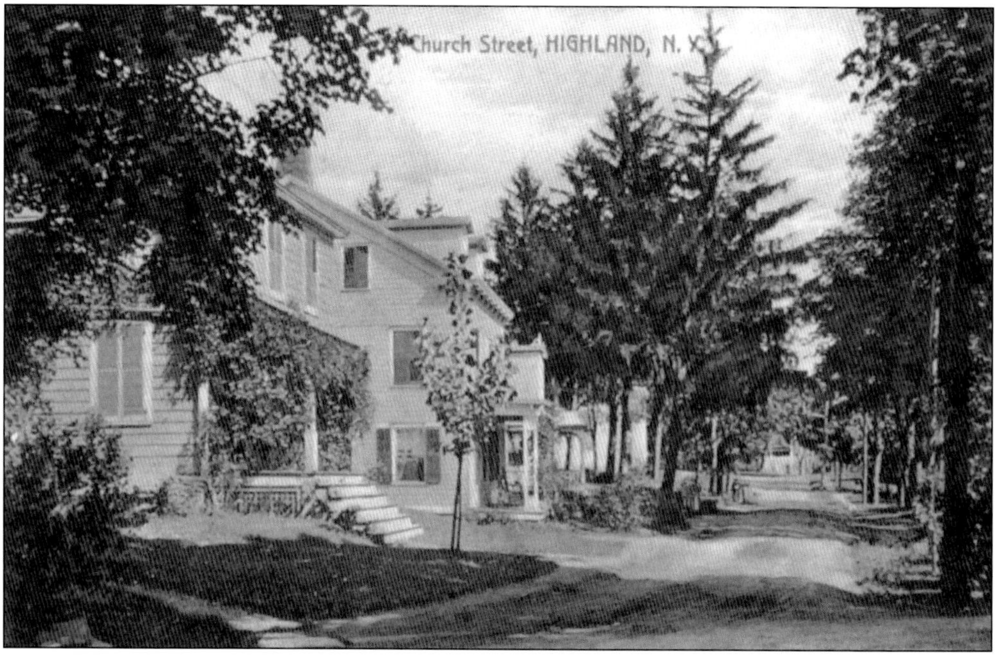

Church Street got its name from the Presbyterian church, which was erected in 1844. When these postcards were made around 1900, the street was a dirt road. In the upper view, one is looking down the street from Vineyard Avenue toward Main Street. Below, one gets a clear view of the church on the left. The present Grove Street on the left side of the church was just a narrow path. The Lloyd town hall now stands on the empty land to the left of the church. Some of the houses on the right side of the street still stand and have changed little since this postcard was made.

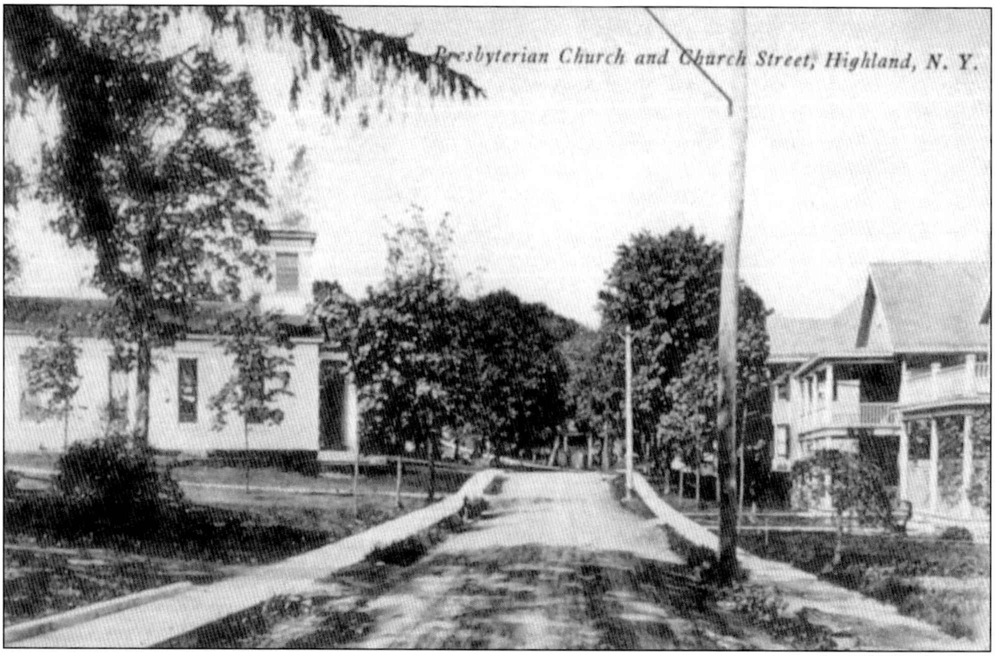

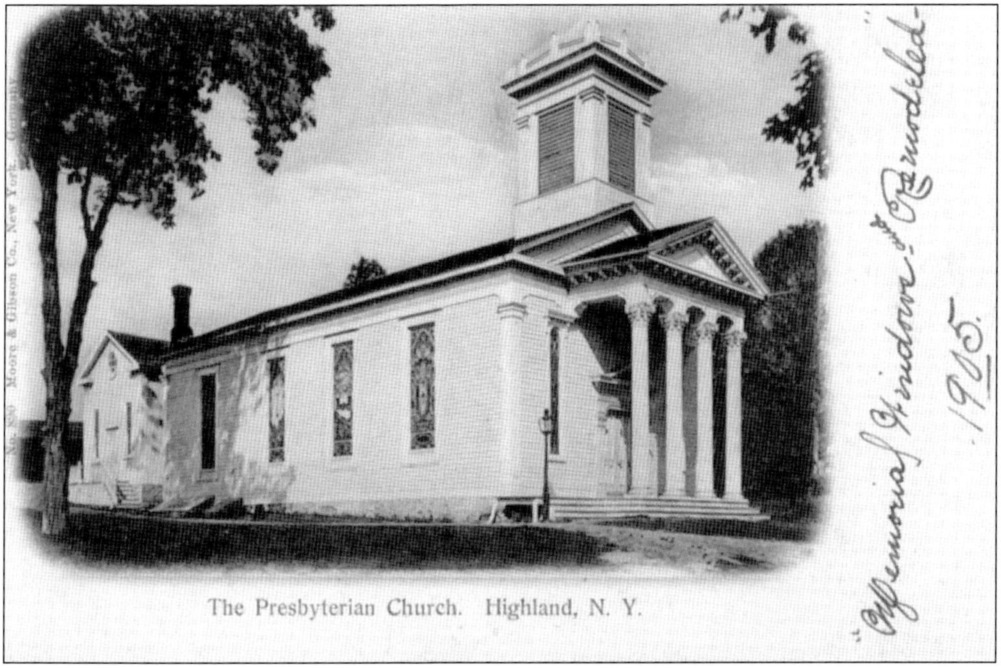

A Presbyterian congregation formed in the Town of Lloyd in 1792, and the first church was erected on the Modena Turnpike (now Route 44/55) near the corner of Chapel Hill Road. The original Presbyterian cemetery is located there. This present church began as a small white building in 1844 and was nicknamed the "White Church." The building was enlarged in 1871, and the fine Greek Revival facade was added. The writing on the upper postcard indicates that it was remodeled again and stained-glass memorial windows were added around 1905. The postcard below was mailed in 1916, but the date that the photograph was taken is unknown. Until 1971, Washington's birthday was always observed as an important patriotic holiday on February 22, Washington's actual birth date.

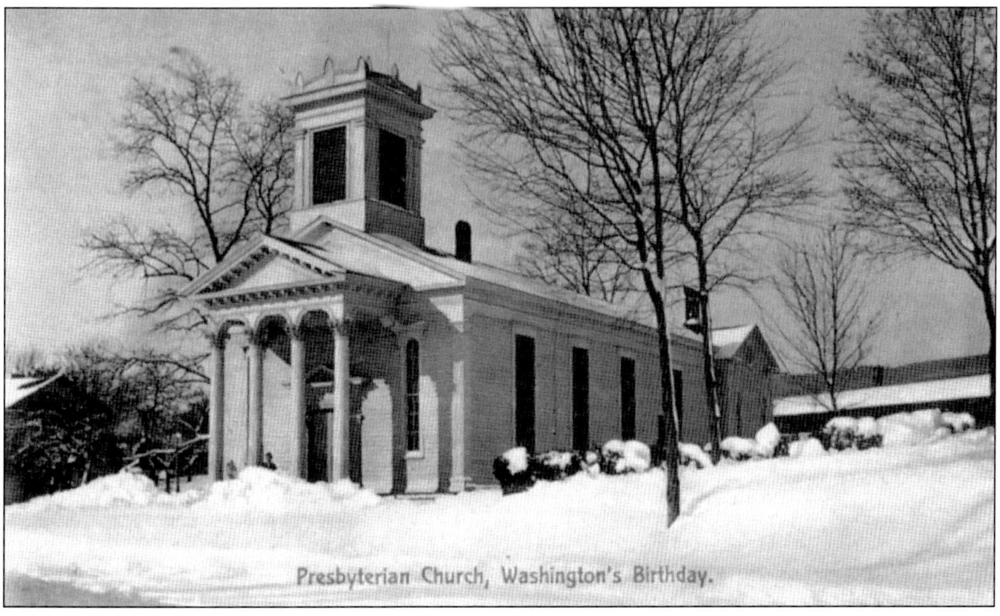

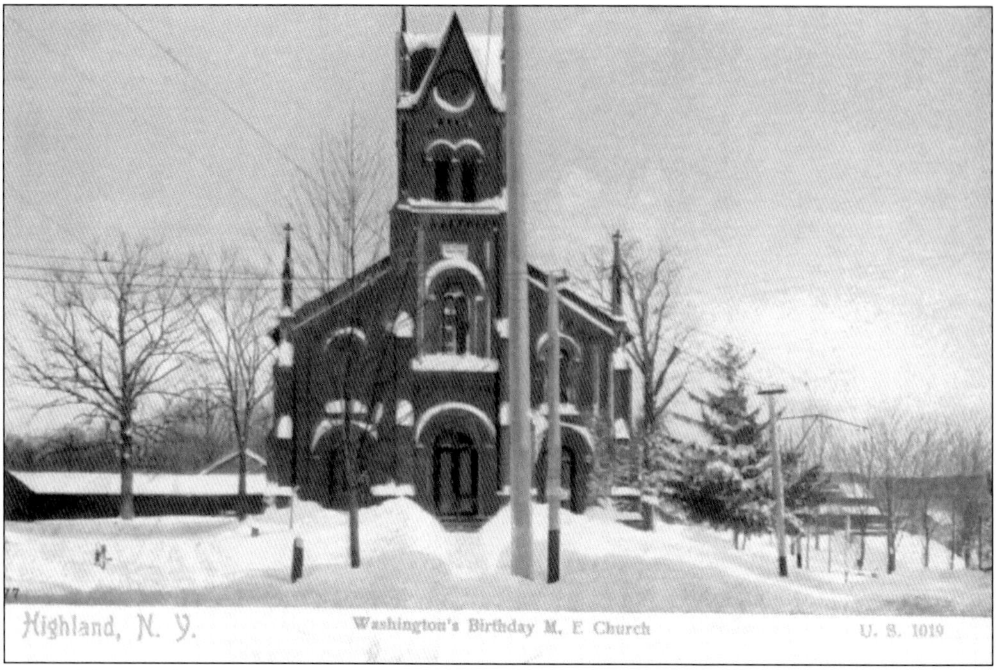

Viewed from in front of the Methodist church, another "Washington's Birthday" scene is pictured here. This card was postmarked in 1908, and it may or may not have actually been taken on February 22. The birthday of the "Father of His Country" also symbolized the coldest part of winter, and this type of snow scene may have been reminiscent of the winter that he spent at Valley Forge with the Continental troops in 1777–1778. The back of this postcard, shown below, is interesting because it was mailed at the Loyd post office (see bottom of page 41). The Loyd post office was established in 1844, a year before the Town of Lloyd was established. The proposed town's name had also been spelled Loyd, but in the final state proclamation, the spelling was changed to Lloyd, perhaps accidentally.

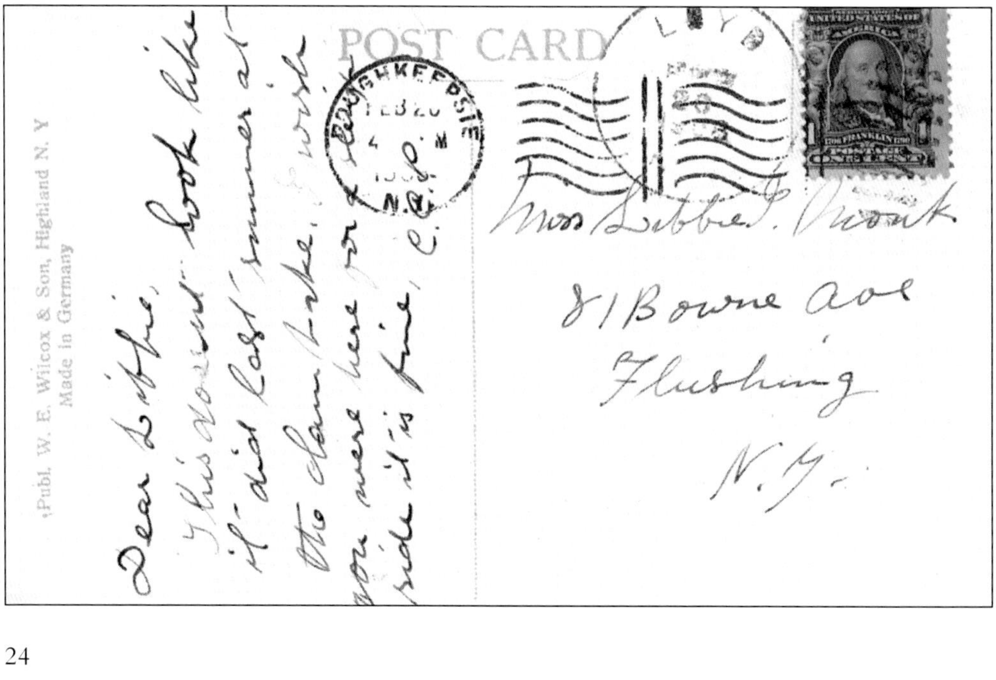

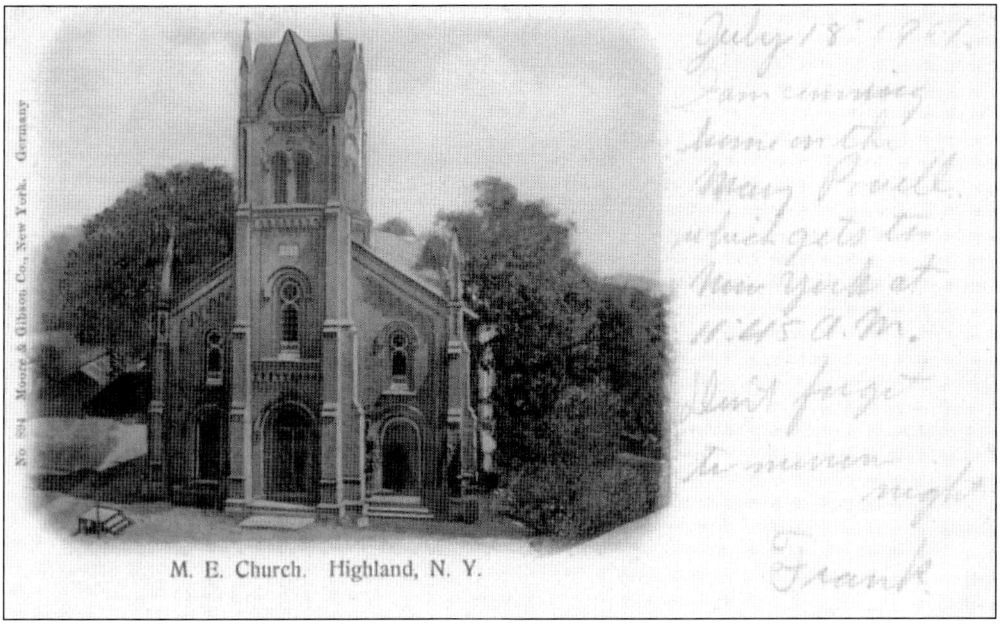

The Methodist church, originally the Methodist Episcopal church, is represented in more postcards than any other Highland building. This 1869 edifice is the second Methodist church on this site. Highland's founder, Philip Elting, donated the land, and a wooden church was constructed in 1821. When the above building was erected, the original wooden church building was moved across the street; it had a second life as a store and offices in the courtyard behind the bank building until it was demolished in the 1960s. The above photograph was taken in or before 1906, the year when the clock was installed in the tower. The growth of the Methodist movement into what was once Highland's largest congregation can be attributed to a long history of ministers known for their character and rectitude, beginning with the circuit rider Rev. Ezekiel Cooper in 1786.

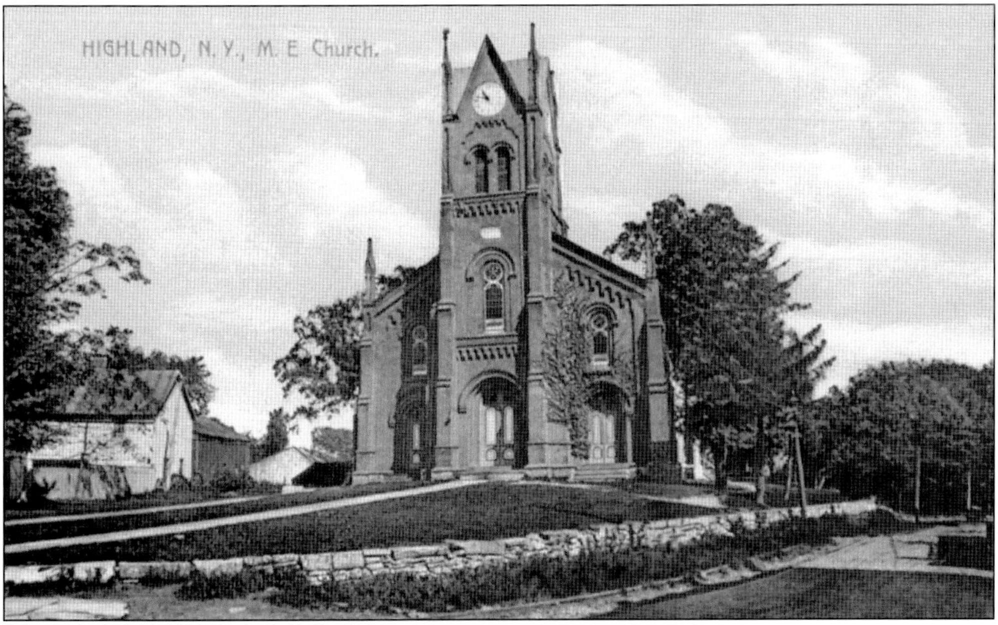

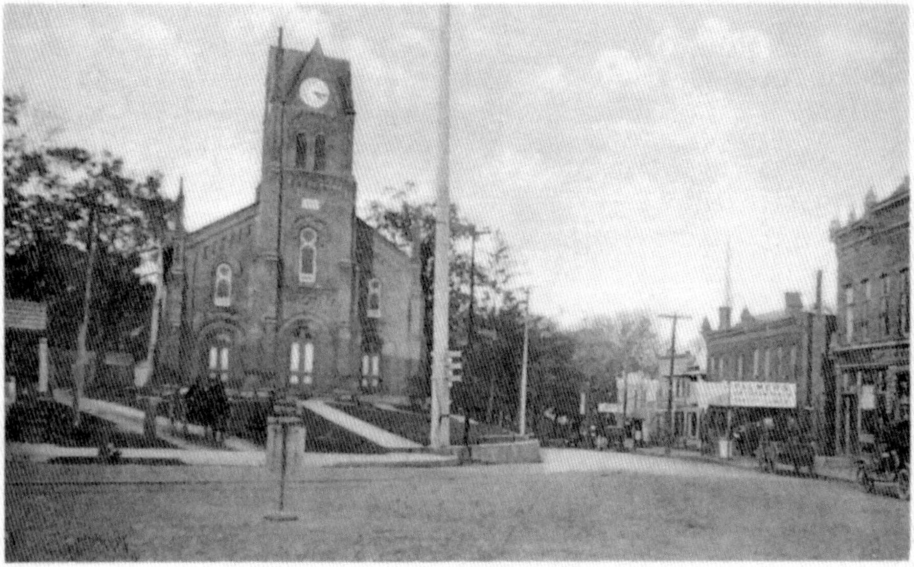

M. E. Church and lower Main Street, Highland, N. Y.

The postcard above gives a glimpse of lower Vineyard Avenue, then part of the New Paltz Turnpike, with its trolley line coming up from the riverfront. Part of Feeter's hardware store in the Rose Building is visible in the far right, which continued to house a hardware store into the 1990s. The next building, to the left of Feeter's, was another new brick building erected after the fire of 1891. Occupied by various businesses over the years, it has been home to Three Guys Pizza, the oldest restaurant in Highland, since 1969. To the left of that is Upright's new hotel, which opened around 1895. The first hotel was on the same site, but it was destroyed in the disastrous 1891 fire. The postcard of the Methodist church below dates from about 1960 and was published in full color.

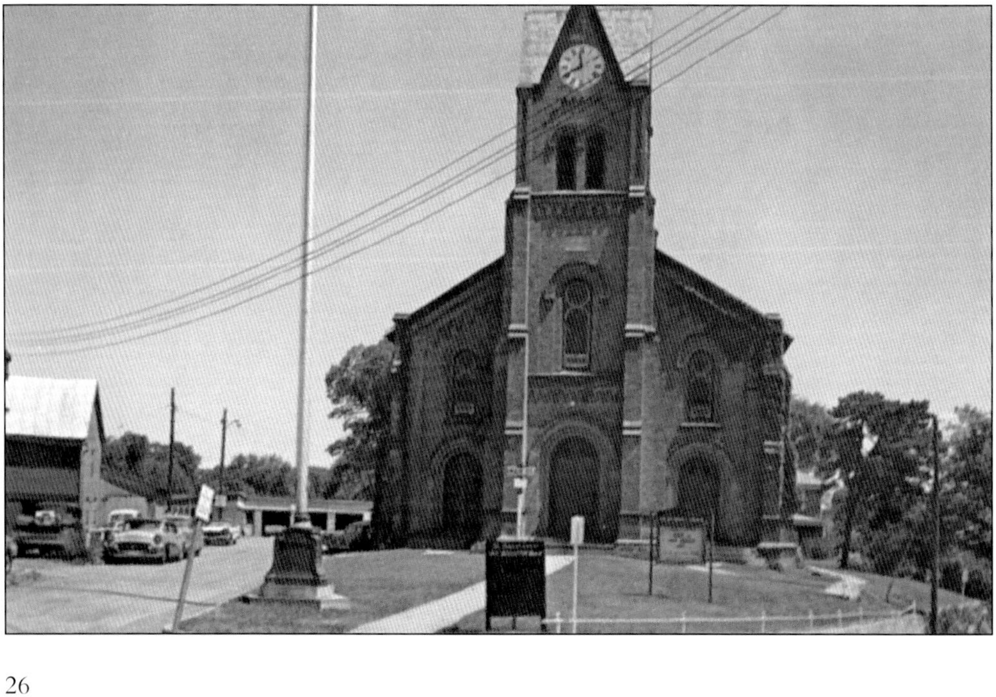

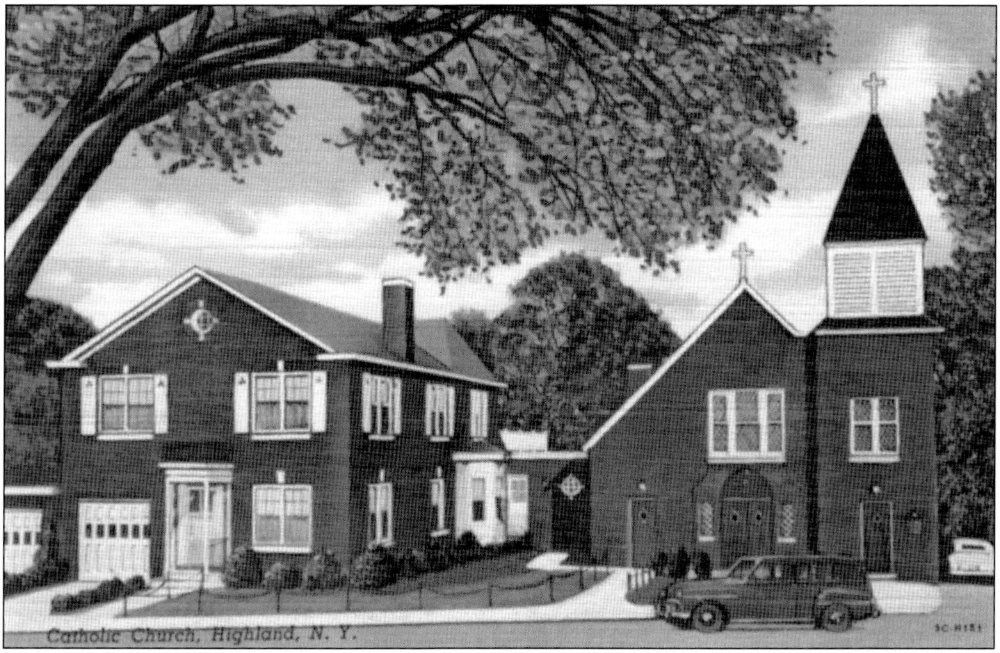

In 1899, St. James Church in Milton started a Roman Catholic mission in Highland, and in 1900, the Church of St. Augustine was erected. The original wood-frame building is shown on the left side of the postcard below. The Highland church continued to be a mission of the Milton church until 1950, when Francis Cardinal Spellman established Highland as a separate parish. Also in 1950, the house to the left of the church was purchased to serve as a parsonage, the church was remodeled, and a redbrick facade was installed on both the parsonage and the church, as seen in the above postcard. The original structure still exists behind the brick facade. Parochial school classes were held in the basement of the church until 1959, when the St. Augustine Parochial School opened on the corner of Philips Avenue and Elting Place.

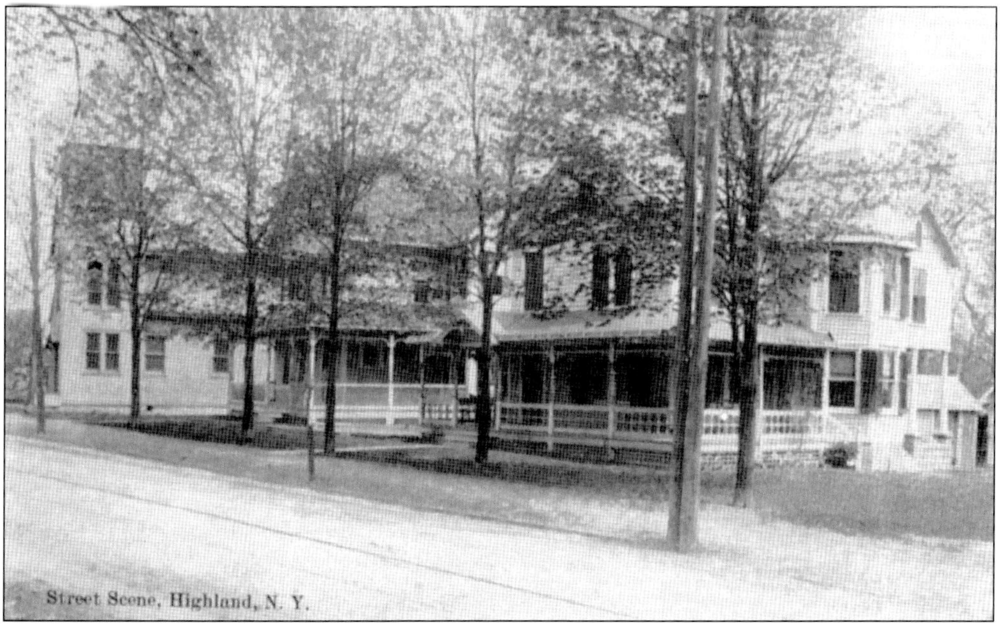

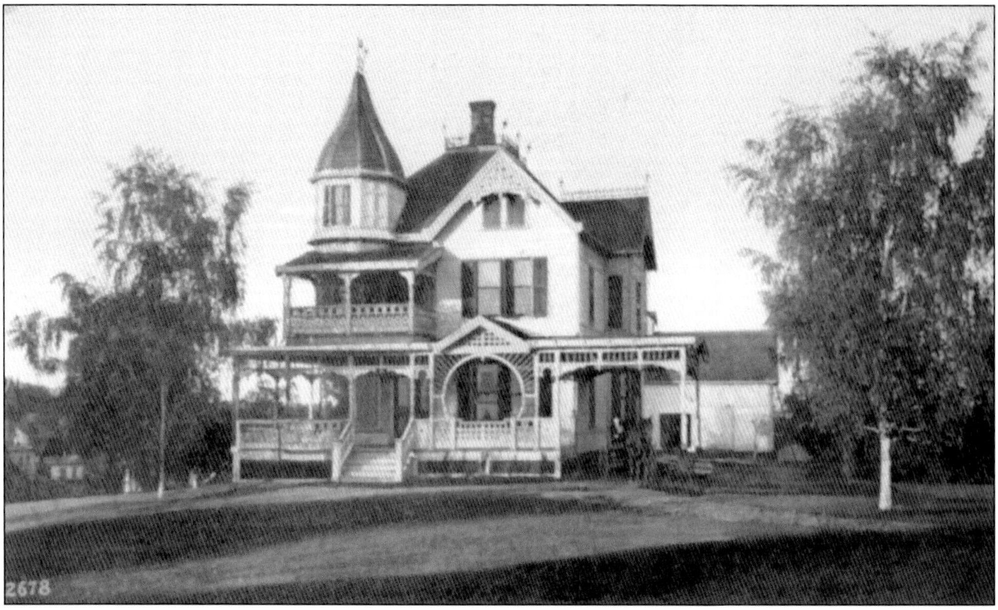

The 1896 Victorian home of Aaron Rhodes was a landmark at the entrance to downtown Highland on Route 9W. It was the town's last surviving example of the Queen Anne architectural style. Despite the efforts of preservationists to have it moved a few feet behind the planned Veterans Park and restored as a museum, veterans groups prevailed, and the state demolished the house to make a parking lot behind the monuments.

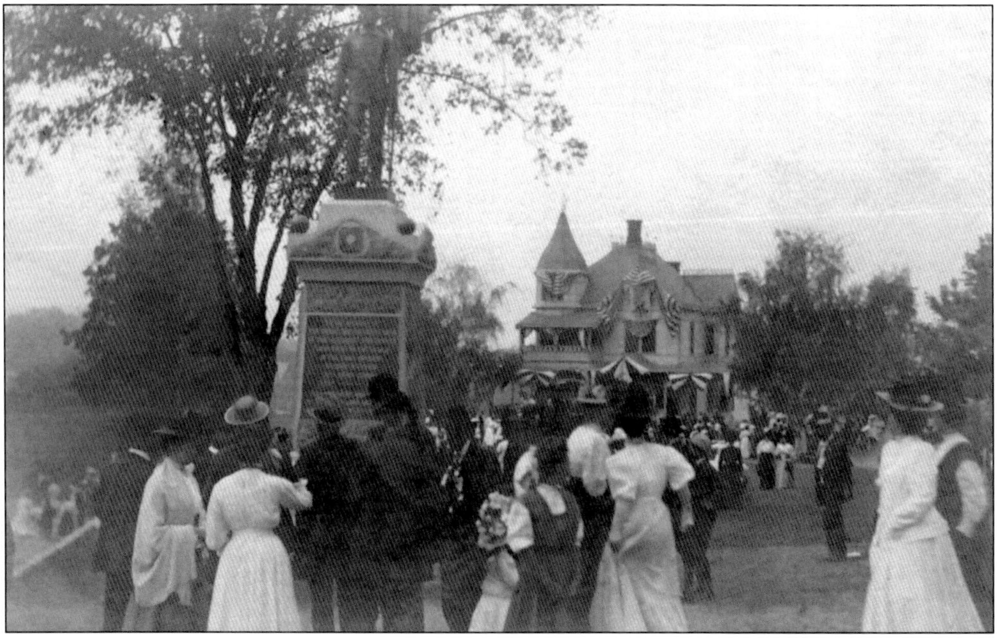

Aaron Rhodes donated the land in front of his house to the town for a monument to Civil War veterans who served in the 156th Regiment of the New York State Volunteer Infantry. Rhodes himself served in the 20th Regiment. His brother, who served in the 156th Regiment, died in the war. This postcard shows the dedication ceremony for the monument, which was held on September 19, 1908.

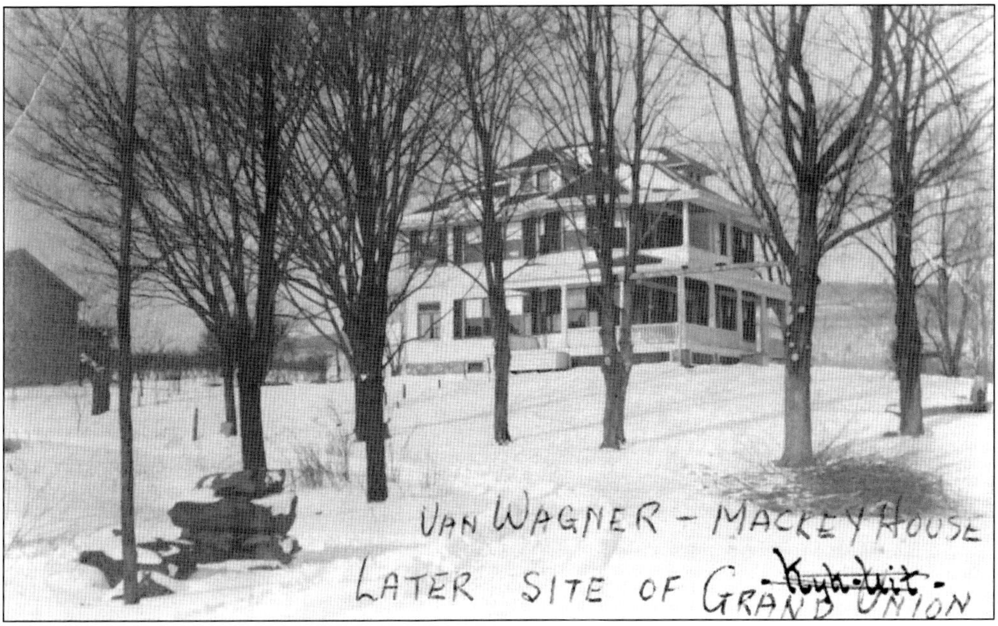

The present Highland Hose Company No. 1 firehouse on the corner of VanWagner Road and Milton Avenue is on the site of the VanWagner-Mackey home, which was named Kyk-Uit. A variation of that name, Kykuit, is the name of John D. Rockefeller's mansion in Westchester County. The name derives from a Dutch expression meaning "lookout" or "high place." (Courtesy of Town of Lloyd Historian's Office.)

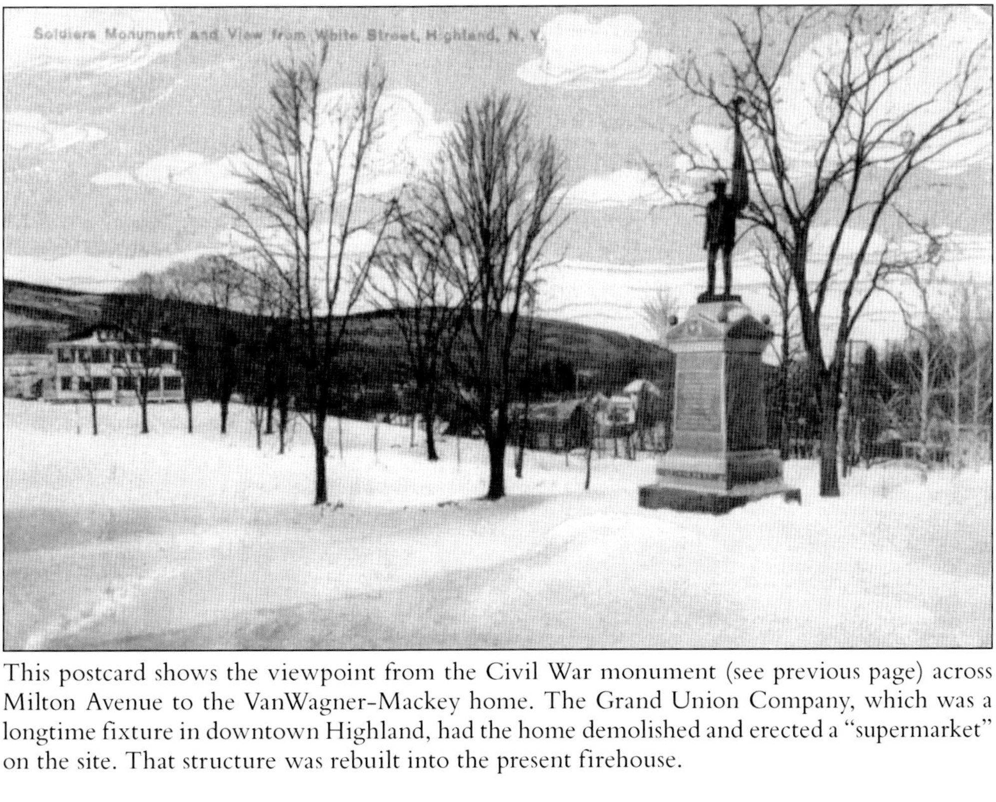

This postcard shows the viewpoint from the Civil War monument (see previous page) across Milton Avenue to the VanWagner-Mackey home. The Grand Union Company, which was a longtime fixture in downtown Highland, had the home demolished and erected a "supermarket" on the site. That structure was rebuilt into the present firehouse.

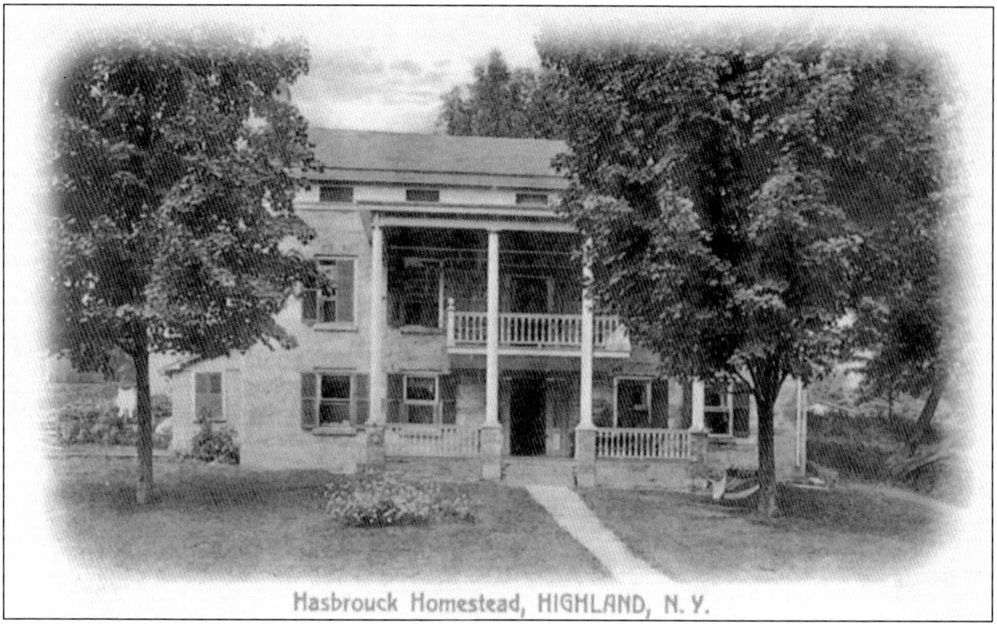

This landmark 1846 Stone House at 121 Vineyard Avenue was built by Col. Jacob Hasbrouck out of sandstone that was quarried behind the house. From the 1930s through the 1950s, it was the home of New York state assemblyman John F. Wadlin and his wife, town historian Beatrice Hasbrouck Wadlin.

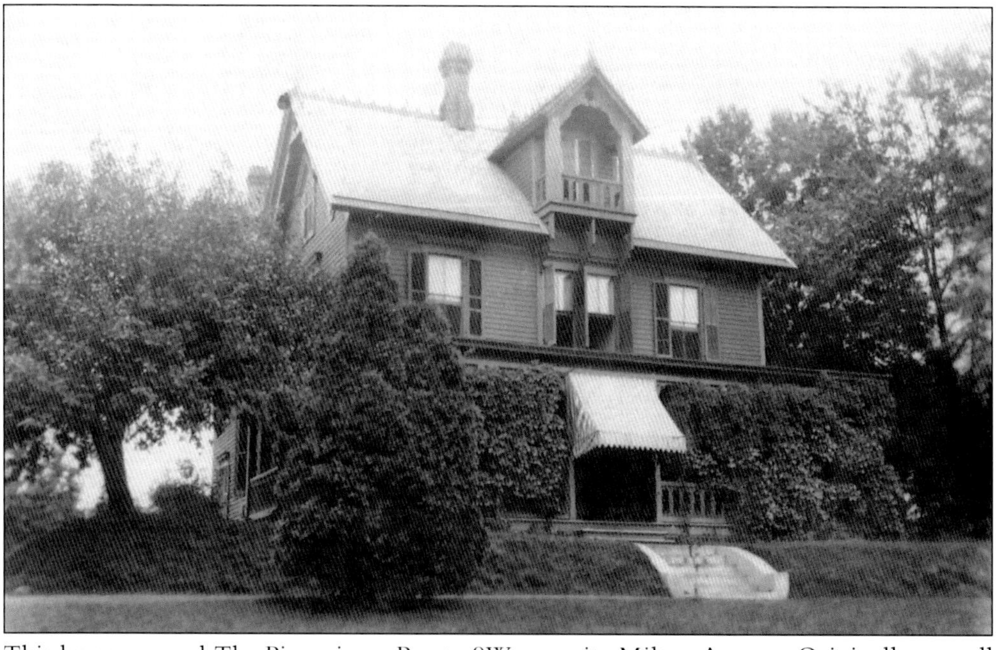

This house, named The Pines, is on Route 9W opposite Milton Avenue. Originally a small Hasbrouck home, it was enlarged in the 19th century. It has been home to two physicians and one minister. Although New York State abolished slavery in 1827, an 1829 deed to this property shows that it was sold for four milk cows and a slave girl.

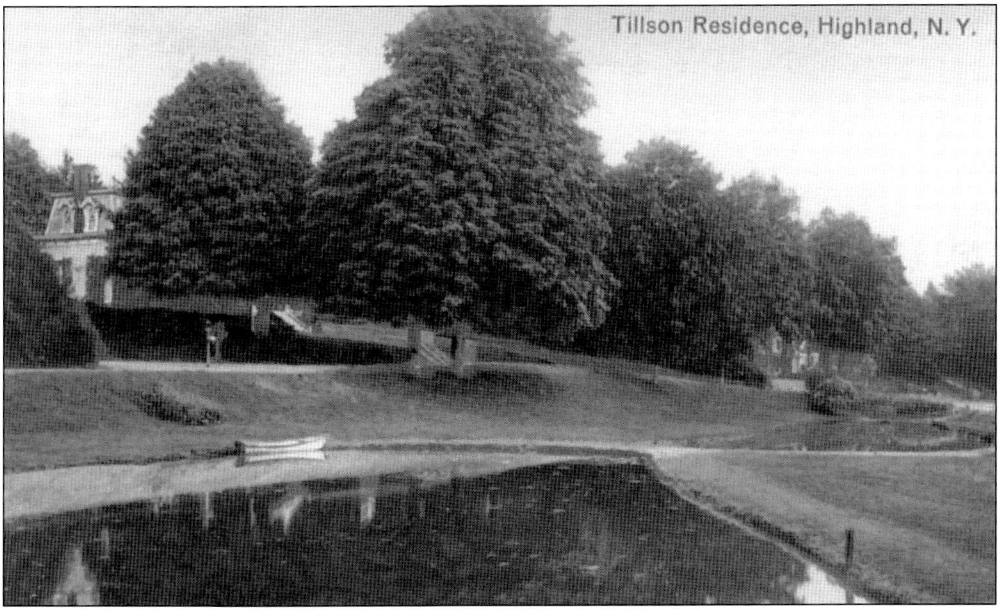

The Lakeledge estate is on Vineyard Avenue across from Tillson Avenue. The second-empire Victorian house seen at the left was built in 1873 by Oliver J. Tillson on the site of a house from the 1700s that had been destroyed by fire. To create the artificial lake seen in the postcard, Tillson rerouted Vineyard Avenue and diverted water from the Twaalfskill Creek. Tillson's orchards, located behind the house, were among the first in Lloyd.

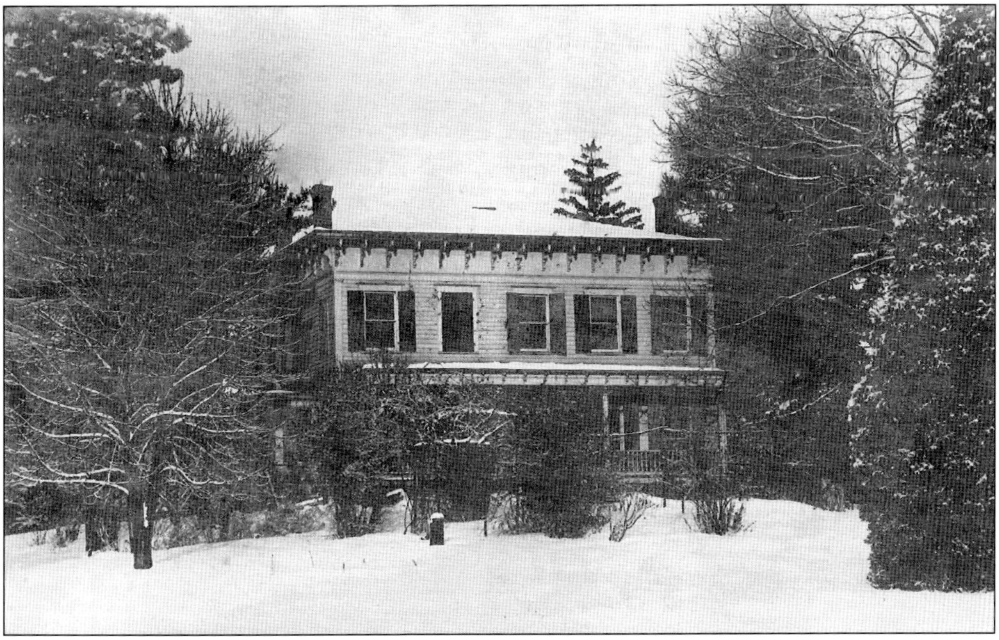

The Ezekiel Elting House is off of Route 9W, between Tillson Avenue and the Hudson Valley Rail Trail (formerly the Central New England Railway), and was built about 1845. It was later the residence of Clarence Elting (born 1860) and, still later, contractor Eugene Ossie, who built many substantial edifices in the 20th century, including the former Highland High School on Main Street (now the middle school).

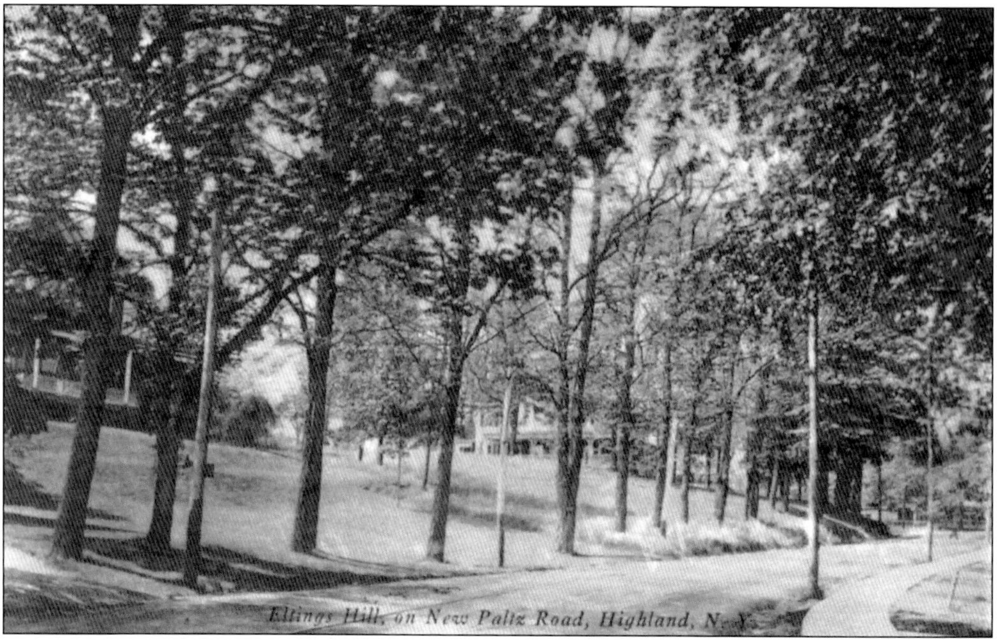

Located on the New Paltz Turnpike (now Main Street in Highland), Elting's Hill was the farm of Highland's founder, Philip Elting. On the right in these two postcards, partially obscured by trees, is the homestead that Elting built in 1817. It was donated to the Adonai Lodge No. 718 Free and Accepted Masons in 1951 and became a Masonic temple. A historical marker has been placed in front of the site by the New York State Department of Education. On the left is a home built for the Elting family in 1897, now the Michael Torsone Memorial Funeral Home. The above photograph is the older one, taken before the stone wall was erected.

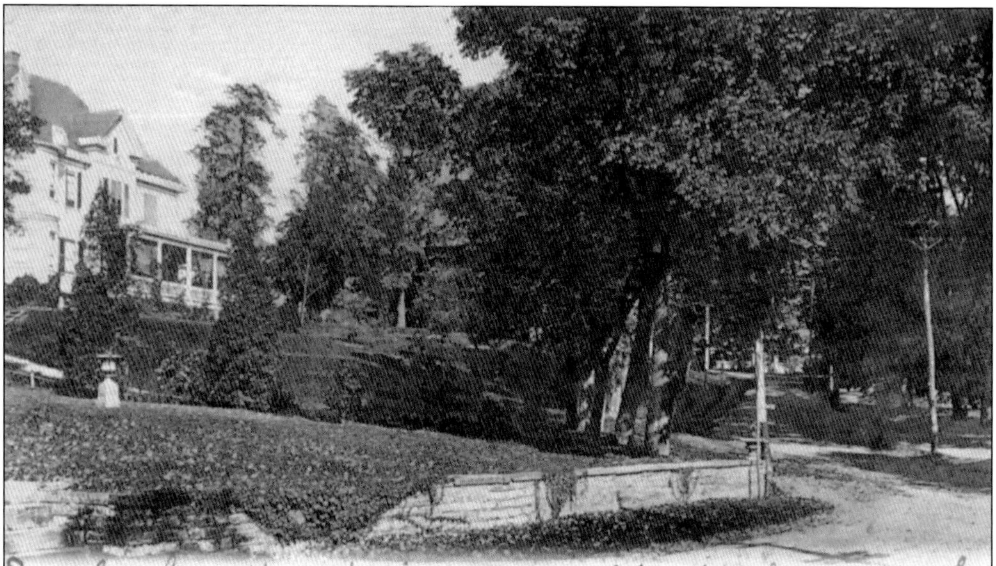

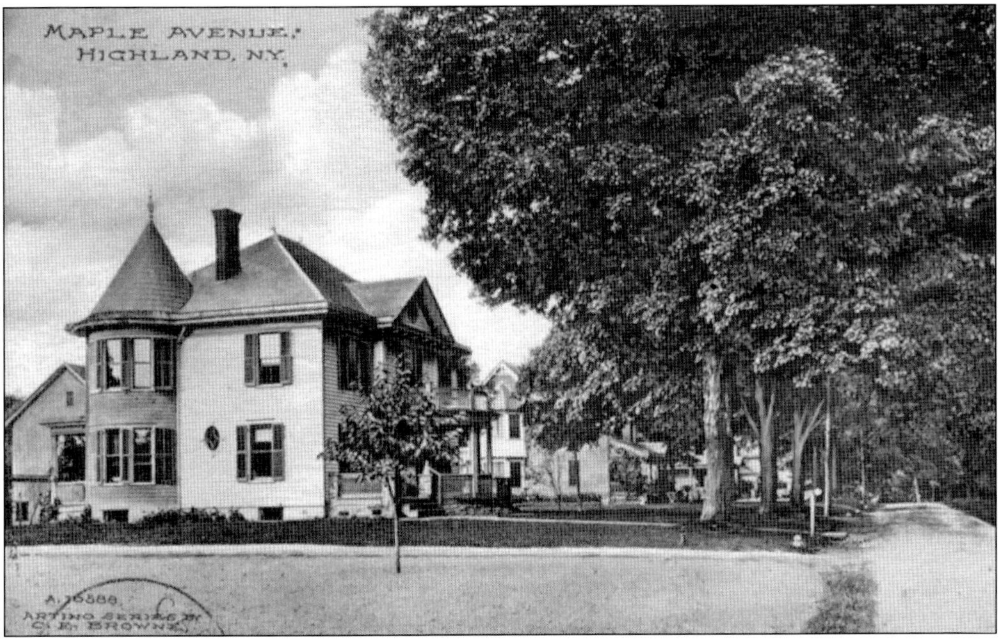

Maple Avenue was the original route of the New Paltz Turnpike from the river to Highland, and then westward to New Paltz. A private enterprise built the turnpike between 1820 and 1832 and collected tolls from users. When this postcard was published around 1900 by Highland photographer C.E. Browne, the turnpike had been rerouted to what is now River Road, which was built to accommodate trolley cars.

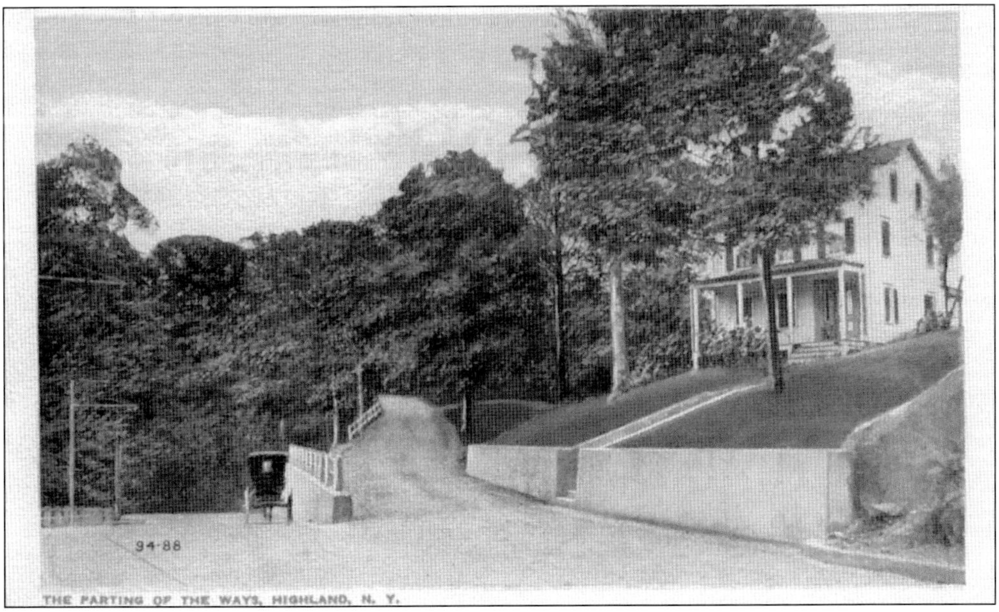

The western intersection of the old turnpike (Maple Avenue) and the new turnpike (River Road) was dubbed "The Parting of the Ways" by a creative postcard publisher. Note the trolley tracks and overhead wires on the left. A tollbooth stood farther west, and the toll for a one-horse wagon was 3¢. After the trolley started to operate in 1897, tolls were no longer collected from horse-drawn vehicles.

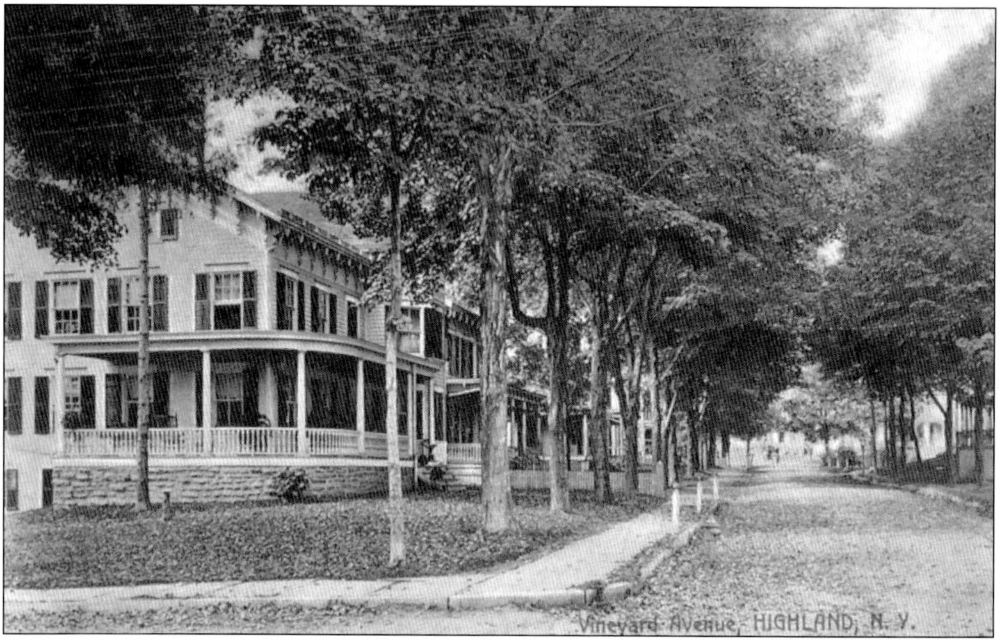

Vineyard Avenue—the principal street in Highland, and probably the longest one—also was constructed by a private enterprise, the Highland and Modena Turnpike Road Company, organized in 1866. Originally called the Modena Turnpike, its name changed to Main Street when it got to downtown Highland. The section that paralleled the Twaalfskill Creek immediately southwest of Highland became known as Willow Way because it was lined with weeping willow trees. The name Vineyard Avenue came into use after numerous vineyards were planted to supply the factory of Schuhle's Pure Grape Juice Company (see pages 40–41). Postcards of street scenes sold well, and the homes on Vineyard Avenue provided ample subject matter. Note the hitching posts for horses in the above photograph.

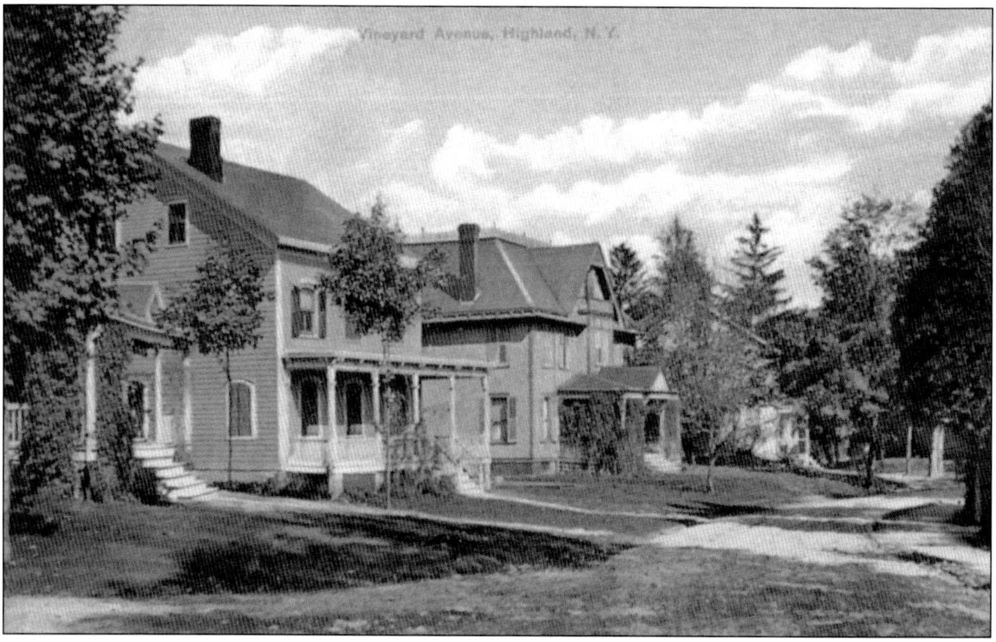

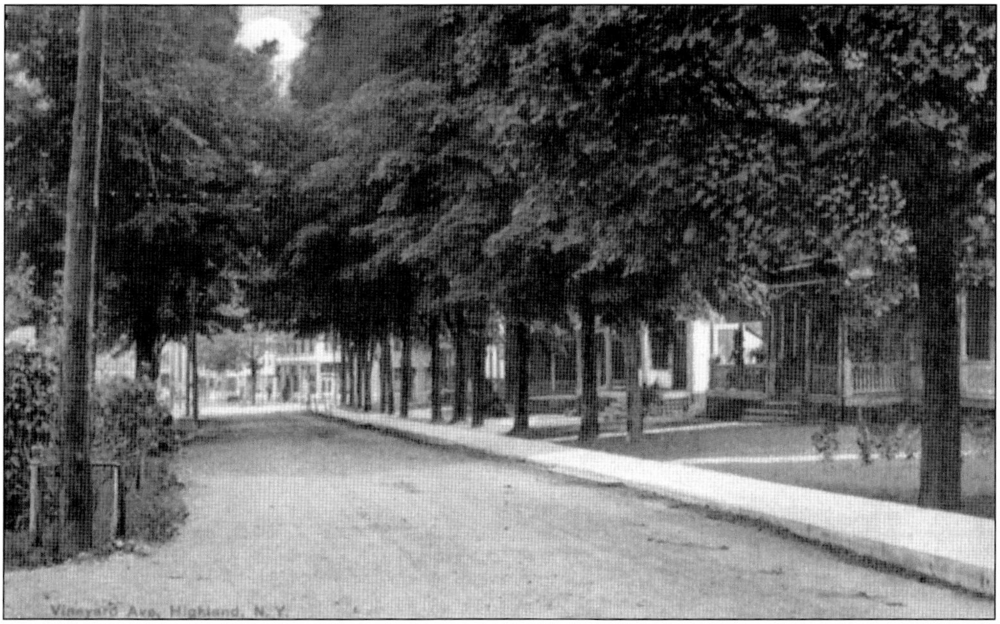

Highland street names have changed over the years. After the name Vineyard Avenue caught on west of the village, the street that is called by that name today in the center of the downtown business district was still called Main Street. Mapmakers decided that Vineyard Avenue ended and Main Street began at the intersection with Church Street. The downtown street that is called Main Street today was part of the New Paltz Turnpike and went by that name. In the above postcard, one is looking toward Highland from the west, and the Kenilworth Building (now a pizza shop) is seen in the distance. Further west of the village, in the postcard below, the neat sidewalk and smooth (but unpaved) road shown above have turned into a footpath and a road full of ruts.

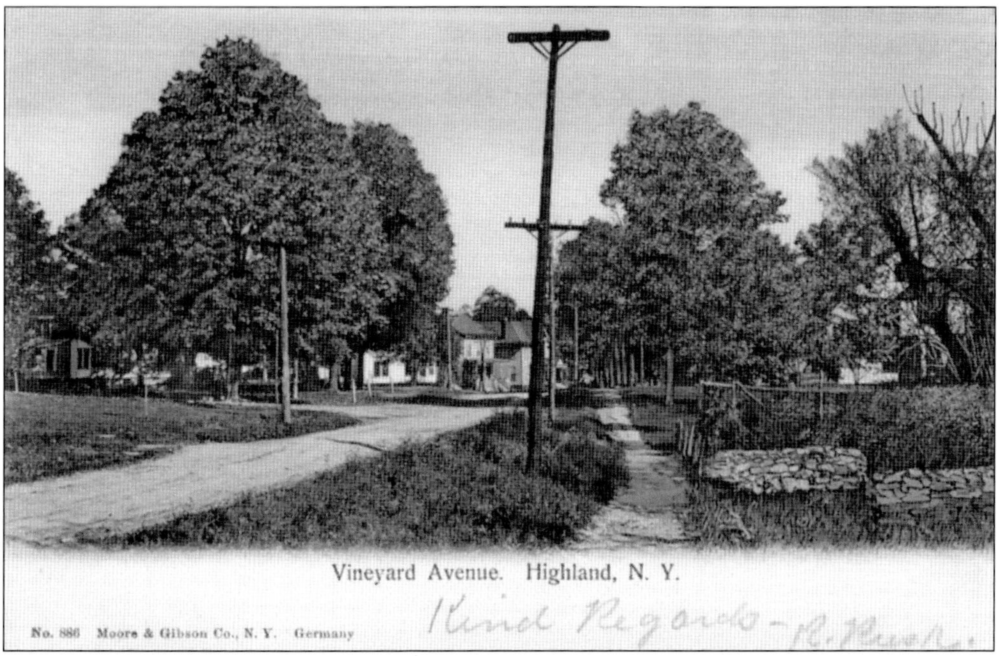

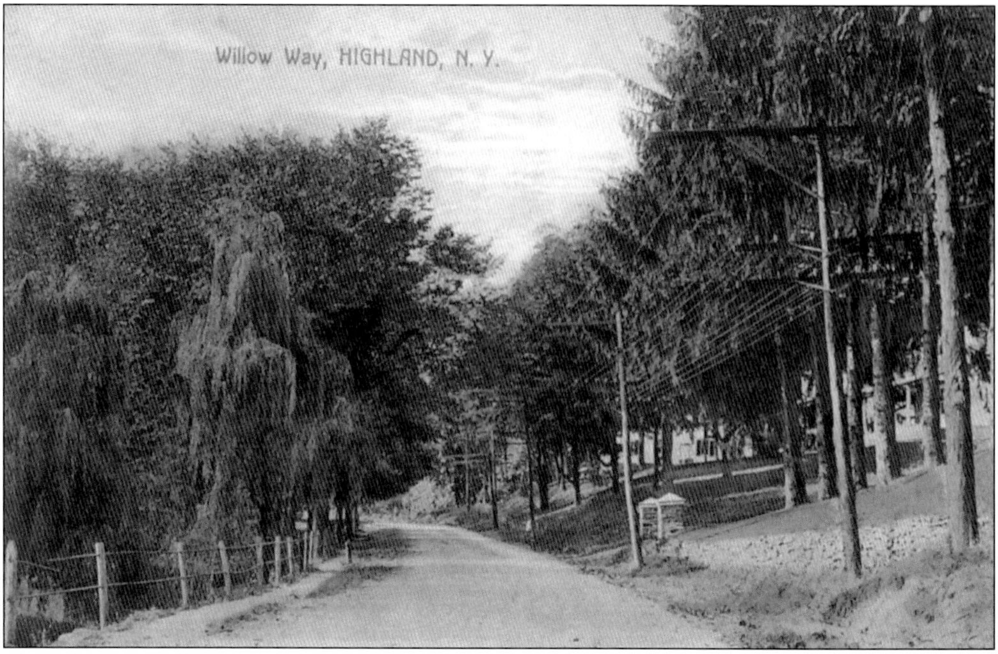

Still further southwest of Highland, the Willow Way part of the Modena Turnpike (near Tillson Avenue) must have been considered to be a very scenic area, judging by the large number of postcards that were published showing views of it. The railing on the left side in the postcard above has been replaced by a concrete wall to protect pedestrians and vehicles from going into the creek that runs alongside the road. The stone wall, pillars, and homes in this photograph make it easy to identify its location today. Willow Brook, now called Twaalfskill Creek, was also named for the willow trees. The bridge seen below was for pedestrians.

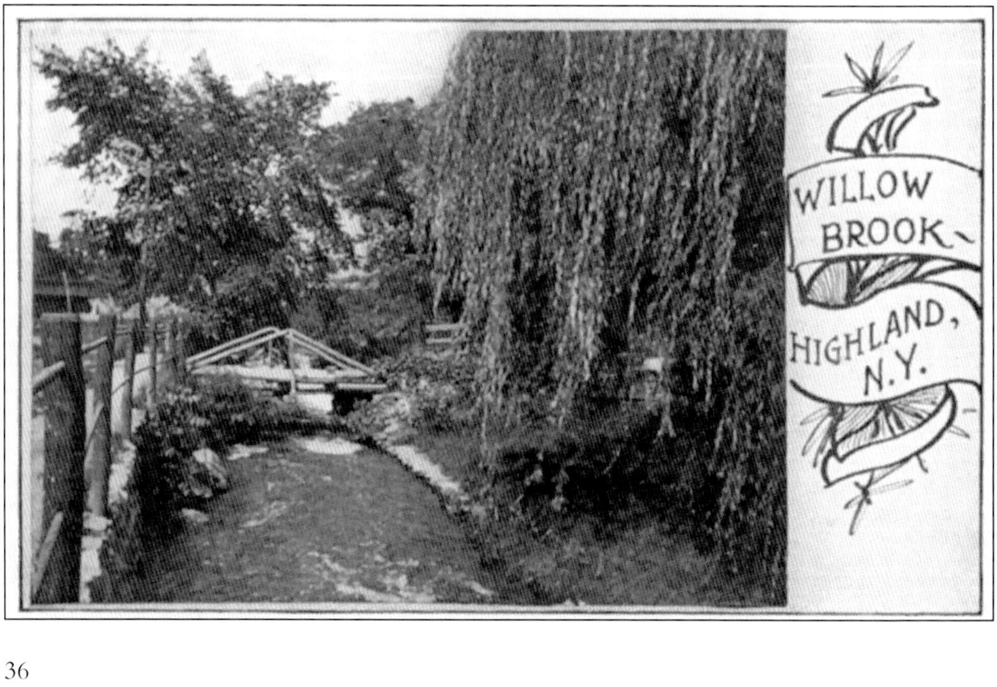

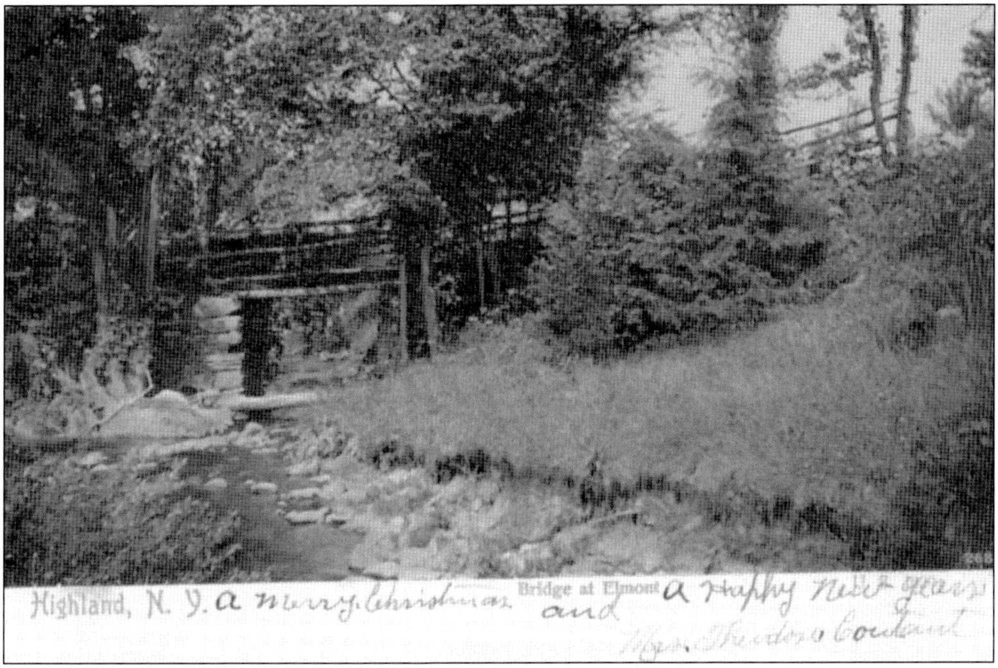

The "Bridge at Elmont" in the above c. 1900 postcard is believed to be the original bridge that carried Tillson Avenue over the Twaalfskill Creek. It is a wooden bridge on stone abutments. In the later postcard shown below, which was postmarked in 1922, the wooden structure has been replaced by a design that closely resembles the bridge that is still there today. This bridge may soon be gone, too, as the town wants to reconstruct the entire intersection of Tillson and Vineyard Avenues. Also shown in this view is a dam that the Pratts built to regulate the flow of the Twaalfskill because of a water-powered sawmill they operated at their lumberyard downstream. (Below, courtesy of Town of Lloyd Historian's Office.)

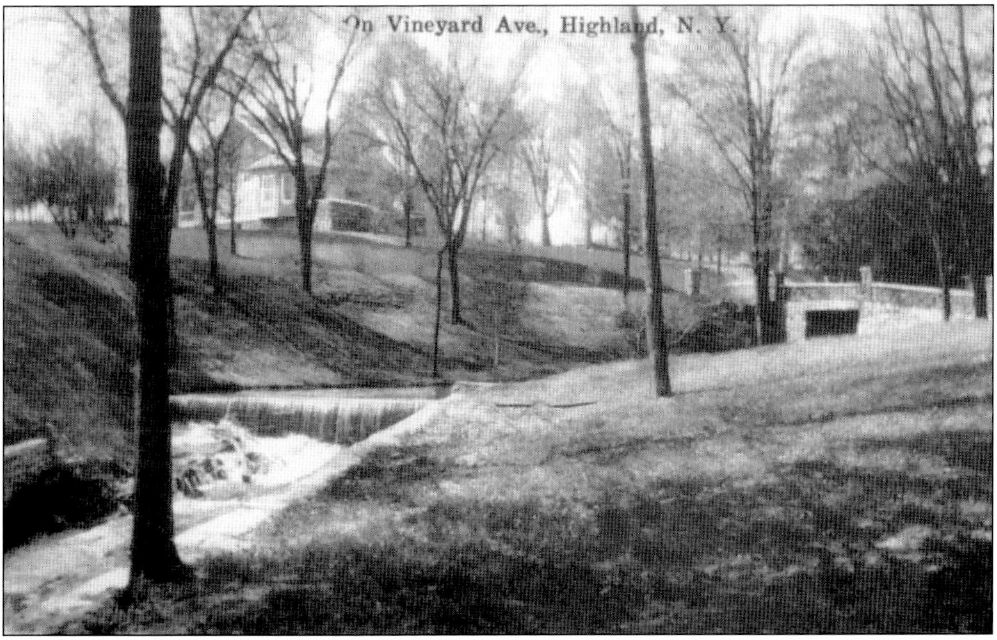

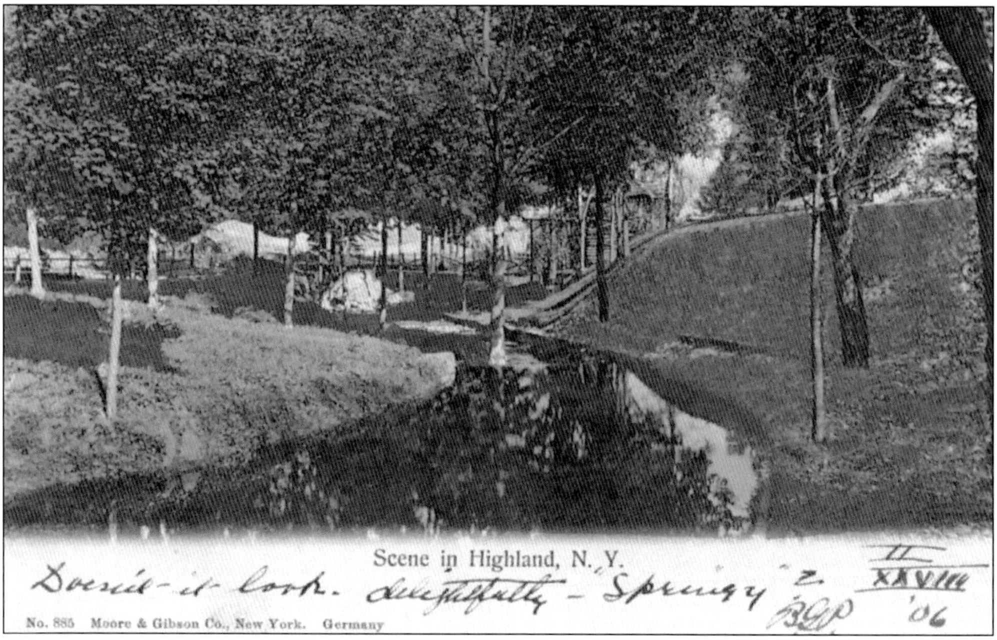

The above image of the Twaalfskill looks from the bridge over Tillson Avenue toward a footbridge that leads to the Pratt estate, west of the George W. Pratt and Sons' lumberyard. In 1906, the writer commented, "Doesn't it look delightfully 'Springy'?" In the postcard below, the footbridge leads to a summerhouse or gazebo. The house behind it on the left was occupied by George W. Pratt Sr. and, later, by his son George W. Pratt Jr. Another son of George W. Pratt Sr., Harcourt J. Pratt, built the Edwardian home that is seen in the background to the right of the gazebo. He went into politics and was elected to the New York State Assembly and, later, the US Congress. His home has been refurbished as the Inn at Twaalfskill Bed and Breakfast.

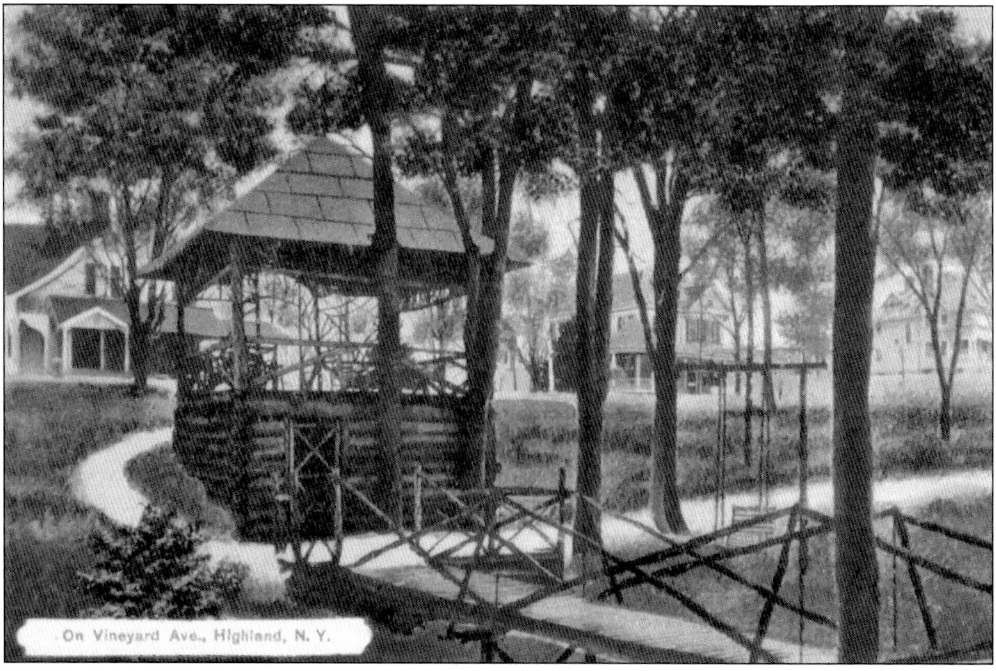

Two

Agriculture and Rural Life

Agriculture was and is the most important business in Highland's history. Agriculture shaped everything, from the skills people developed to settlement patterns to the love of the land that has kept so much of the town rural. Farming in many ways made possible the area's number two industry today—tourism (which is discussed in the chapter on tourism and recreation). Some attractions include apple blossoms in the spring, "you-pick" orchards in the fall, and yearlong great hiking with fabulous views of rolling hills, magnificent forests, and untouched wetlands. In addition, these two businesses—agriculture and tourism—both continue to contribute to the rural life.

The indigenous people were farming in the Hudson Valley long before Hudson's 1609 voyage. An apple orchard is said to have existed along what is today South Street at the western edge of the township. Many of the Italian craftsmen and laborers who came to help build the stone piers for the Poughkeepsie-Highland Railroad Bridge found the land in Highland much to their liking. They bought or rented farms and started growing currants, apples, pears, peaches, and grapes in great abundance. Highland's businesses were initially clustered along the waterfront for access to transportation. Then, beginning in the mid-1800s, commerce spread out from the Hudson. There were destructive fires at the waterfront business establishments, and new small centers of commerce that included stores, churches, post offices, and schools flourished as more and better roads made it easier to visit, live, or work at a distance. As rural life became less isolated, more and more families chose it, whether or not they actually farmed. In some instances, the family's main income was as boardinghouse proprietors, enabling the owners to enjoy the rural life without the difficulties of nature's fickle side.

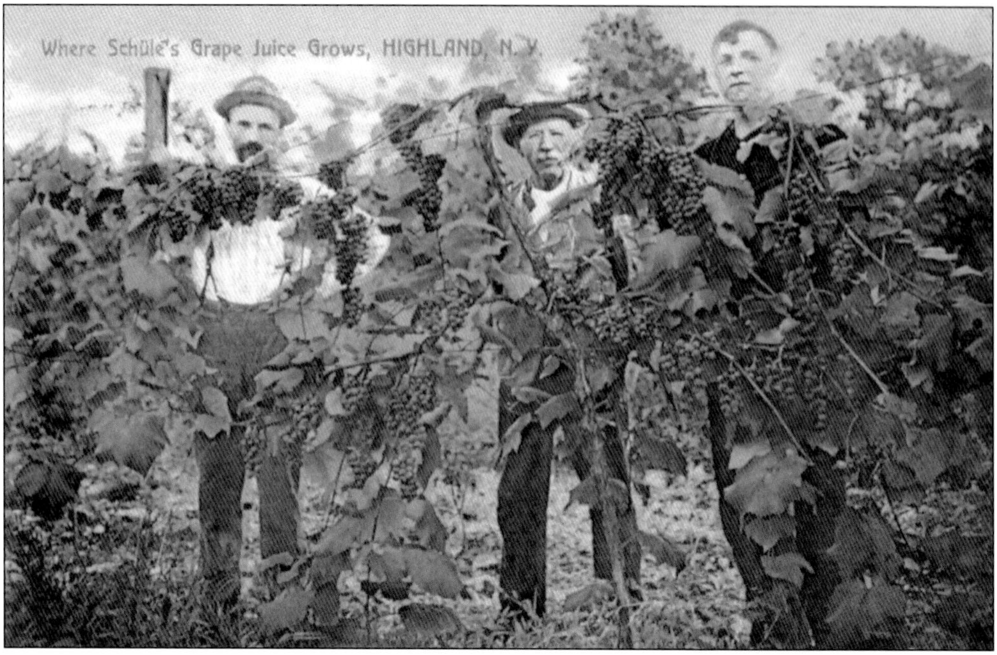

Possibly no other business grew as large in Highland as Schuhle's Grape Juice Company. In the above image, founder John Schuhle appears on the left. After selling the business in 1919, John experimented with making vegetable juices. He died in 1936 and is buried in the Alan Sheeley plot of the Loyd Cemetery; his grave has no marker.

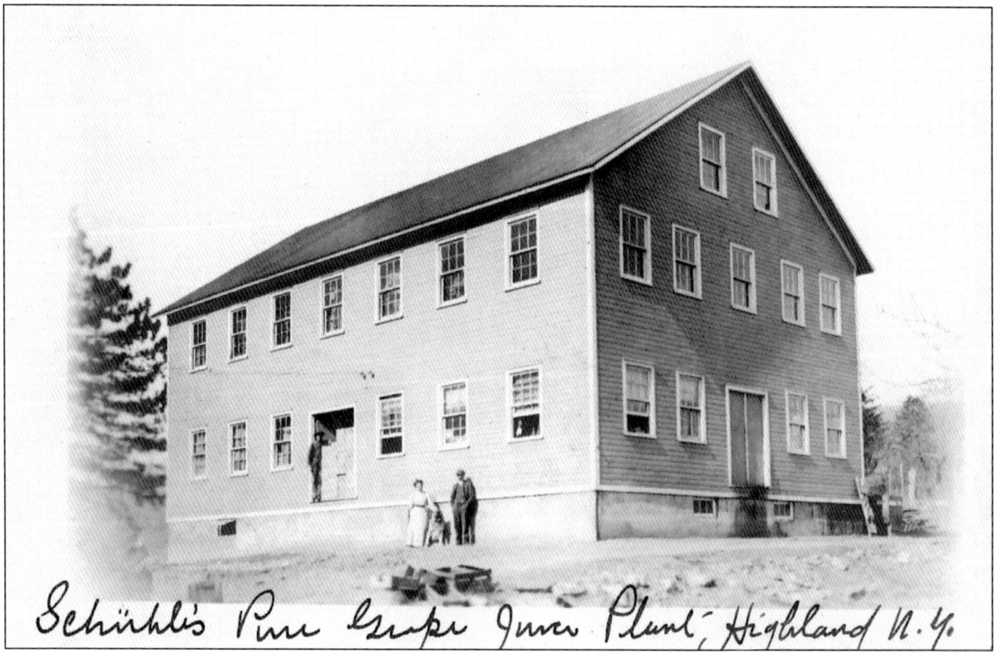

Schuhle's Highland business was born in 1906, when he visited the area to purchase grapes for his business in Connecticut. He moved to Highland, and in 1907, the family built the first of its Highland plants, as commemorated in this postcard. The Schuhle family added to the building in 1911 and again two years later. (Courtesy of Gail Russell.)

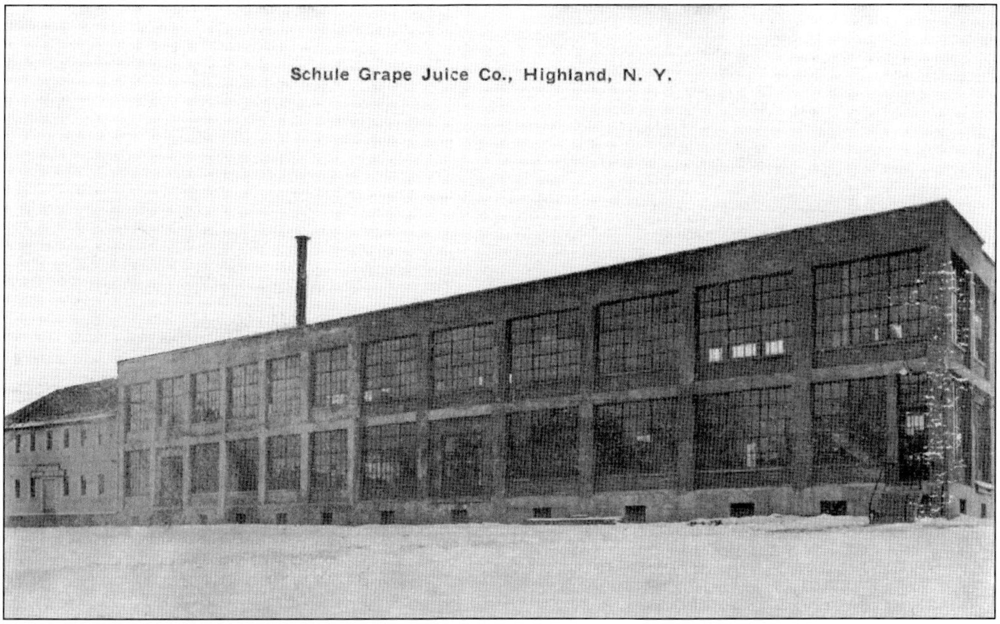

The postcard above shows the Schuhle factory after the 1911 addition. Schuhle sold it to the United Drug Company in 1919. In 1951, it was sold again to the Rexall drugstore chain, which used it to manufacture chocolate syrup. The smell of chocolate percolated throughout the village. Later, a printing company used the buildings for storage. The facility stands on Vineyard Avenue south of Reservoir Road. (Courtesy of Town of Lloyd Historian's Office.)

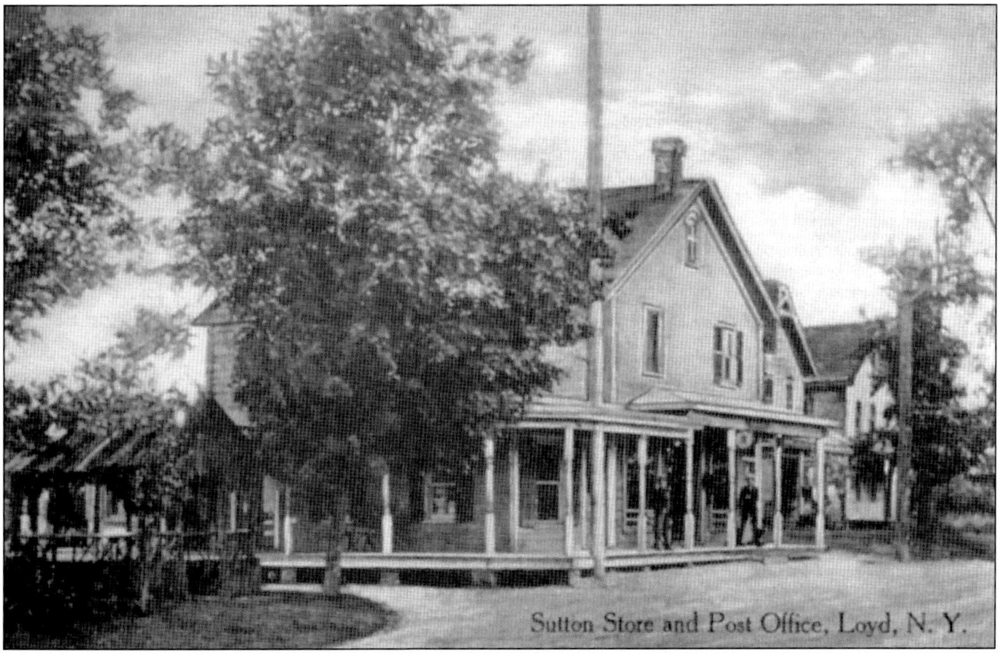

The hamlet of Loyd was on the New Paltz Turnpike and the Highland-New Paltz trolley line, where today's Route 299 crosses Old New Paltz Road. Sutton's provided the all-important services: store and post office. The trolley power station was located nearby in what is today the No. 2 Highland Fire Station.

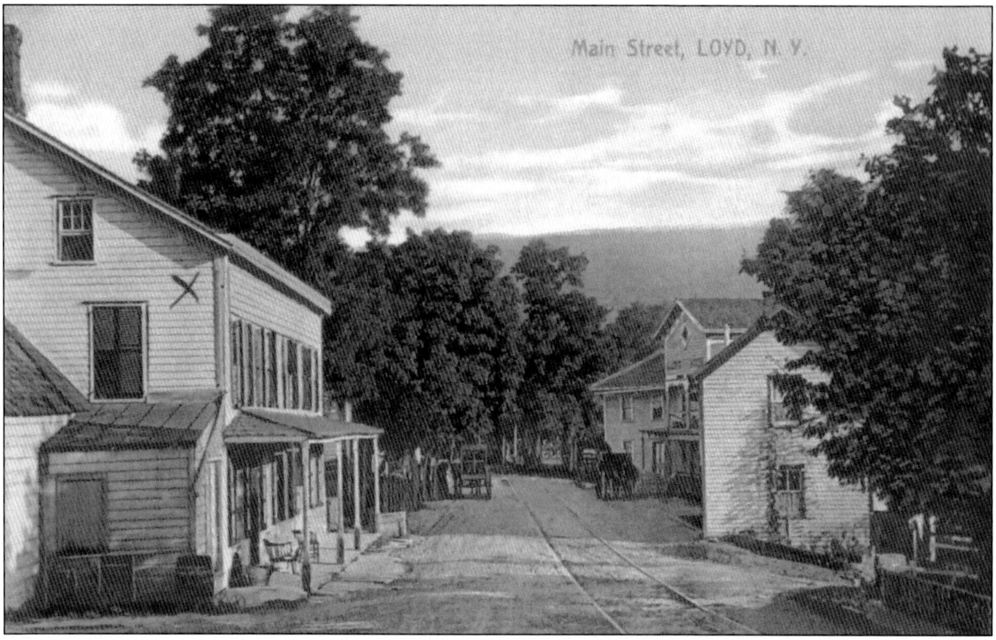

On the Highland–New Paltz trolley line, Centerville (noted here as "Loyd") was a popular place for farmers to shop without going into the villages of Highland or New Paltz. Centerville was at the intersection of Riverside Road, Pancake Hollow Road, and the New Paltz Turnpike. The postcard below, which was mailed in 1911, tells that the sender, Mrs. Churchill, was the owner of the store marked with an *X*. Illinois Mountain is in the background. A 1913–1914 ledger from Churchill's store was recently donated to the Town of Lloyd historian's office, and it shows transactions of credit-using customers. Many family names entered in the ledger are found today on streets and buildings. A large number of the customers' descendants still live in Highland.

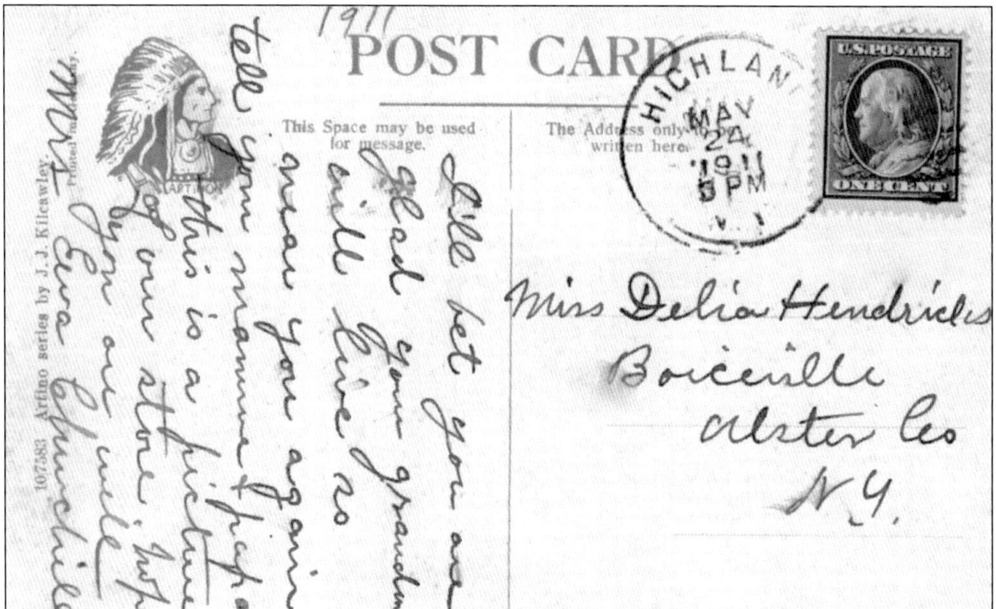

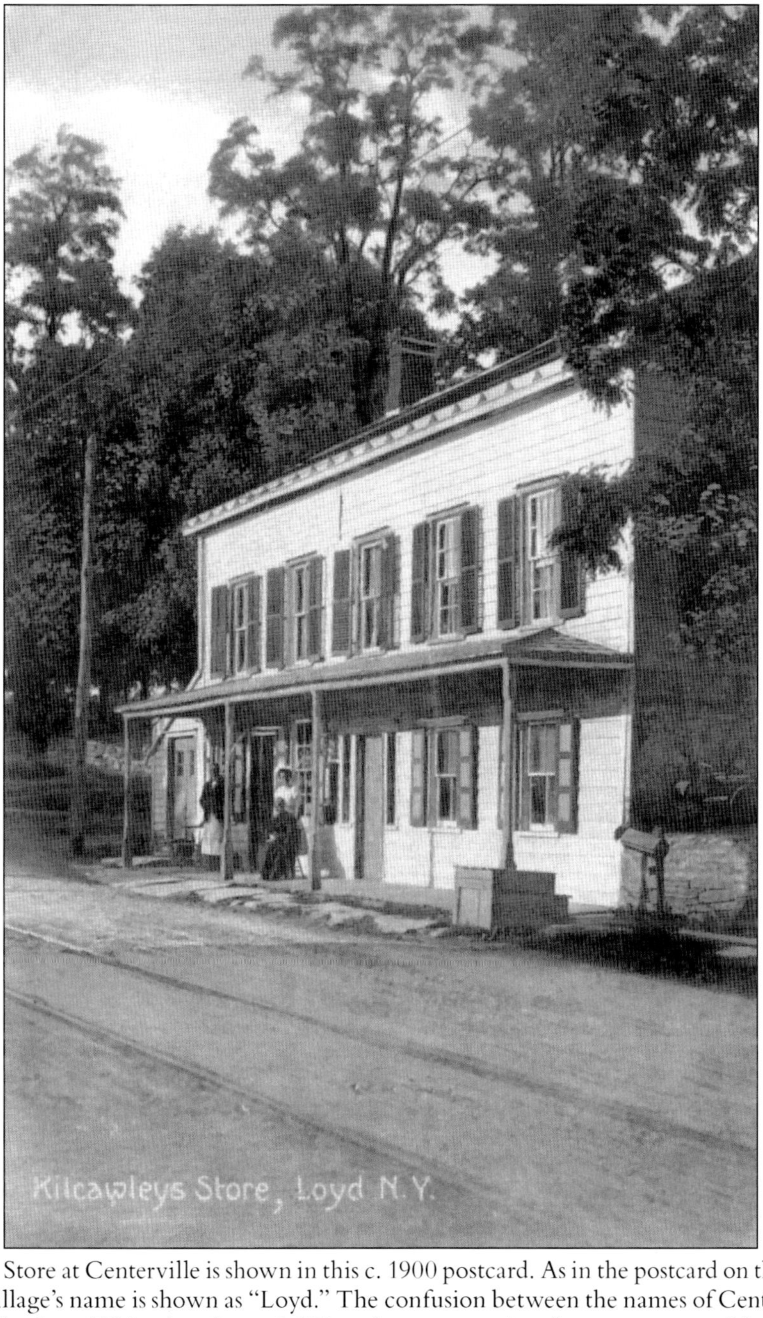

Kilcawley's Store at Centerville is shown in this c. 1900 postcard. As in the postcard on the previous page, the village's name is shown as "Loyd." The confusion between the names of Centerville and Loyd dates back to 1894, when James J. Kilcawley was appointed as postmaster of the Loyd post office. That post office then moved from its original location in Loyd to Kilcawley's Centerville store, but it moved back to Loyd again in 1905. After the Kilcawleys, the store was operated by B.C. Churchill and his wife. It belonged to Frank Madlener in the 1950s. When the Town of Lloyd seceded from the Town of New Paltz, Centerville was the site of a meeting where Lloyd's government was organized on May 6, 1845. The meeting took place at Lyman Halstead's hotel, not far from the site of this store. That building is still standing today and is now an apartment house. It is marked with a New York State Educational Historic Marker.

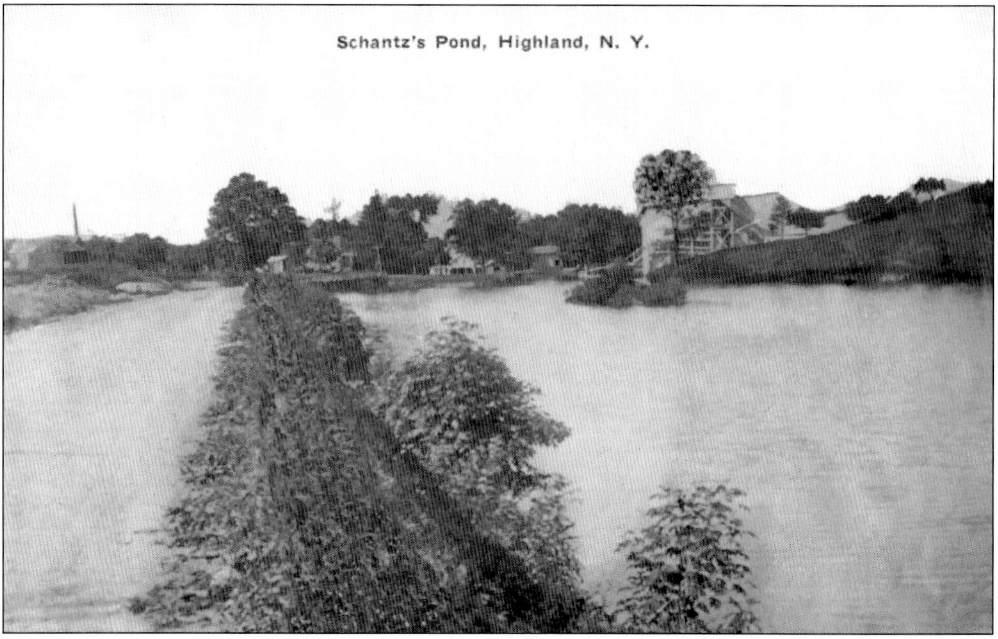

Above, the icehouse at the north end of Schantz's Pond is visible on the right side of the card. Vineyard Avenue Ice, started in 1913 by John Valentino, cut 15,000 tons of ice a year from Schantz's Pond, just south of the town center of Highland. For 5¢, one could buy 25 pounds of ice, and 100 pounds of ice cost 15¢. The family delivered some of the ice in a horse and wagon to the Chodikee Lake establishments. Route 44/55 runs along the left of the postcard. An ice customer would place the sign below in his window. The iceman would deliver the amount of ice indicated at the top of the card, in this case 10 pounds. The nine-by-nine-inch card is bright yellow with red printing, easily visible from the road for the benefit of the iceman. (Above, courtesy of Gail Russell.)

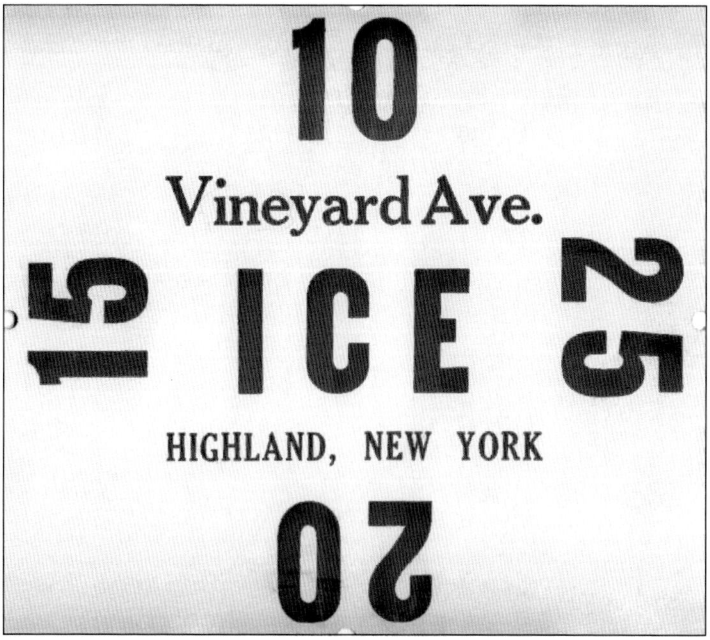

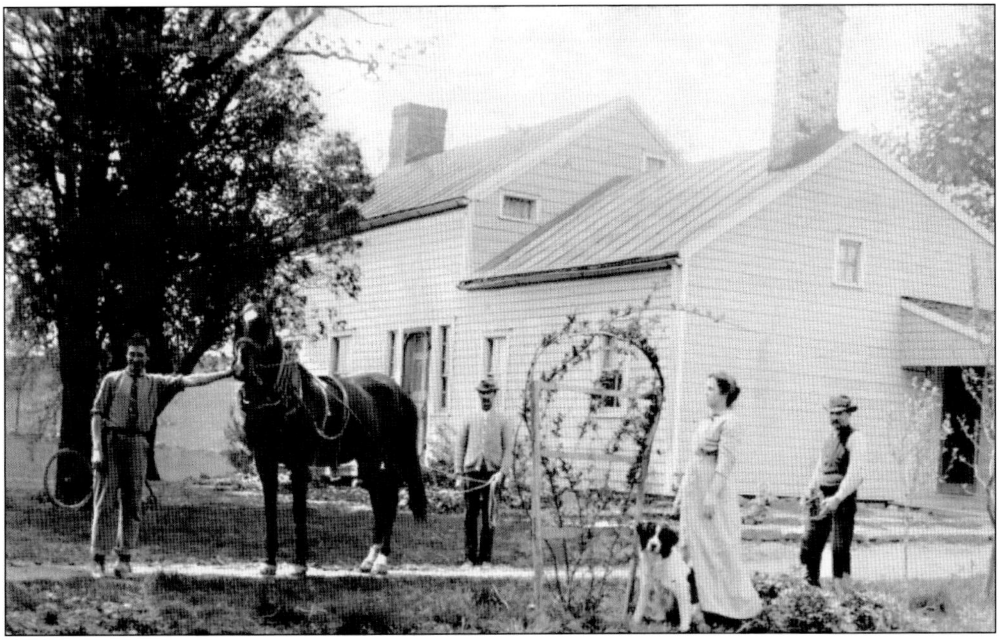

The Kisor family's wealth is apparent by their lovely house, dog, and horse. Their farm was on Kisor Road, off what is now Route 299. Kisor Road was later the location of Hotel Ottaviano, which is pictured on page 62 as Hotel Grandee. (Courtesy of Town of Lloyd Historian's Office.)

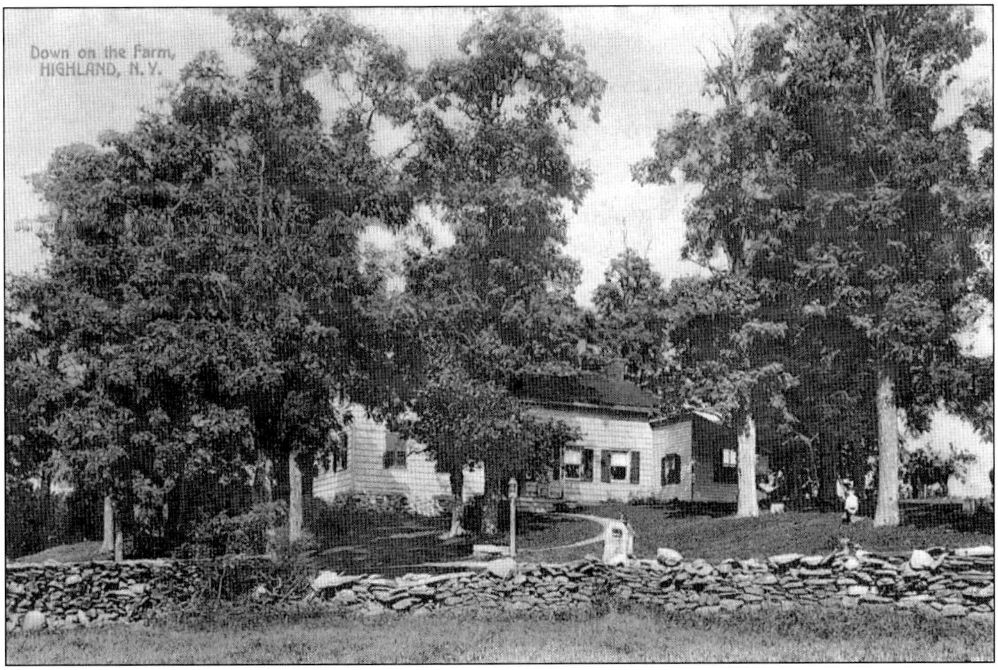

This card was sent from Highland to New York City at 7:00 a.m. on August 1, 1912. (Imagine a post office open at 7:00 a.m.!) Note the high stone walls. Highland was and is a rocky place. Farming required the removal of stone, and making walls was a practical and attractive use for the stone. The card's simple message reads, "Best regards. J.H.M." The location of this farmhouse is unknown.

Agnes Weiler, nicknamed "Bobbie," left Germany with her parents in 1936 and immigrated to Palestine, which was under British mandate. Her father, David Weiler, had been a lawyer in Munich. In Palestine, they became farmers, growing and selling vegetables and eggs. Agnes married Herbert Wolf; in 1948, the Weiler-Wolf clan, now with the Wolfs' two young children, came to America. They left Palestine on the last ship before the State of Israel was declared. They would not have been able to leave the country after that because Israel was immediately at war with all of its Arab neighbors. They purchased a farm on Plutarch Road, and to make ends meet, they offered rooms and three meals a day for a farm vacation. Agnes's mother did the cooking, and David Weiler, according their grandson Albert, provided "the shmooze." Charges for all of this were $5 per day. Bobbie Wolf wrote of her life in Germany, immigrating to Palestine, and immigrating to the United States. She became a schoolteacher late in life and penned the play *A Man Under Her Bed*.

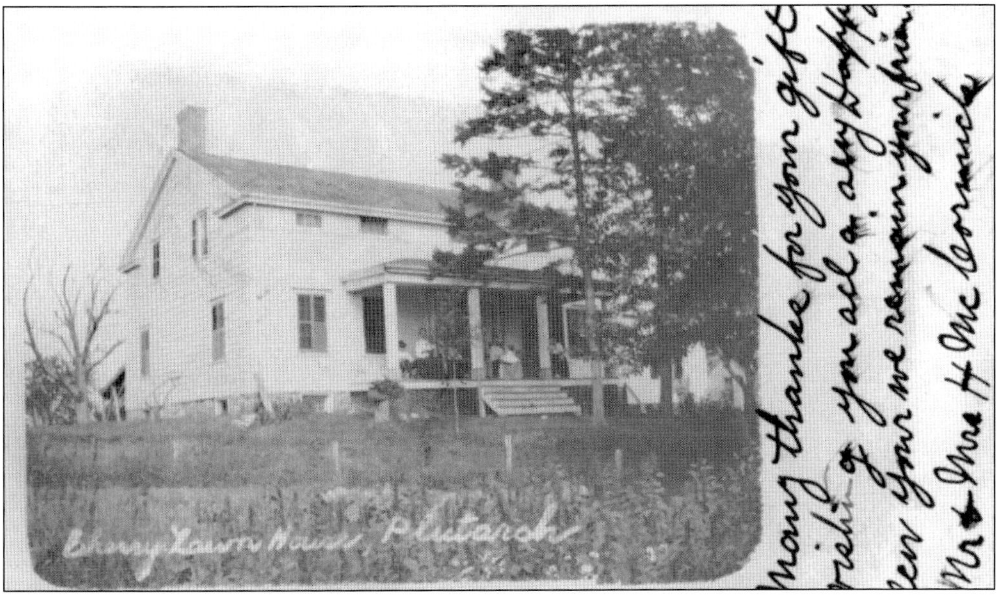

In the late 1930s, this home on North Eltings Corners Extension Road was purchased by Charles and Marie Buttennandt. Charles had been a butcher before buying this house, and he settled into farming, raising dairy cows and chickens. Their chicken operation became the most highly mechanized in Ulster County. (Courtesy of Town of Lloyd Historian's Office.)

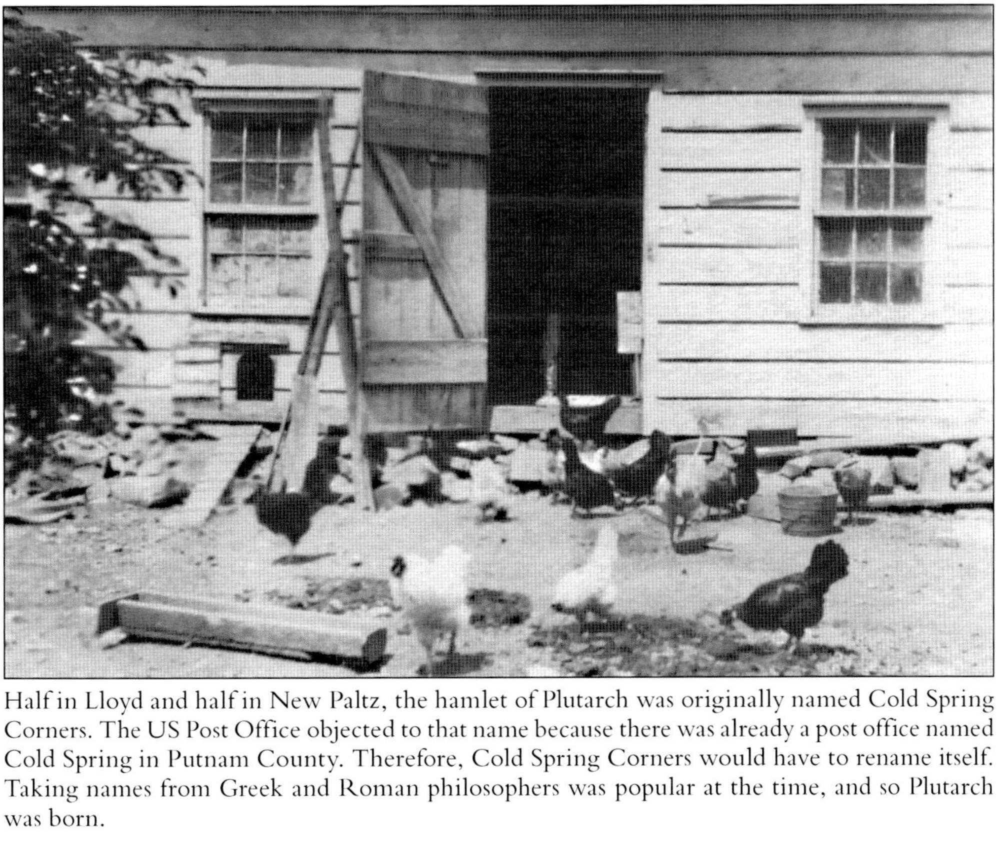

Half in Lloyd and half in New Paltz, the hamlet of Plutarch was originally named Cold Spring Corners. The US Post Office objected to that name because there was already a post office named Cold Spring in Putnam County. Therefore, Cold Spring Corners would have to rename itself. Taking names from Greek and Roman philosophers was popular at the time, and so Plutarch was born.

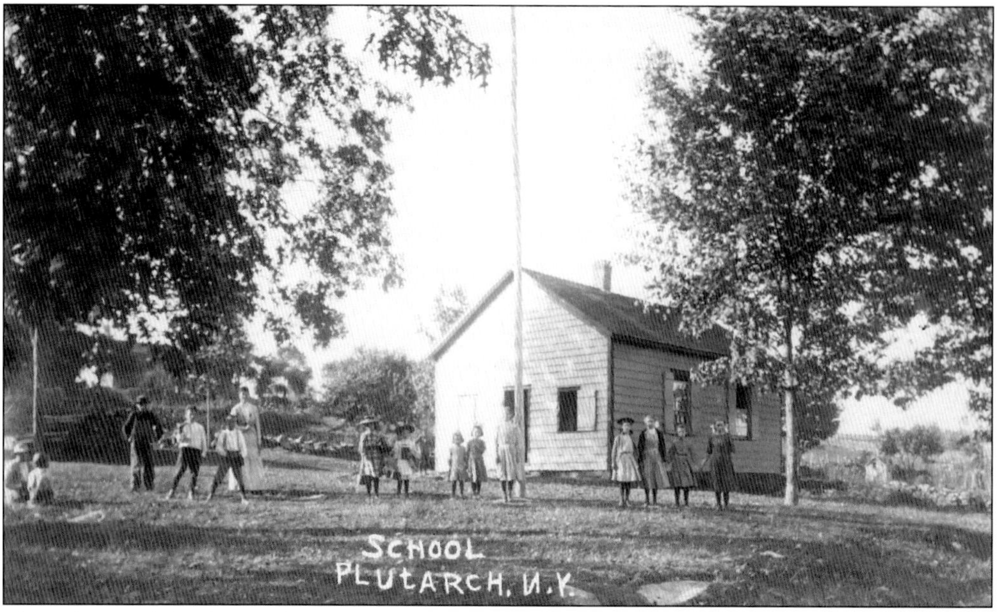

Plutarch Road divides the hamlet of Plutarch. On the Town of New Paltz side is the school, which today serves as headquarters for the Plutarch Sportsmen's Club. The school was heated with wood in a stove lovingly tended each morning by Emily Finkenstadt, who lived in the house next to the school. The school had boys' and girls' outhouses. This card reads, "This is our old school house where I learned my small bits of worldly wisdom. Oct 20, 1910."

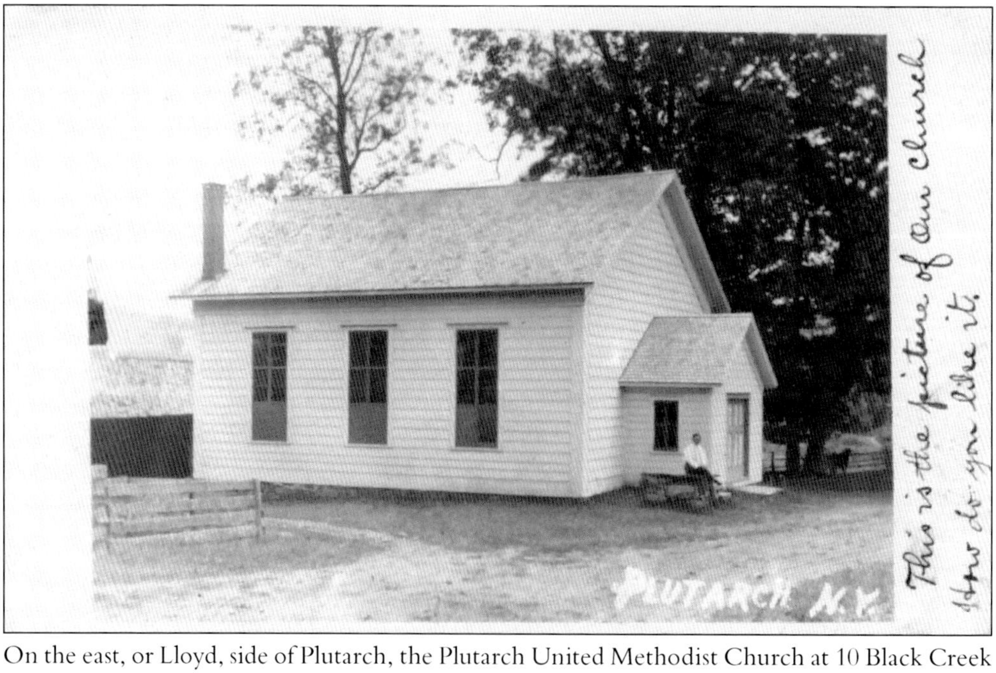

On the east, or Lloyd, side of Plutarch, the Plutarch United Methodist Church at 10 Black Creek Road was a spiritual and social agency for the area residents. Its Strawberry Festival was one of the biggest family social events and drew hundreds from miles around. Local women prepared their best dishes and helped to raise funds for the small institution. Festivals are still held one day every June. Church services are held Sunday evenings at 7:00 p.m.

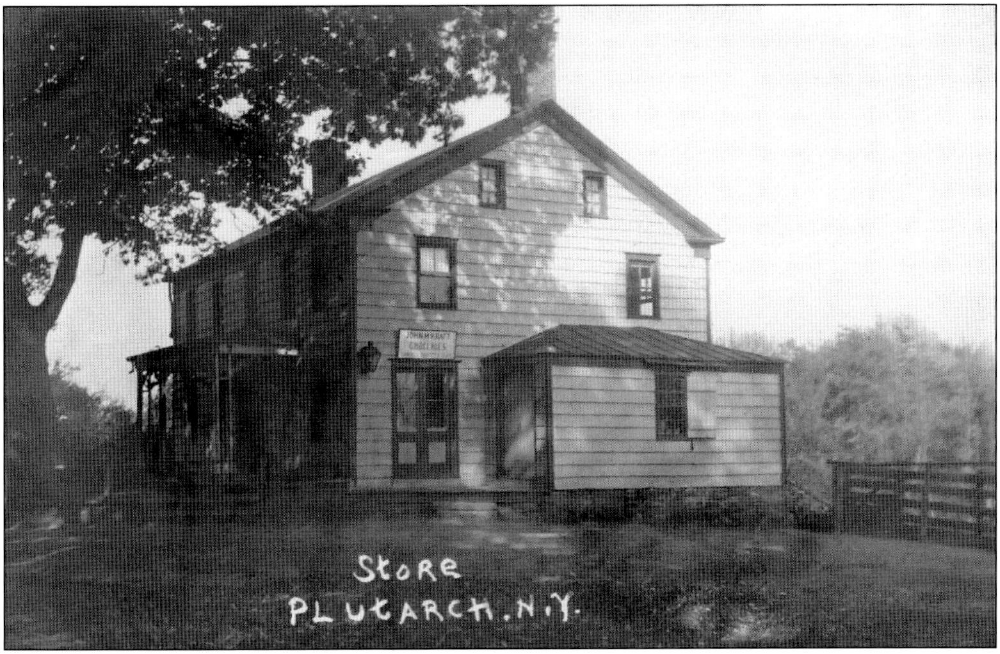

Also on the Lloyd side of Plutarch Road, this house still stands today. At the time that the postcard was made, the building served as the Plutarch Store. Later, it added the Plutarch post office in the small addition shown here. "This is our house and store," writes the sender in 1910.

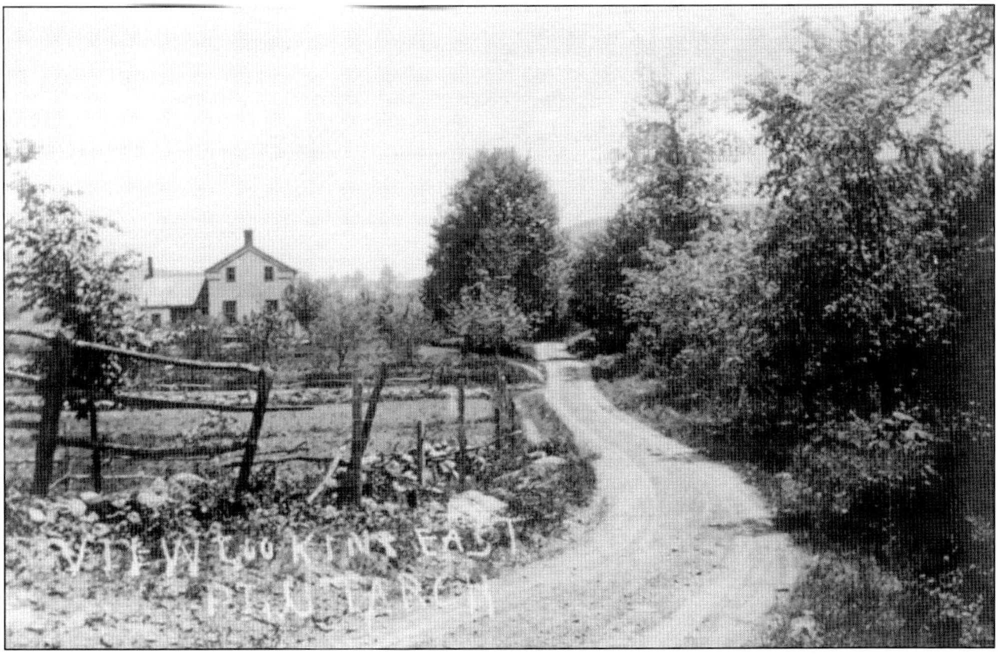

Nellie Lilberg's house on Black Creek Road in Plutarch still stands today. Lilberg is long gone, the road is paved, the fences are a memory, and the fields are now forests. Black Creek Road is on the Lloyd side of Plutarch Road. This image is looking east from the intersection.

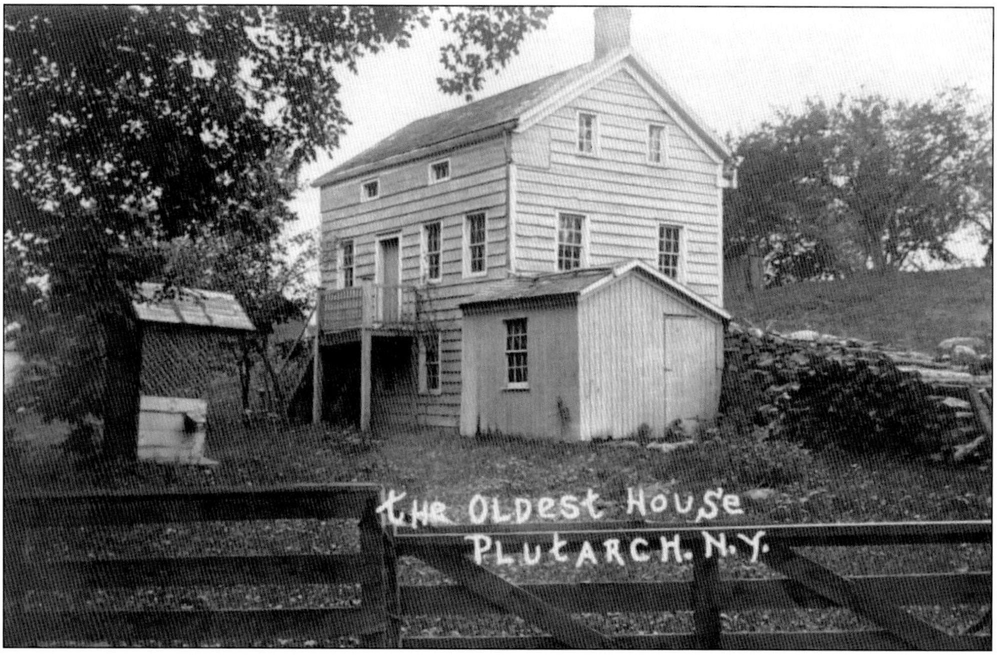

The oldest house in Plutarch is at the southwest corner of the intersection of Van Nostrand and Plutarch Roads. It looks very different today. Below is a view of the Plutarch Road intersection from Black Creek Road. The buildings are, from left to right, the blacksmith, the store and post office, and the United Methodist church. Probably the most distinguished person to have lived in the area was the world-famous walker Edward Payson Weston, who lived on what is now Weston Road (off Plutarch Road). His feats of walking incredible distances in record times were chronicled in every major national and international newspaper in the late 1800s and early 1900s. As with today's sports figures, he made his money with endorsements.

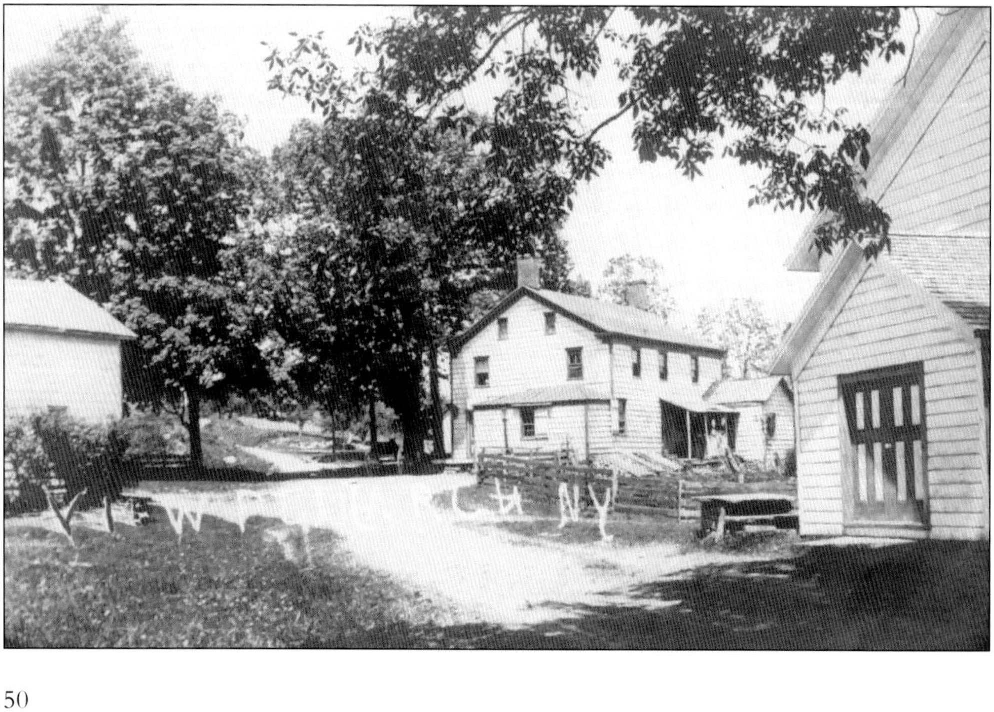

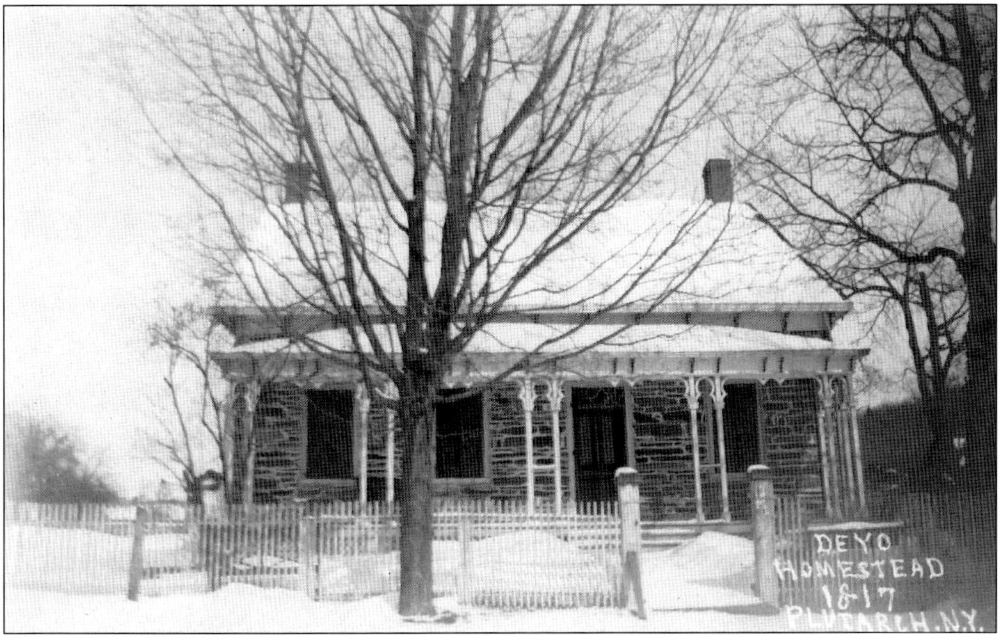

Still part of the Plutarch hamlet, but near the intersection of North Eltings Corners Road and Black Creek Road, stands the 1817 Deyo home. The Alessi family was the last to actively farm this land, and much of the land has been sold off and developed into many home sites. Today, the Deyo house looks very much the same as it does in this postcard, but now other buildings have closed in on it.

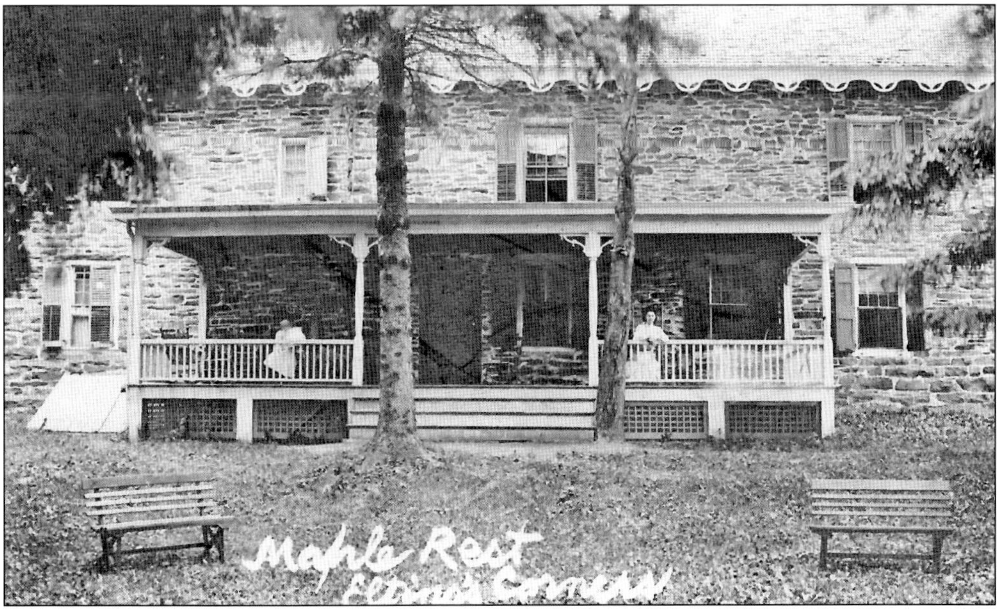

Maple Rest, built by Josiah Elting, was a lovely boardinghouse at Eltings Corners. It was a popular tourist destination located not far from the intersection shown on page 53. As with so many other Highland boardinghouses, it was on the trolley line. It burned down and was not rebuilt. This real-photo postcard dates from about 1905.

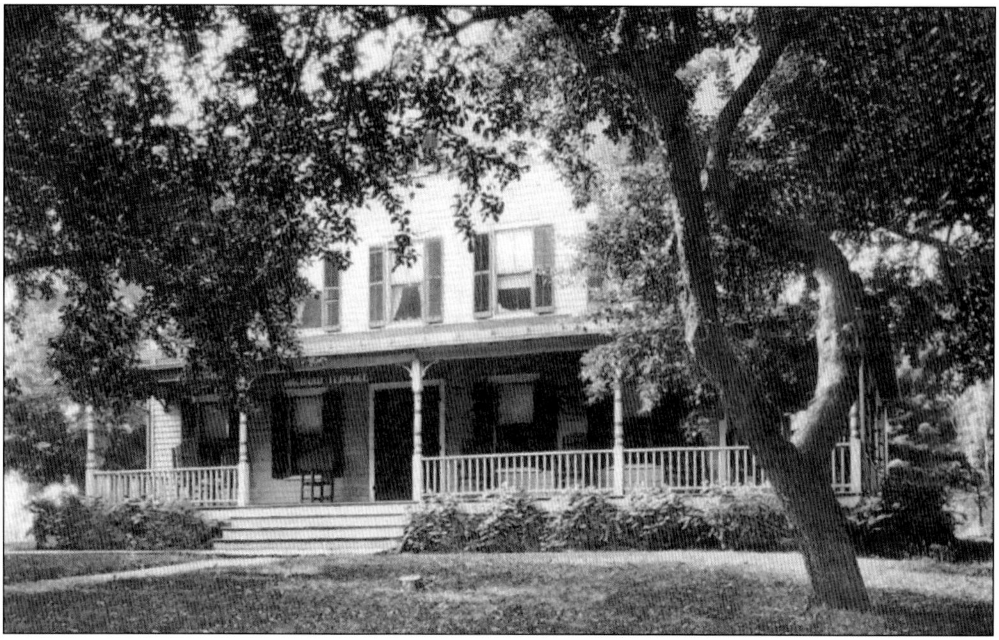

Orchard Terrace boardinghouse advertised itself as "on the trolley line." Transportation was an important consideration for drawing tourists. The house was later owned by the followers of Father Divine, a black charismatic leader in the 1930s. His followers had houses all over the United States. The building at Eltings Corners burned down in 1936.

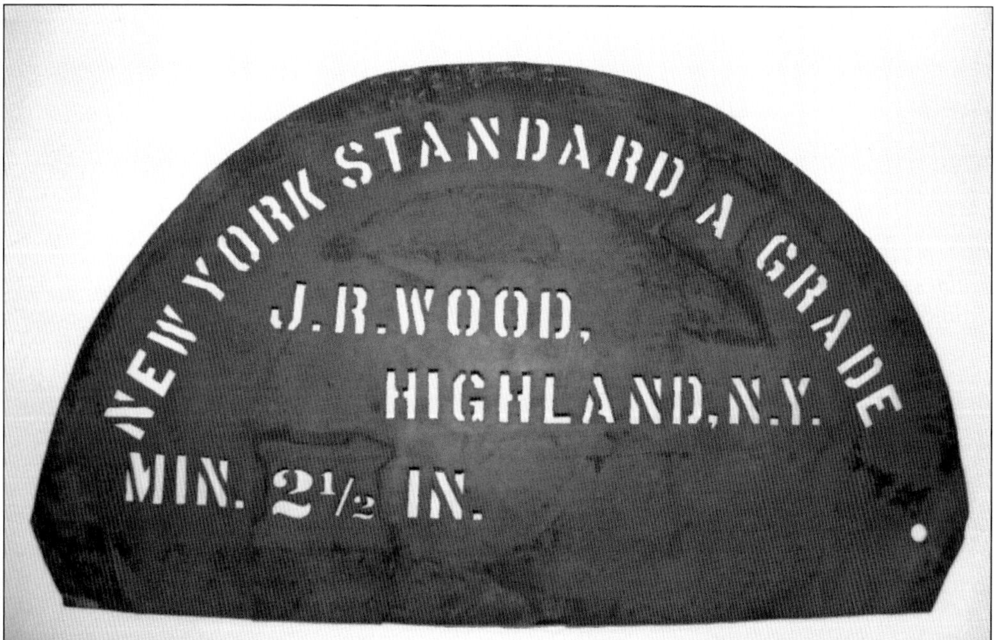

This tin apple-barrel template was used for stenciling the size and grade of J.R. Wood's fruit. It demonstrates the ingenuity of the time: the size (two and a half inches) and the grade (A) were changeable. Different grade and size apples could be marked for shipping using the same basic template. The template is about 14 inches across, just right for most barrel heads of the time.

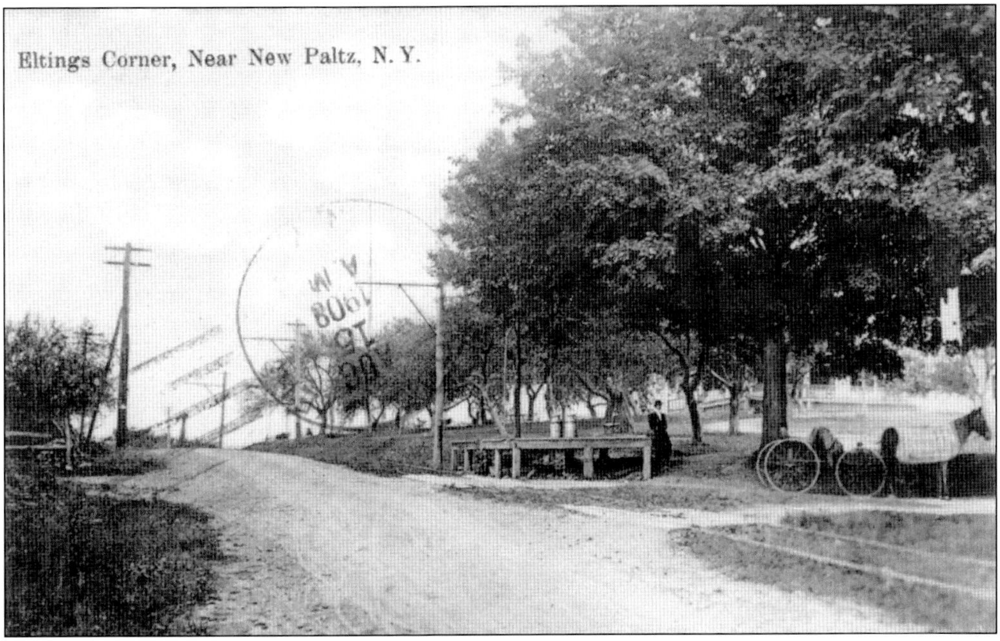

Eltings Corners Road, named for Josiah R. Elting, crosses the New Paltz Turnpike left to right on this postcard, which was postmarked Highland, August 15, 1908. The Highland–New Paltz trolley stop has some milk cans awaiting transport and someone waiting to pick up a passenger. Later, the intersection was called "Zannucci's Corners" for Joe Zannucci's Hardware Store and residence. Both buildings still stand. Behind the carriage is Orchard Terrace.

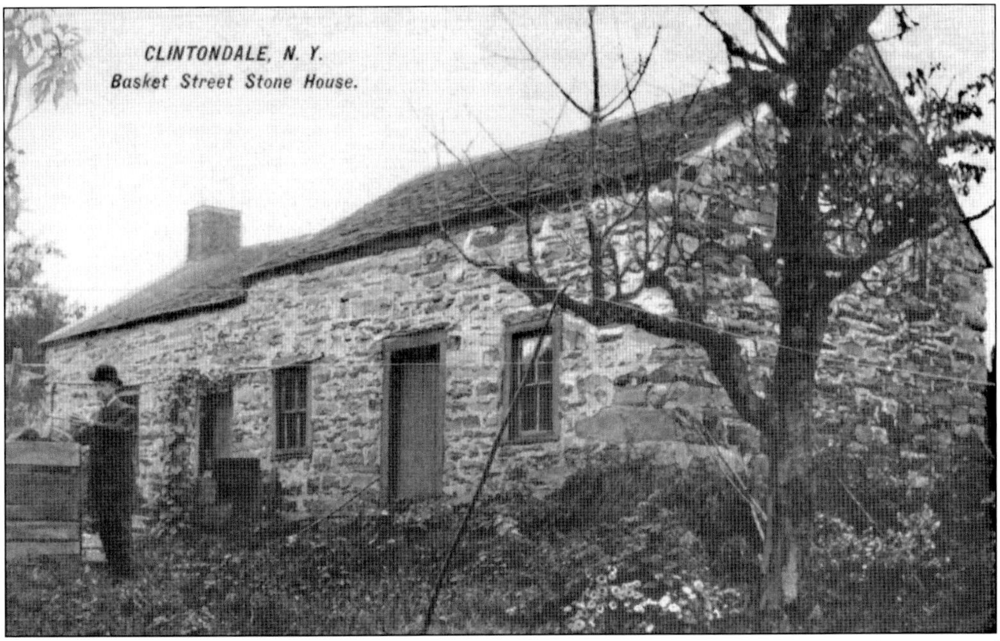

According to Beatrice Wadlin's *Times and Tales of the Town of Lloyd* (Highland), the Town of Lloyd historian's office has a basket made by native people that came from the Basket Street area. Other authors suggest that Basket Street was the site of a later basket-making group. The house pictured here was located on Basket Street near the intersection with Pancake Hollow Road.

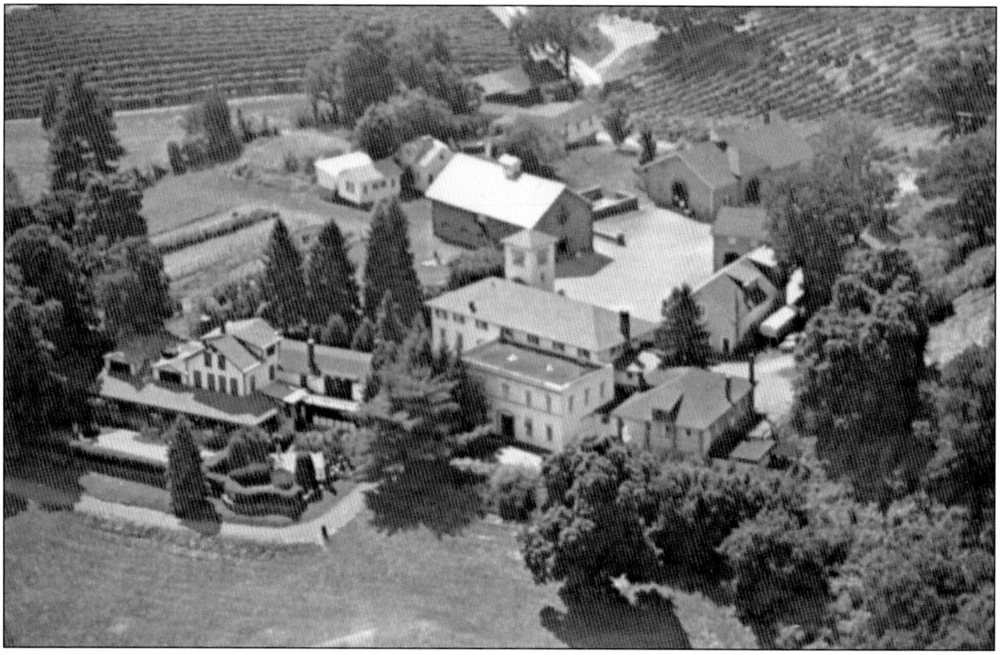

Located on a bluff above the Hudson River, Hudson Valley Wine Company's vineyards, buildings, and wine tastings were popular attractions. Reminiscent of a Tuscan village, it once hosted a World War II reenactment of the invasion of Italy by American troops. Located on Blue Point Road, it is currently closed. Owners are considering reinvigorating its history as a "wine village" with housing and shops on some of its acreage. The property is the burying place of Revolutionary War soldier Jonathan Tompkins. His family included four signers of the Articles of Association in 1774, and they owned the property at the time of the American Revolution.

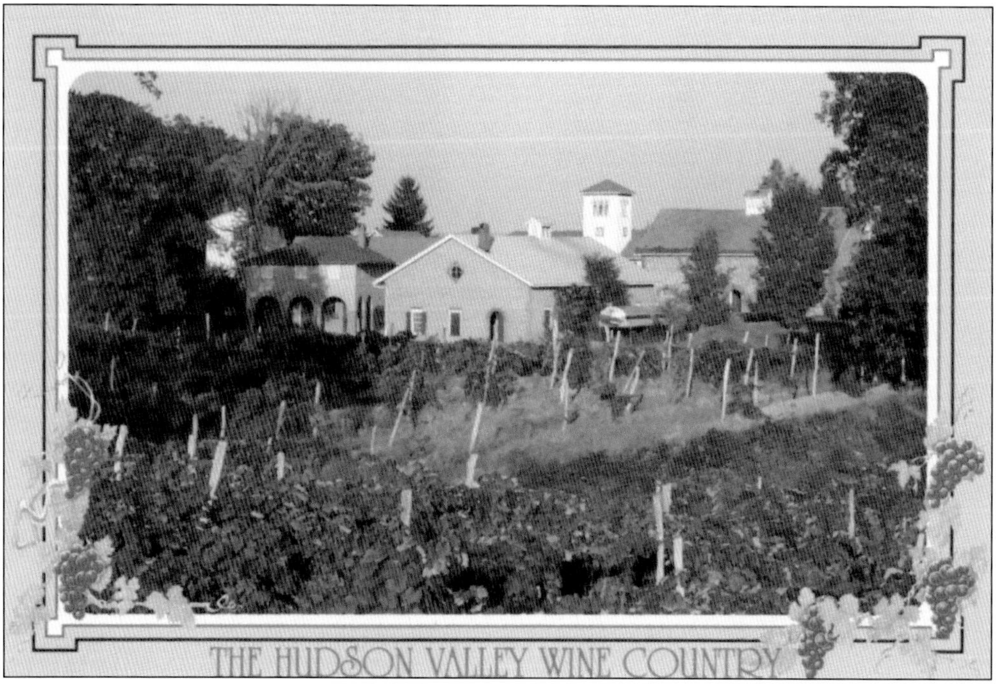

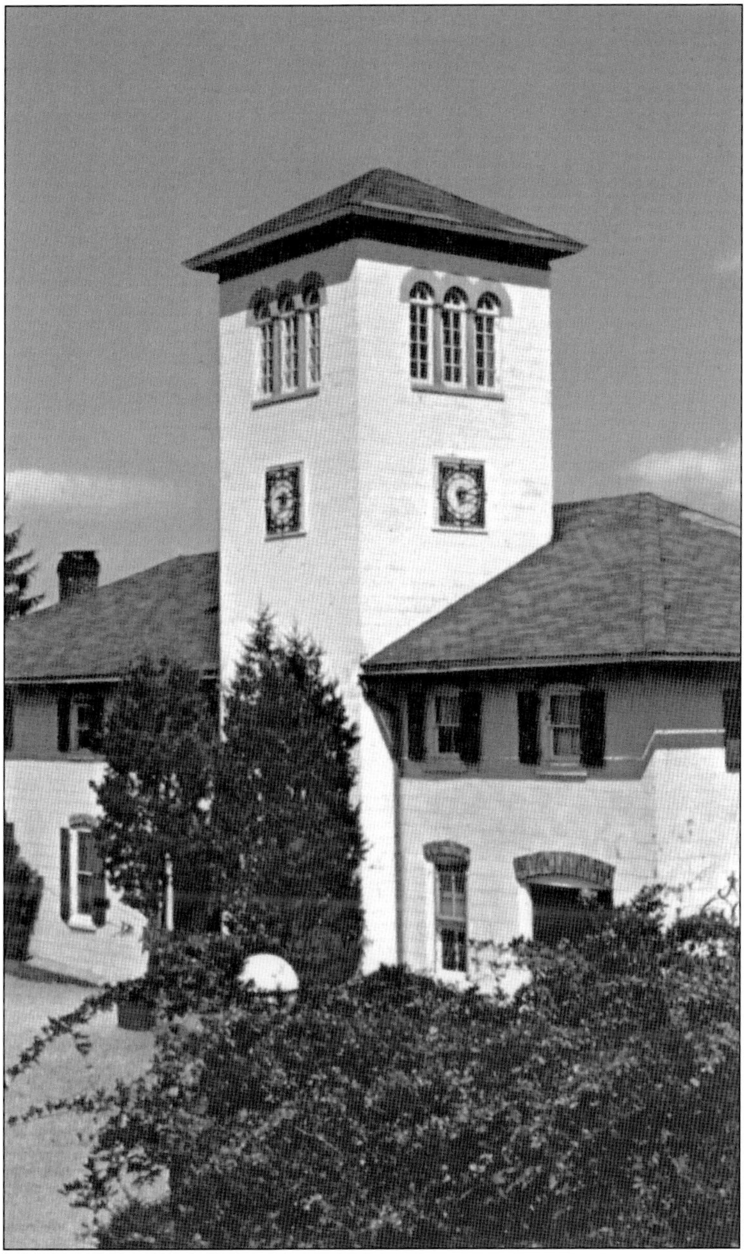

According to a public relations piece from the 1970s, the wine village was built by Alexander Bolognesi, whose family had been making wine in Italy for 400 years. Immigrating to America in 1888, they first ventured into banking and only later into the wine business. They survived Prohibition by making altar wines for religious use. After Prohibition was repealed, they gained a reputation for fine American wines (23 varieties) and champagnes. The 253 acres were covered with vineyards. Hudson Valley Wine Company wines were aged in white oak casks imported from Europe. The casks were shipped in pieces and assembled at the winery by the father of one of its last winemakers, Sam Williams. A series of tunnels went between buildings. The property had one of Highland's three Hudson River ports. It also had a kiln, probably for lime, at the time of the Revolutionary War.

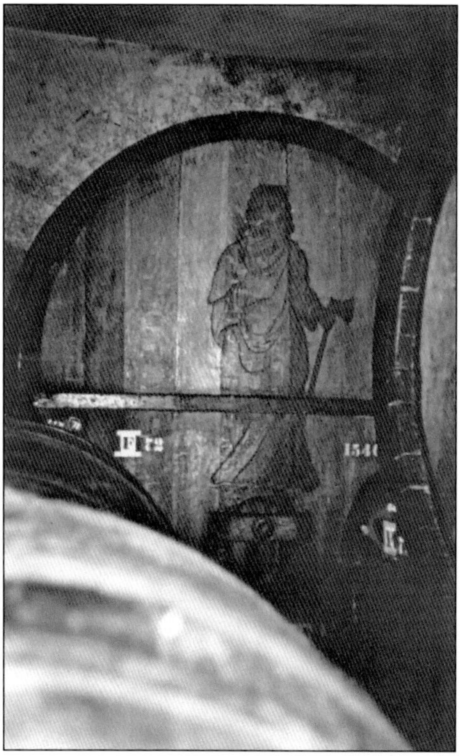

"Premium wines, estate bottling since 1907" proclaims this Hudson Valley Wine Company card from the 1960s. "Birthplace of American Viniculture" refers to the Hudson Valley, not necessarily the Hudson Valley Winery itself. This 400-year-old cask features a carving of the patron saint of wine, Saint Vincent. "We are told he chose to enjoy the wine of the earth over the pleasures of heaven," the card explains.

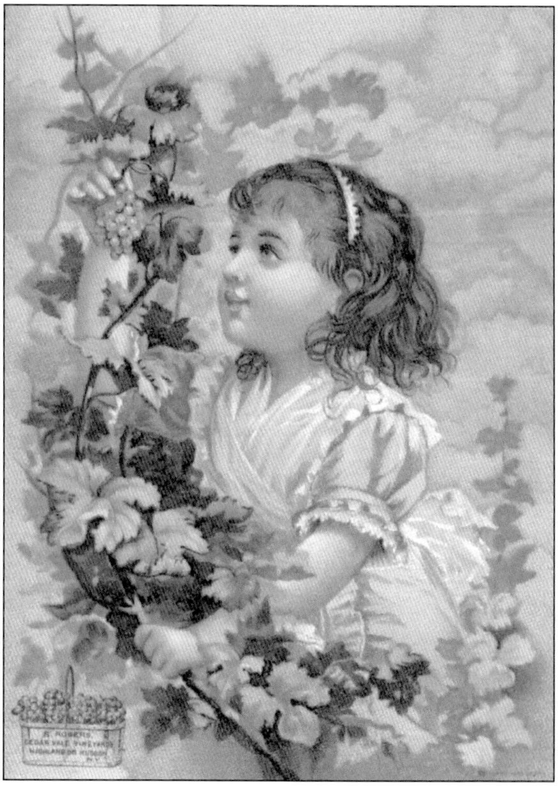

This lovely trading card reads "S. Rogers, Cedar Vale Vineyards, Highland On Hudson, N.Y." The "On Hudson" address was common to a number of places at the time, including Bellevue Villa On Hudson (see page 87), Milton On Hudson, and Highland On Hudson.

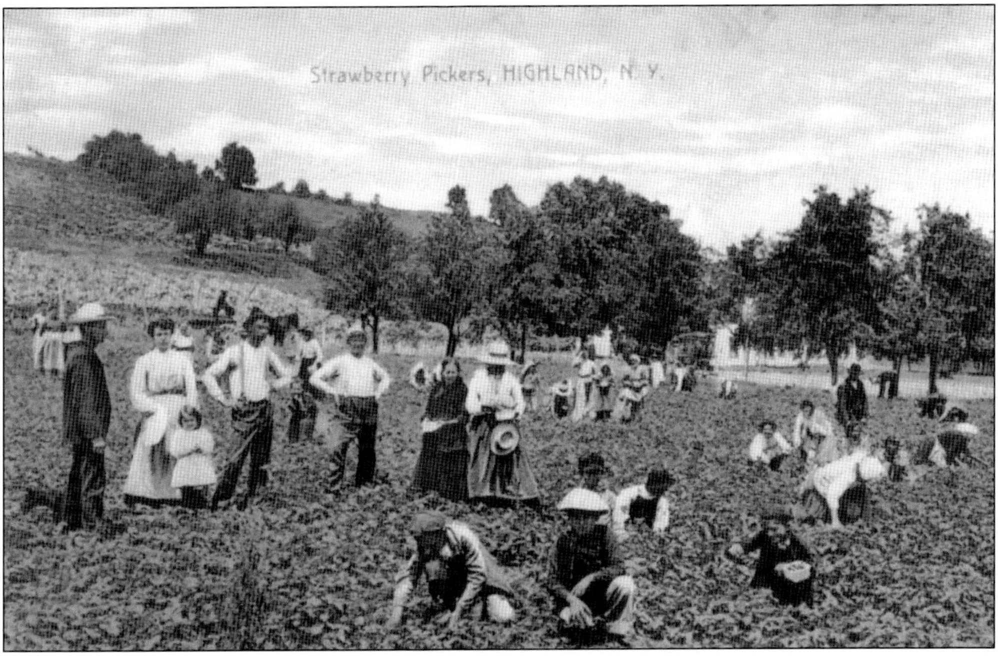

Highland resident and future Chevrolet automobile dealer Louis Smith stares out at the viewer from the bottom center. Although strawberries did not store and ship as well as other fruit, Highland strawberries were shipped by train all over the eastern United States and Canada. Today, pick-your-own sites for strawberries make it an important local crop and the main draw for many festivals.

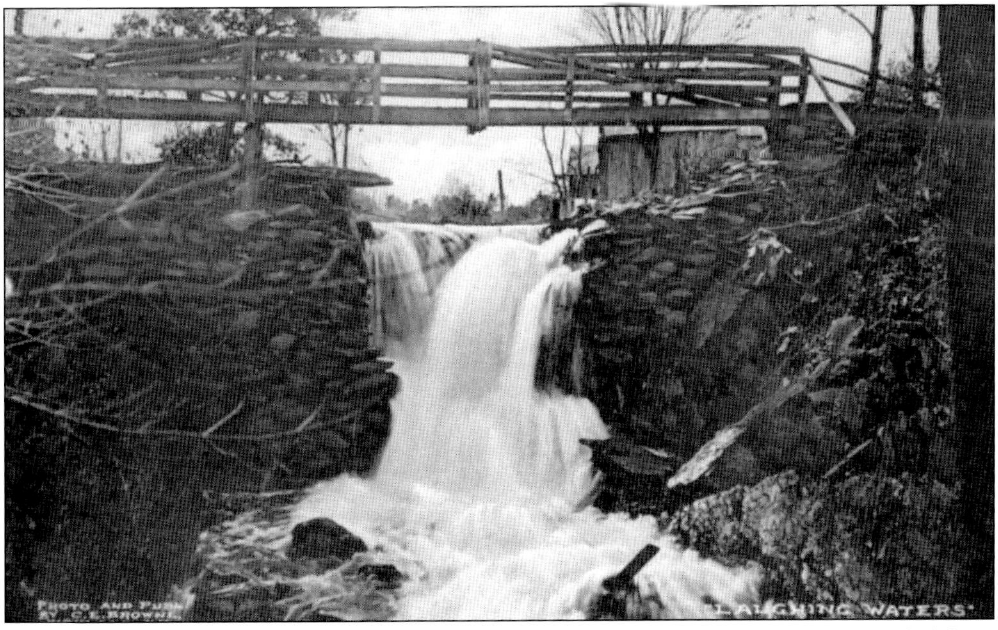

Photographed and produced locally by C.E. Browne of Highland, this card was mailed from Highland in 1907. The site of the "Laughing Waters" falls may have been Schantz's Pond, but it is impossible to be certain because Ulster County and the Town of Lloyd had many millponds that were created by damming streams.

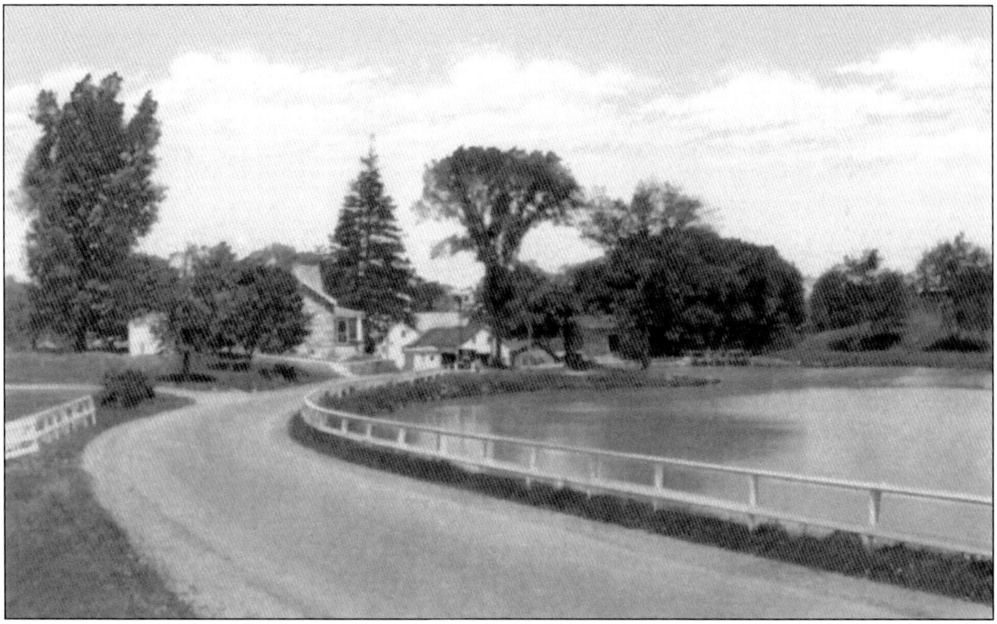

Visible on the left of this 1940s postcard is the Schantz house (later the Gaffney house). Built in 1760 by Hendrick Deyo, legend has it that native people who dined there asked that the pewter plates they used be put on the mantel forever. The house is on Vineyard Avenue and, as of this writing, belongs to Scenic Hudson. The plates are not there.

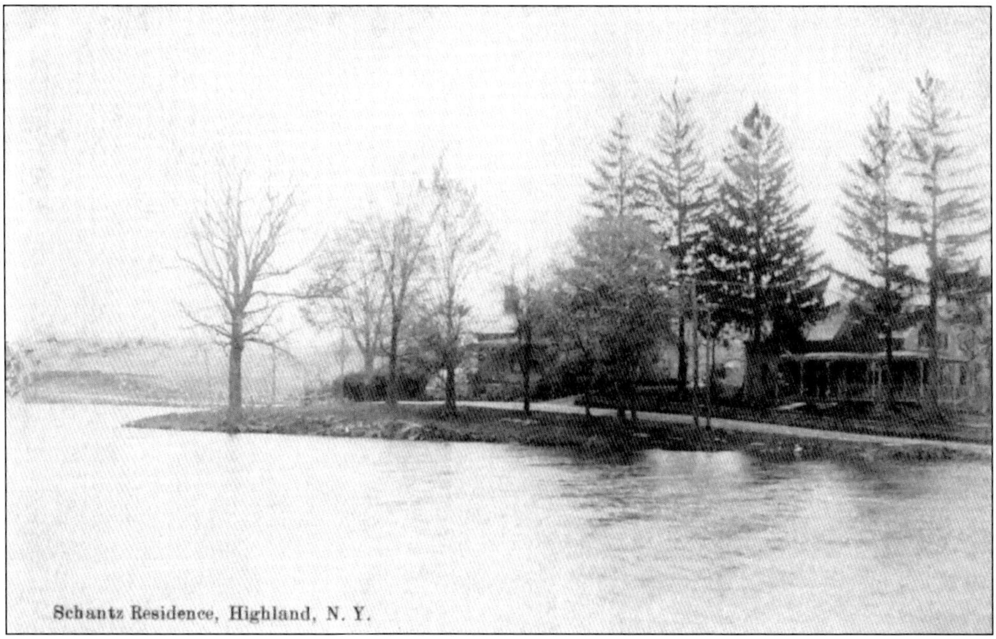

Another view of the Schantz residence (Hendrick Deyo 1760 house) from the dam at Schantz's Pond is pictured here. From the early 1900s through the early 1960s, ice was cut from this pond for use in produce storage (see page 44 for more about the Valentino family ice business).

Three

Tourism and Recreation

With millions of people suddenly able to afford and enjoy the leisure provided by the economic growth of the Industrial Revolution, tourism flourished in the Hudson Valley. The region was endowed by nature with all the calming wonders of flora, fauna, and water, and postcard images became a popular way to share them. In many instances, advertising was a by-product, but in some instances it was a card's only purpose. From the earliest cards with undivided backs to today's high-gloss photo cards, the fascination continues, but only for the moment. Technology now allows the tourist and resident to snap a photograph and e-mail it anywhere in the world at no cost, signifying that soon, postcard communication may disappear.

Beginning in the late 1800s, tens of thousands traveled up the Hudson. They came either by steamboat or railroad and continued their journeys inland to amusement parks, hundreds of boardinghouses, and the spectacular mountain hotels for a weekend or to spend their vacations. Today, most of those glorious hotels are gone. Although bed-and-breakfast establishments have taken the place of boardinghouses, they still offer the same intimate connection to the area's bucolic scenery and recreation as their earlier counterparts. Amusement parks are gone, but new amusements, such as dude ranches and annual festivals, have cropped up, and hiking and biking have never been more popular.

Highland's agricultural roots are still bringing life to farming, tourism, and recreation as nature enthusiasts find their way to obvious treasures, such as the Hudson River, Hudson Valley Rail Trail, and Walkway Over the Hudson. Just as many come for the smaller gems such as quiet tree-lined roads or a great blue heron fishing for dinner in a roadside pond.

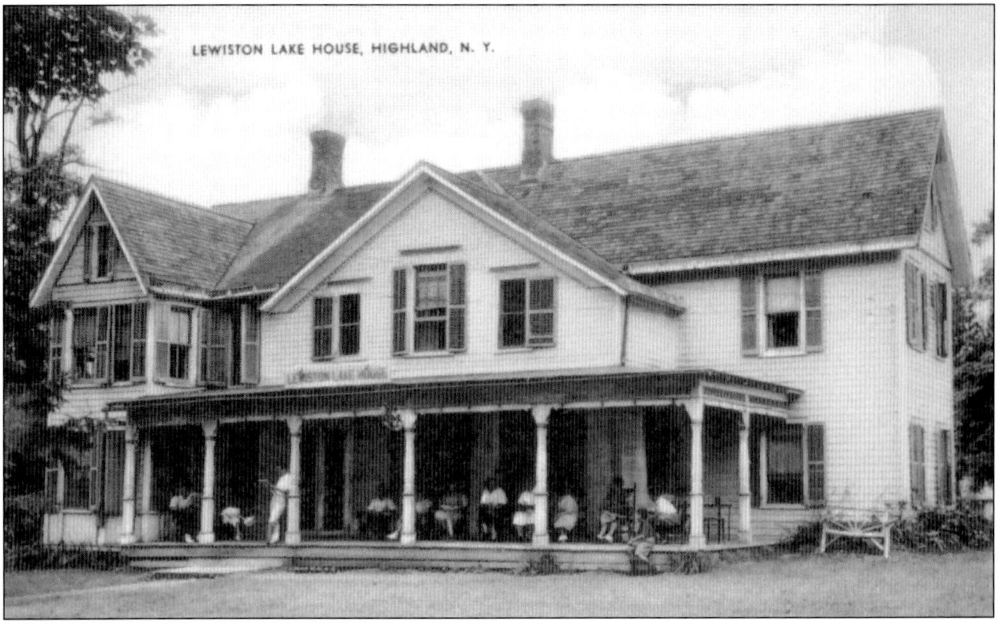

Almost every residence with extra bedrooms became a boardinghouse during the late 19th and early 20th centuries. Although some were for itinerant laborers, most were for vacationers. Often, the same people came year after year, and some eventually moved to the area permanently. Lewiston Lake House, on Vineyard Avenue near Chapel Hill Road, accommodated 40 guests. The owner, Mrs. Bloomer, charged guests $7 to $10 a week and provided food, bath, hot and cold water, steam heat, and a piano. Below, boarders enjoy the small lake under the willows. Barns are visible above the boaters. Today, this house is a private residence.

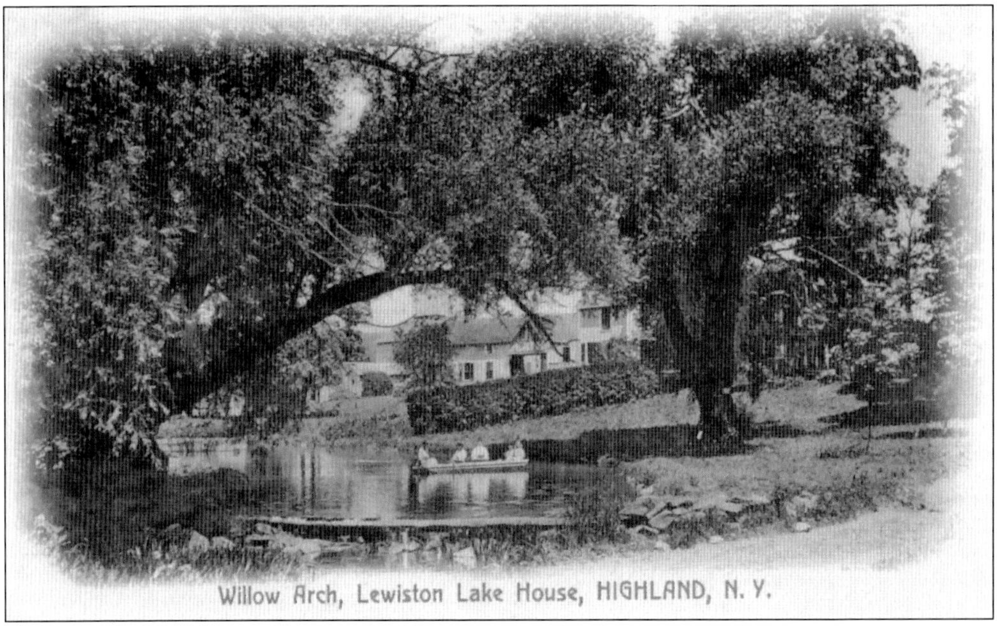

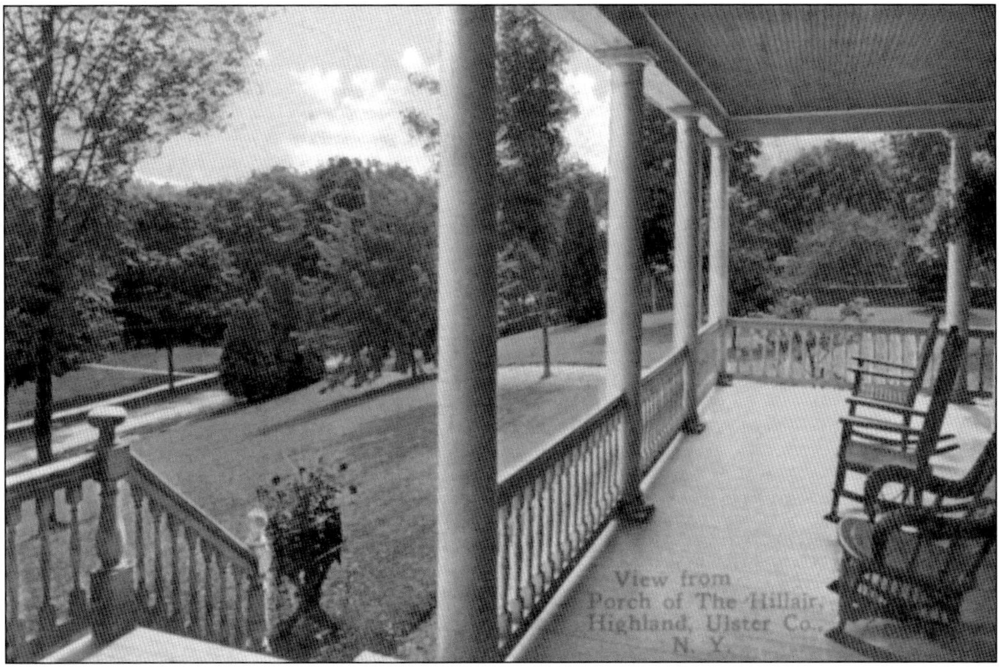

The Syracuse University crew members often stayed at the lovely Hillair House when they came to Highland to participate in the Intercollegiate Regattas on the Hudson River. Now a private residence, the Hillair, located on Grand Street, still has the lower portion of its tower on the north end of the building. The view from the Hillair porch was of the lovely stone Episcopal church on the opposite side of Grand Street. The church remains as it looked when this card was produced. Today, the Hillair property backs up to Route 9W on the west. One often sees the county named on postcards, possibly because the traveling populace at the time did not possess easier ways to navigate the state.

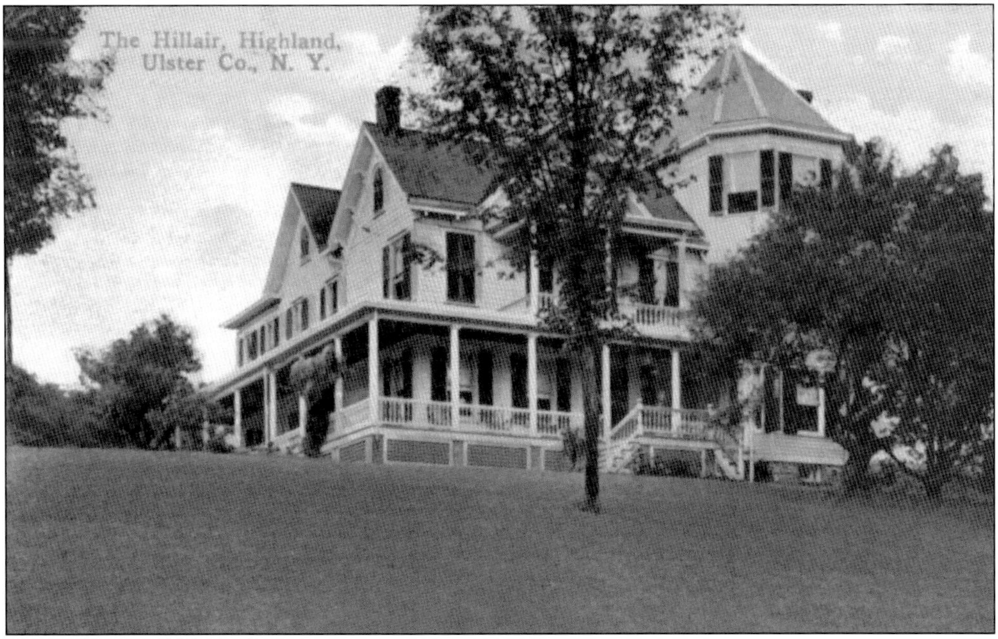

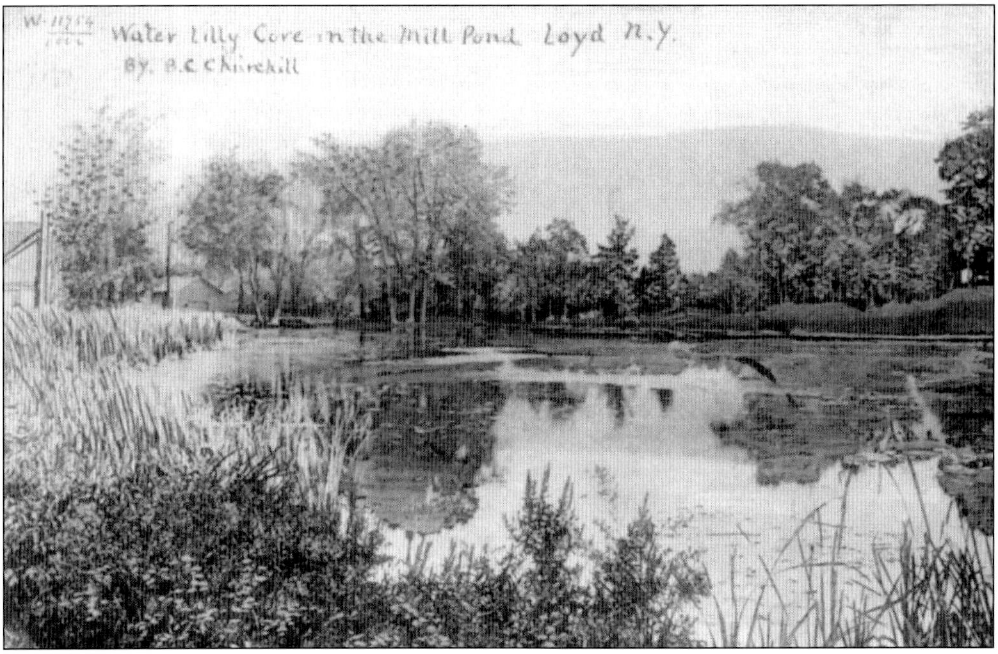

Water and views of water are abundant in Highland. The area's rocky geography is a series of north–south ridges that shape natural lakes and streambeds. Along River Road, the rock upheaval that formed the ridges is very evident. Glacial activity smoothed out the tops of the ridges and deposited glacial moraine gravel and soil that make the land so productive.

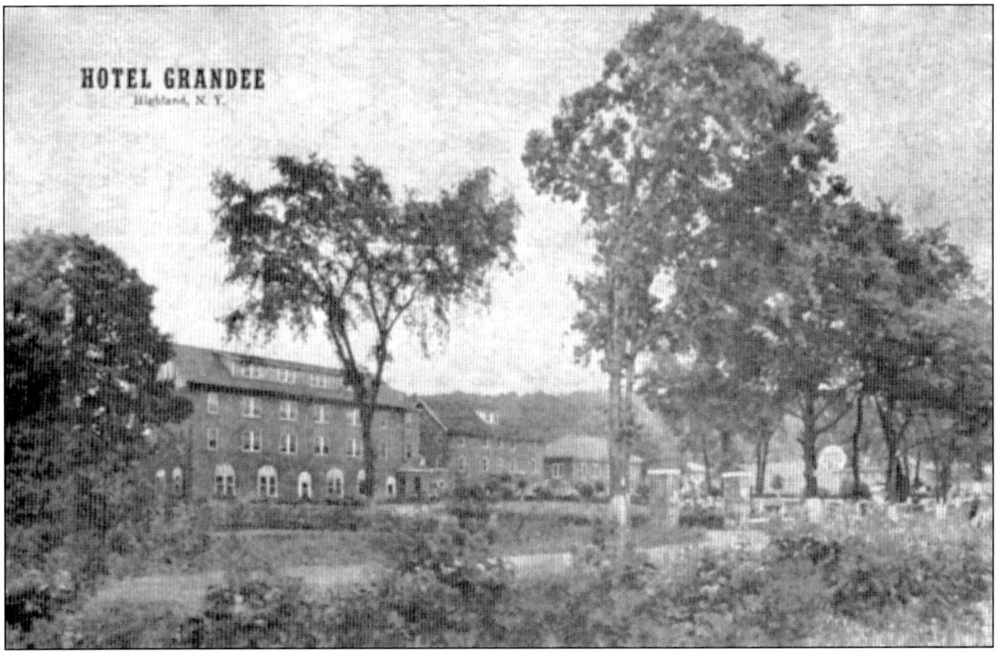

Located on Kisor Road, Hotel Grandee was built in the mid-1930s by John Ottaviano and originally named Hotel Ottaviano. One of its chambermaids was from the Kisor family, pictured on page 45. The Grandee was later owned by an assortment of ethnic and religious groups and was razed in the late 1990s. Today, this land is a private cemetery.

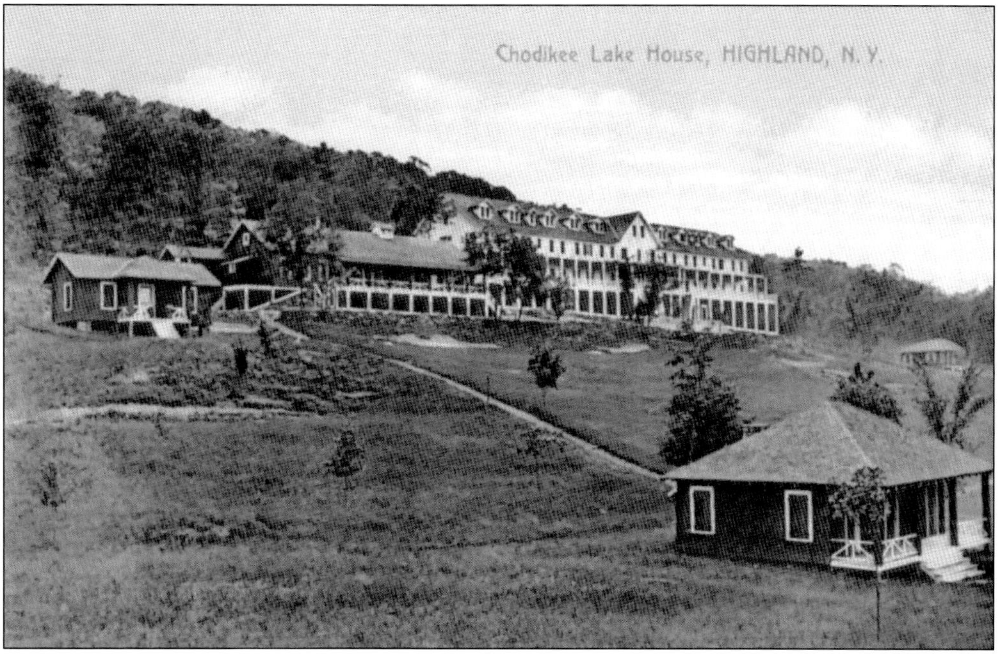

Chodikee Lake, located on the road of the same name, was a tourist mecca from its earliest days. There are many spellings for the lake, including Shatakee, which is close to the native words for the area, meaning a "signal-fire place." John Rose had the first permanent dwelling there, and it was replaced with a hotel by a man named Storms. Other buildings were added as its use changed from tourism to education to its present use as a fenced-in New York State detention facility. No buildings in these images remain today. The Chodikee Lake Hotel's 1913 advertising booklet states, "This is a beautiful fruit growing country, affording special opportunity for kodaking," referring to that wonderful invention, the camera. In addition to tennis, baseball, croquet, and other sports, the hotel had a nine-hole golf course.

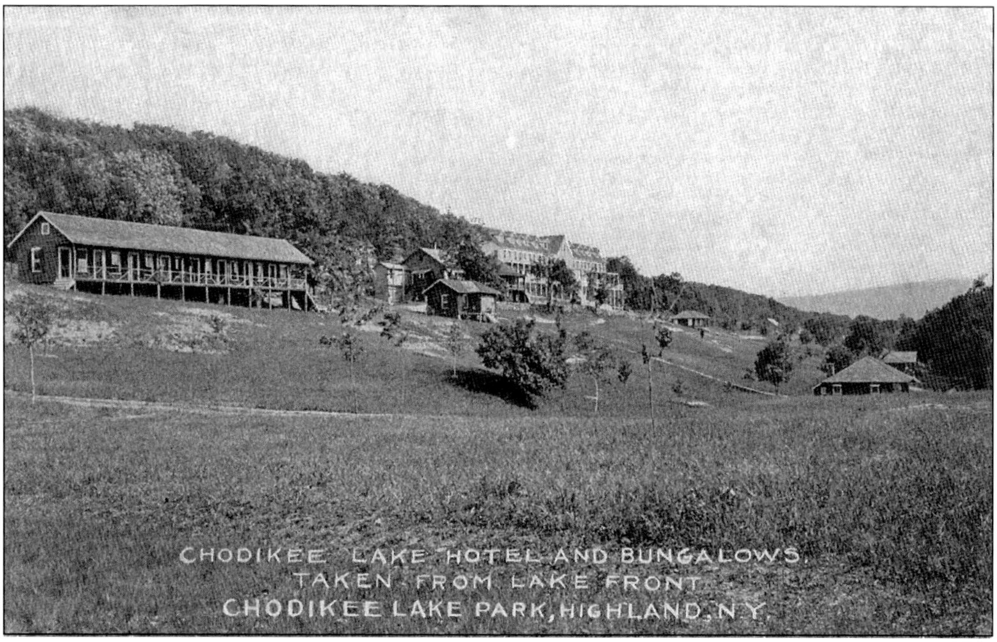

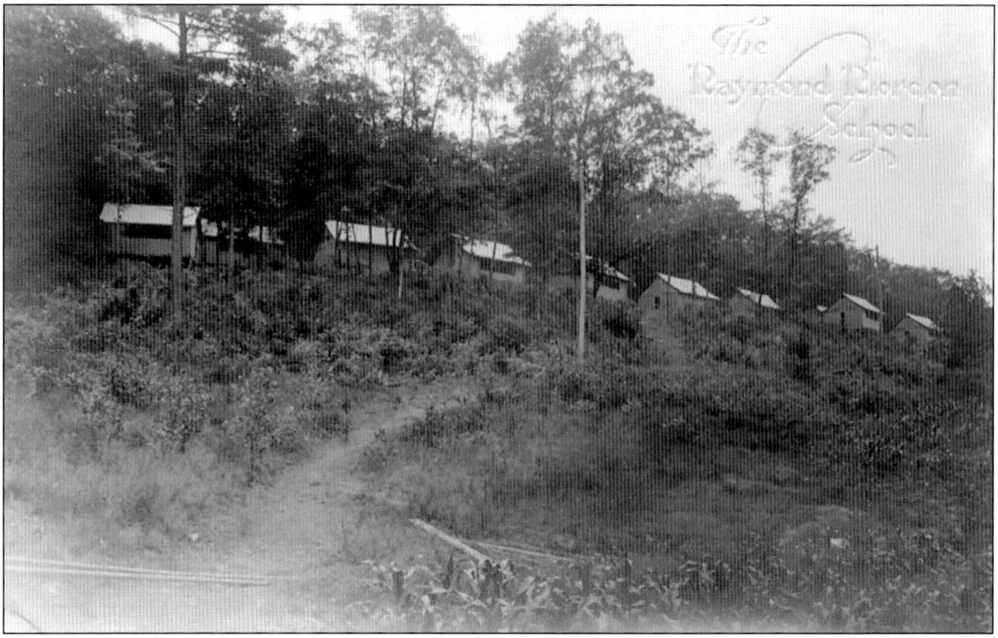

Camps and schools by many names were situated on the shores of Chodikee Lake, including Camp Highland and Camp Stuts, the Raymond Riordan School, and the New York State Detention Facility for Youth, among others. The area offered boating, fishing, ice skating, acres of woods, and many kinds of accommodations, from tents to full-service hotels. Today, the New York State facility is on the east shore, and the west shore offers a Department of Environmental Conservation boat launch. The lake is known for fishing, kayaking, and birding.

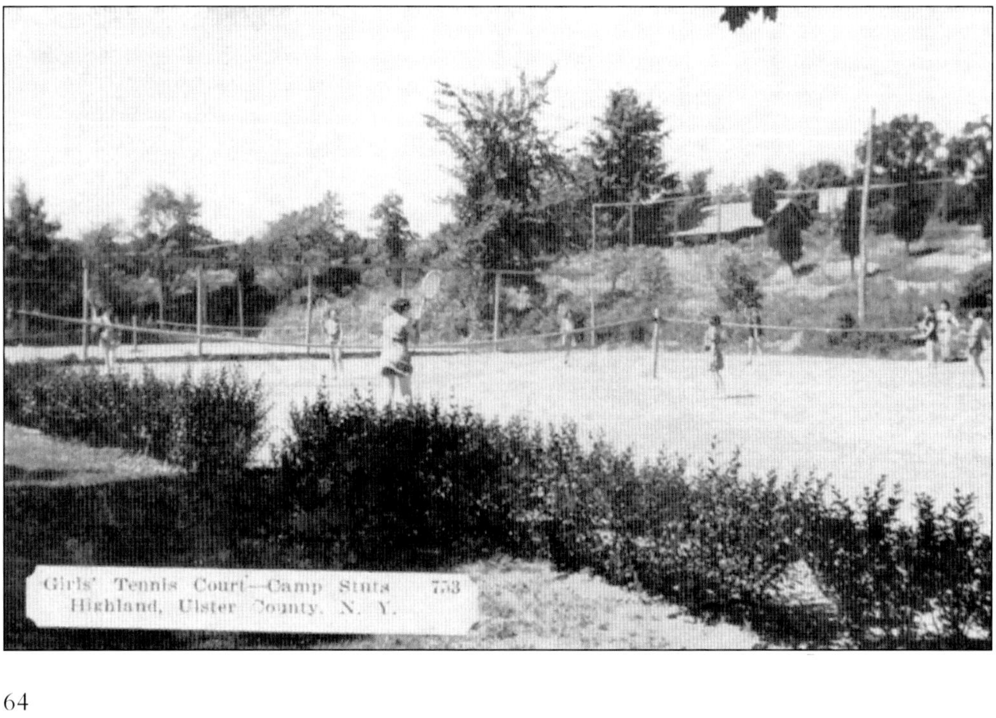

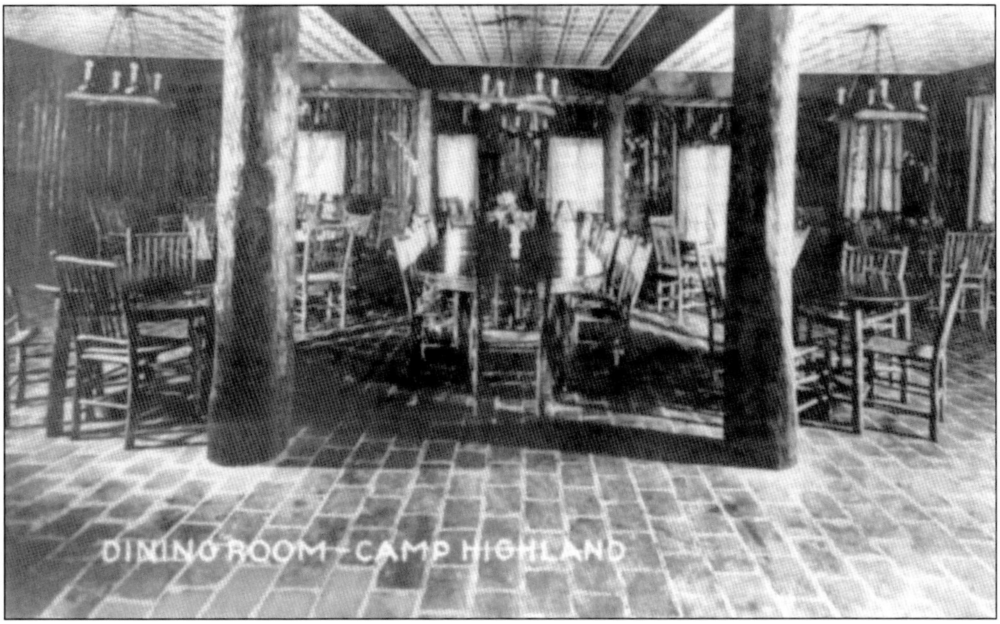

Over time, the buildings at Chodikee Lake had many uses and many masters. One of the most famous was on the board of trustees of the Raymond Riordan School—Gustav Stickley, furniture designer of the Arts and Crafts era. The Riordan School operated as a private school from 1913 to 1947, educating young men from well-off families in the European tradition of a boarding school. It is possible that the chandeliers shown here and some other furnishings of Camp Highland came by way of Stickley. Photographs of Riordan School show some of the same furnishings. The bungalows of Camp Highland are pictured below.

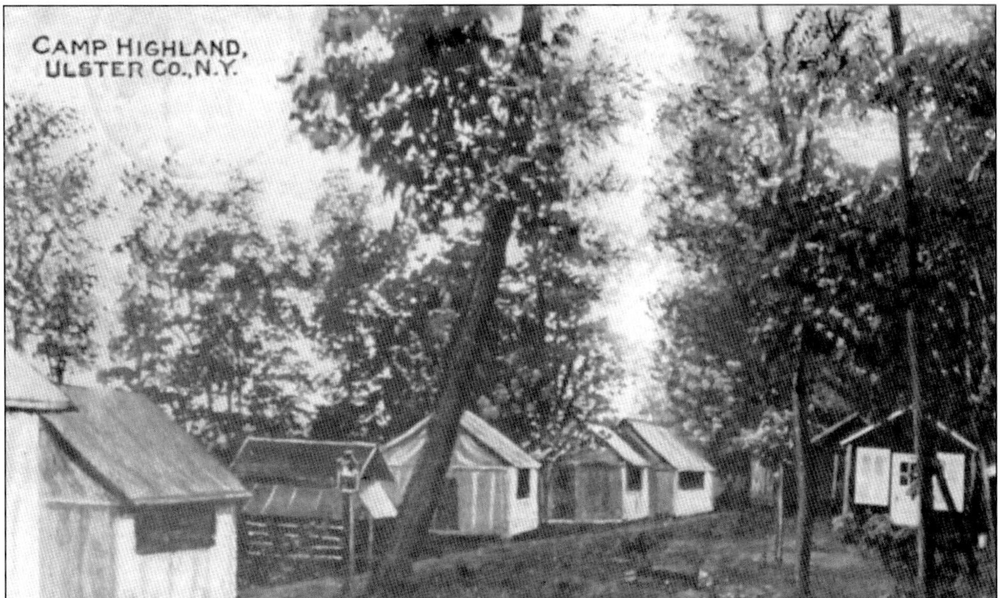

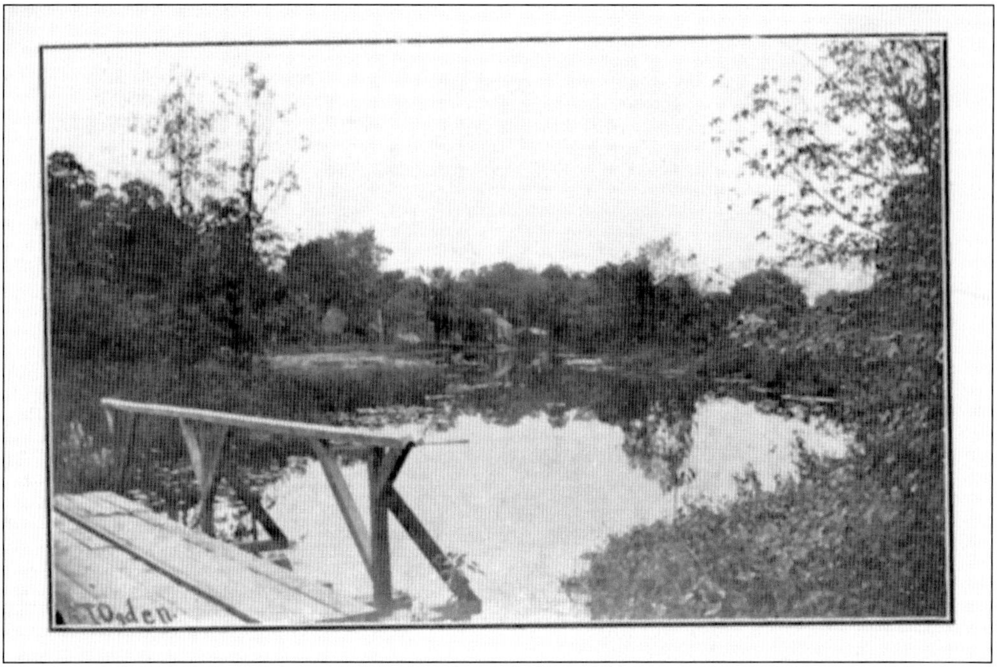

Places that renewed visitors were everywhere in Highland. Postcards let tourists take a bit of that renewal with them or send it to others. From the calm of millponds to the thrill of hiking cliffs above the Hudson, tourists found it enchanting, and until the automobile offered them sights farther afield, they literally came to Highland by the boatload.

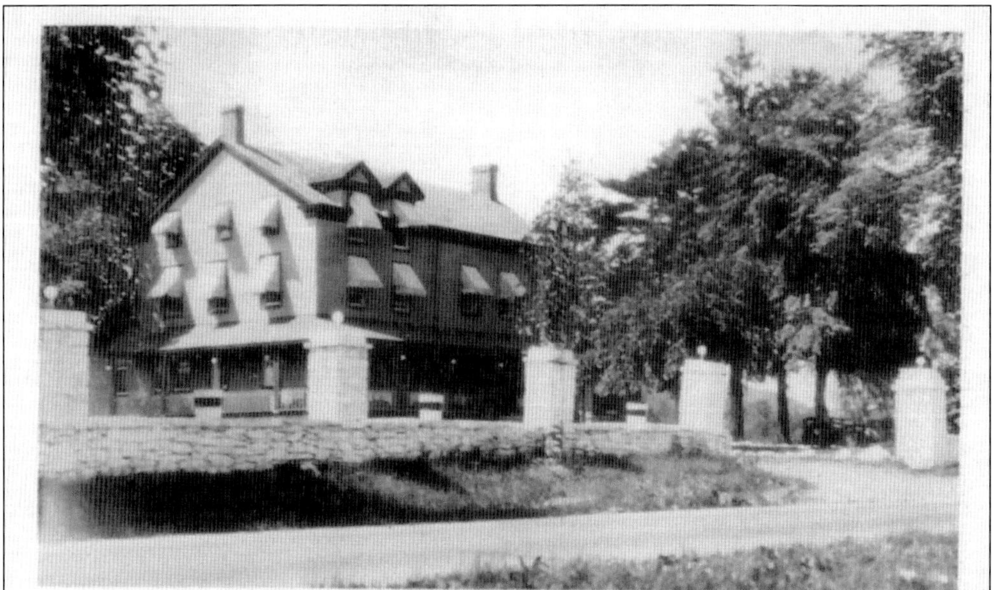

One of the many hotels that catered to the world-weary from New York City, Hotel St. George, offered rest and relaxation, not to mention that it was close to transportation. Women and children often spent the entire summer, while the men traveled back and forth on weekends. They worked during the week to keep the family in places such as the St. George.

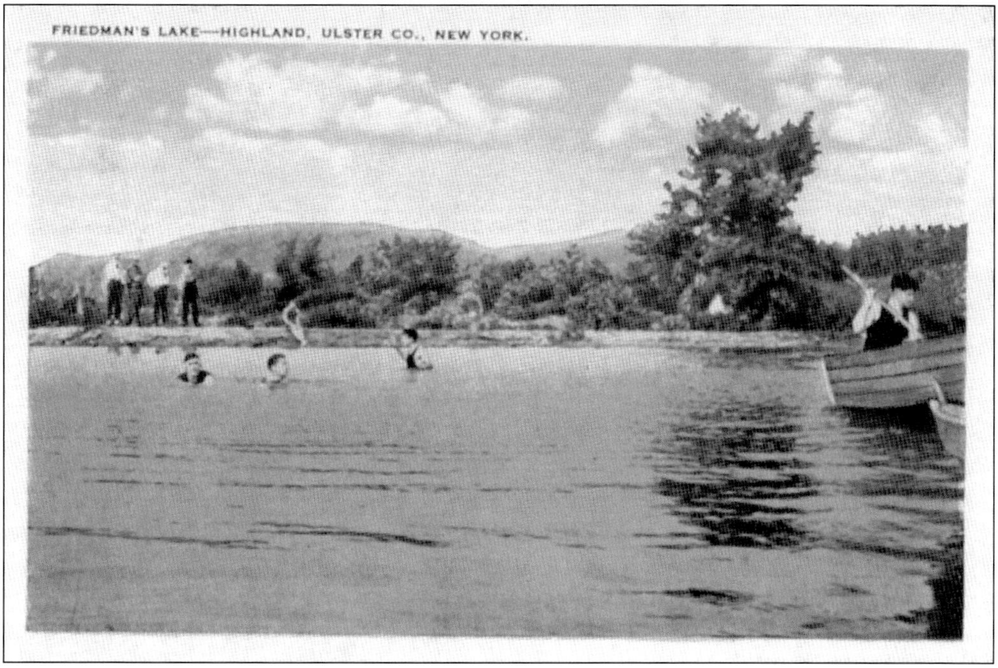

This early Friedman's Shady Lawn Lake House ad offers "Rowing, Swimming, Fishing, Tennis, Ping Pong, Hand Ball Courts, Mountain Trails, Horseback Riding, Private Baths and Showers. European Plan $1.50 and up. American Plan $4.00 a day." The lake is now part of Rocking Horse Ranch, the number one family resort in New York State.

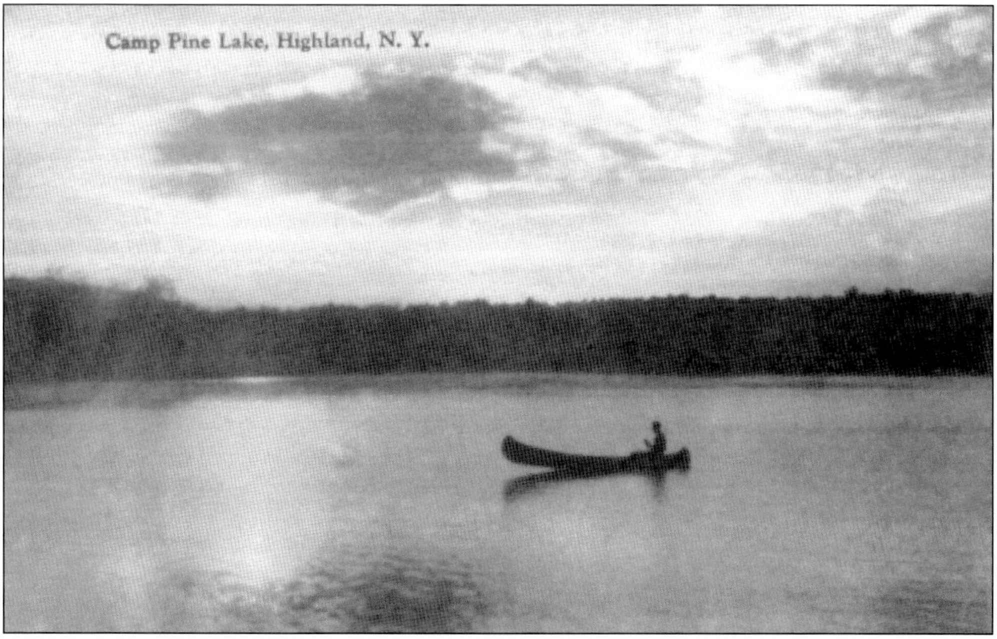

The shoreline of this placid lake helps identify this card's image as Chodikee Lake. Many camps came and went on its shores, and not all have left a record of their existence. Some of the camps were on the west side, such as Camp Stuts, which offered tennis and horseback riding (see page 64).

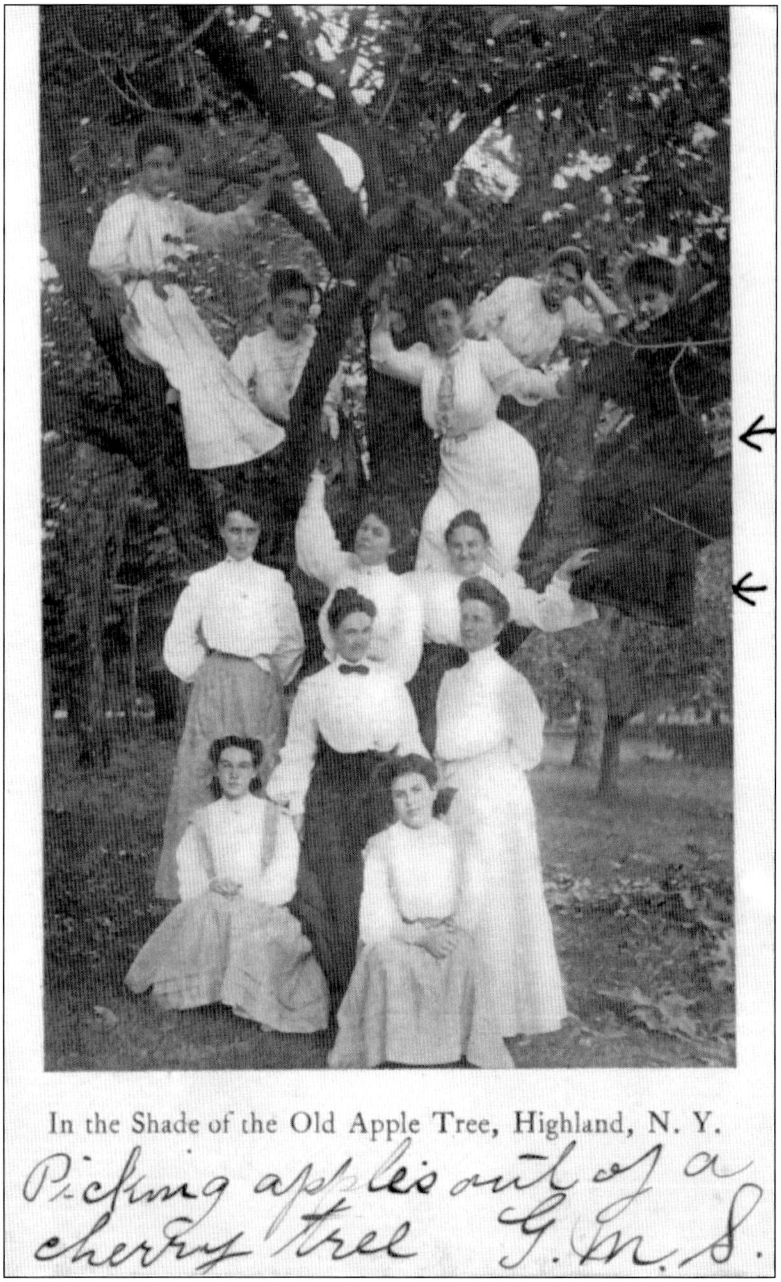

This is one of many postcards featuring the same 7 to 12 well-dressed Highland lassies. It is appropriate for Highland that they are in an apple orchard. The cards carry messages between the women and, sometimes, to others outside of their group. Other cards show them at a variety of locations, including one on a hay wagon and another at a gazebo. Sometimes, they are dressed in elaborate costumes. These women were probably from the more well-to-do Highland families. In this card, the women indicated by the arrows are Martha Cluet Schantz (upper arrow) and Grace Margaret Traver Schantz (lower arrow). The Schantz family name crops up often in these pages, as family members were entrepreneurial spark plugs for a number of businesses and professions in the town. The other women are unidentified. (Courtesy of Gail Russell.)

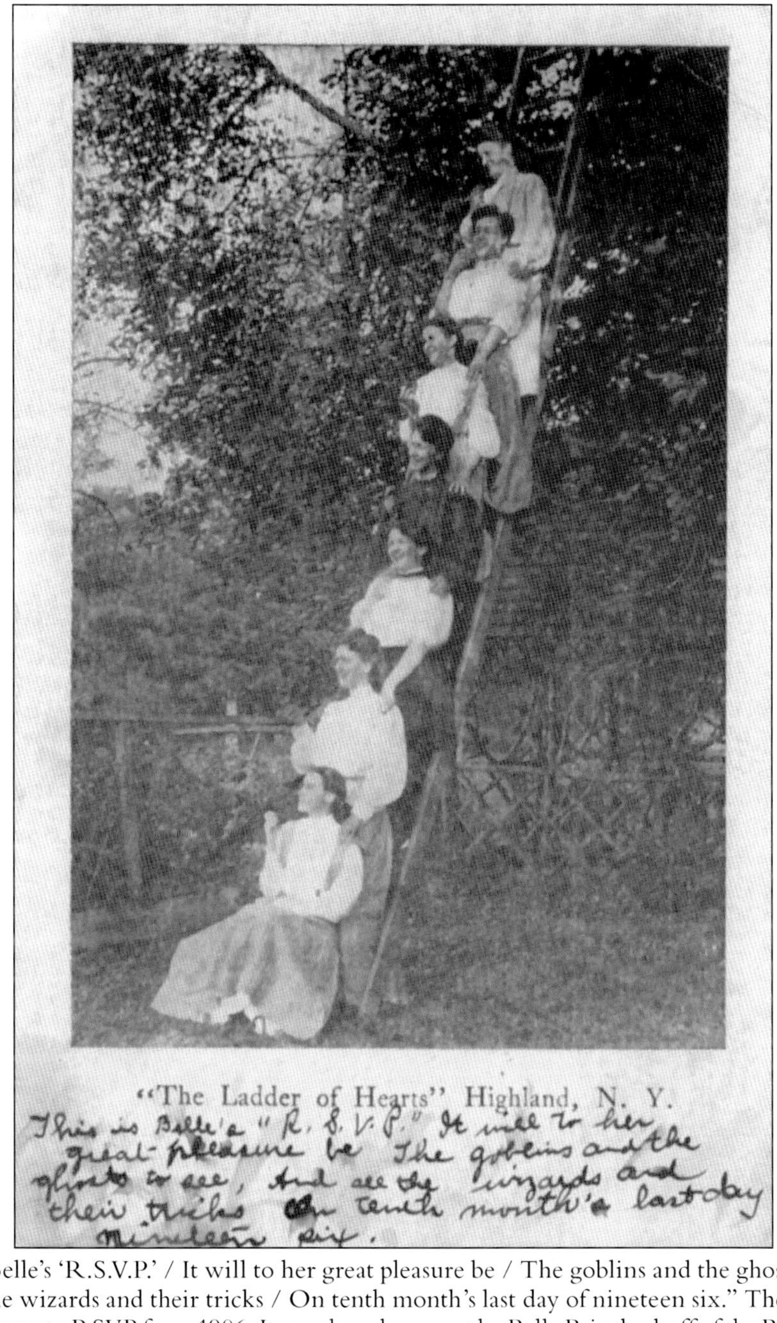

“This is Belle’s ‘R.S.V.P.’ / It will to her great pleasure be / The goblins and the ghosts to see, / And all the wizards and their tricks / On tenth month’s last day of nineteen six.” The poem is a Halloween party RSVP from 1906. It may have been sent by Belle Brinckerhoff of the Brinckerhoff Ferry Company family. The Brinckerhoff ferry, which ran from Highland to Poughkeepsie until 1941, is shown on page 80. The advent of photography was a boon to American costume history because it gives a thorough record of the evolution of style as well as affluence. In order to have the luxury of private postcards, these women must have been among the privileged elite of their era. Note that both this photograph and the one on the previous page may have been taken on the same day—the woman at the bottom left on page 68 is wearing the same clothing as in the bottom of the card on this page.

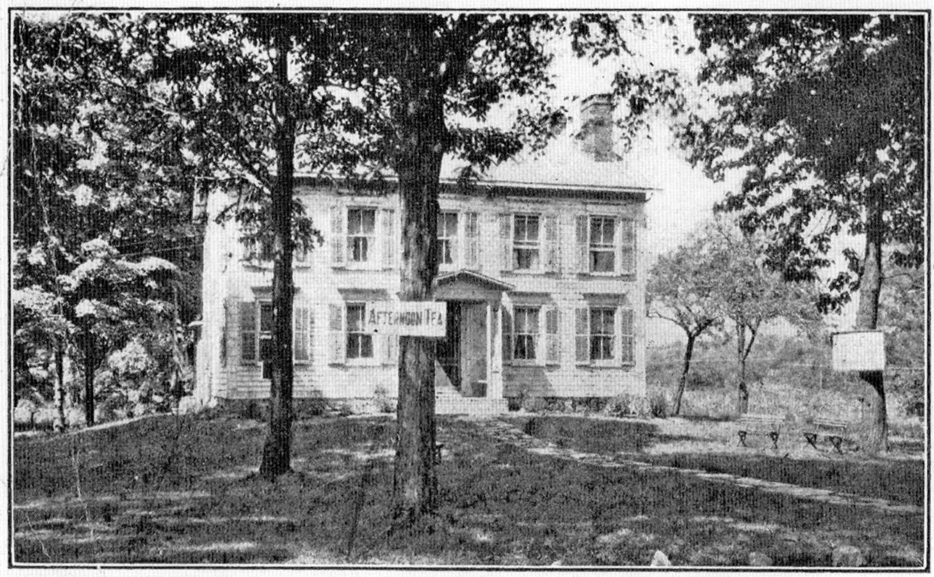

X78 Maple Tree Inn on N. Y. & Albany State Road, Highland, N. Y.

Today's travelers often choose to stay at places off the beaten path in order to avoid traffic noise and fumes. This is made possible by accessible electronic information that makes finding lodging and dining simpler and instantaneous. In the days of the places pictured here—Maple Tree Inn on the New York and Albany State Road and the Brookside Farm on the Highland–New Paltz trolley line—travelers' information was visual; it had to be seen. Therefore, almost all accommodations were on important transportation routes: the river, the trolley, railroads, or major roads.

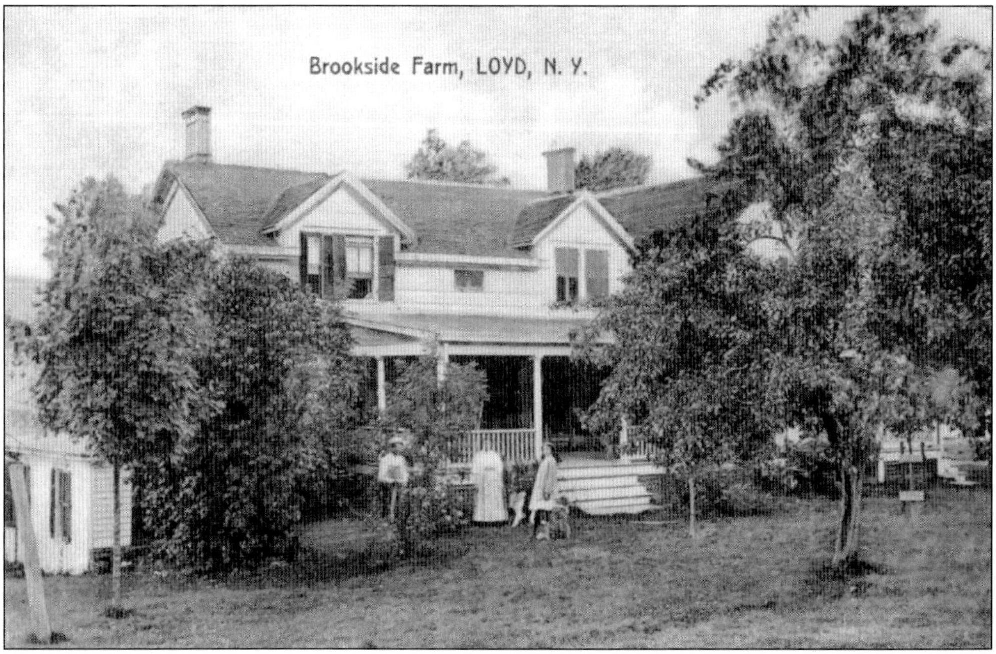

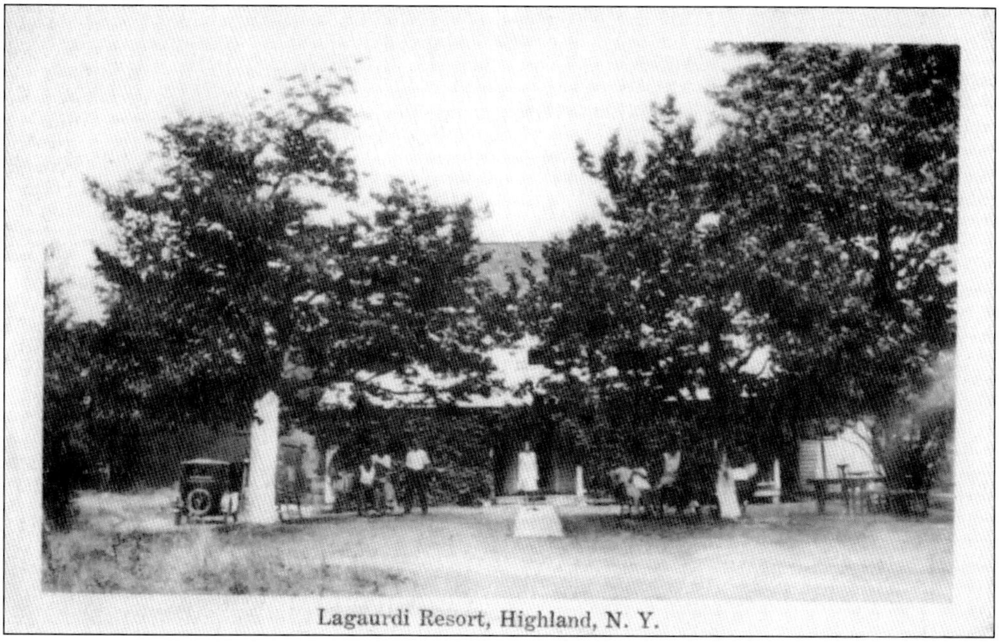

Lagaurdi Resort, Highland, N. Y.

Names of resorts, such as Lagaurdi, often gave a clue to the expected ethnicity of the clientele, but that was not always true. The Maple Crest, sounding roundly American, advertises itself on the reverse of the card below as follows, "The Leading Italian-American Hotel in Ulster County. Swimming, Bocci, Baseball and all other Sports on premises. Dancing. Bar. Movies. Excellent Italian American Cuisine." This card was postmarked in 1958. Other popular resorts of the 1930s, 1940s, and 1950s in Highland included the Hotel Di Prima on North Road, which today is The Would restaurant.

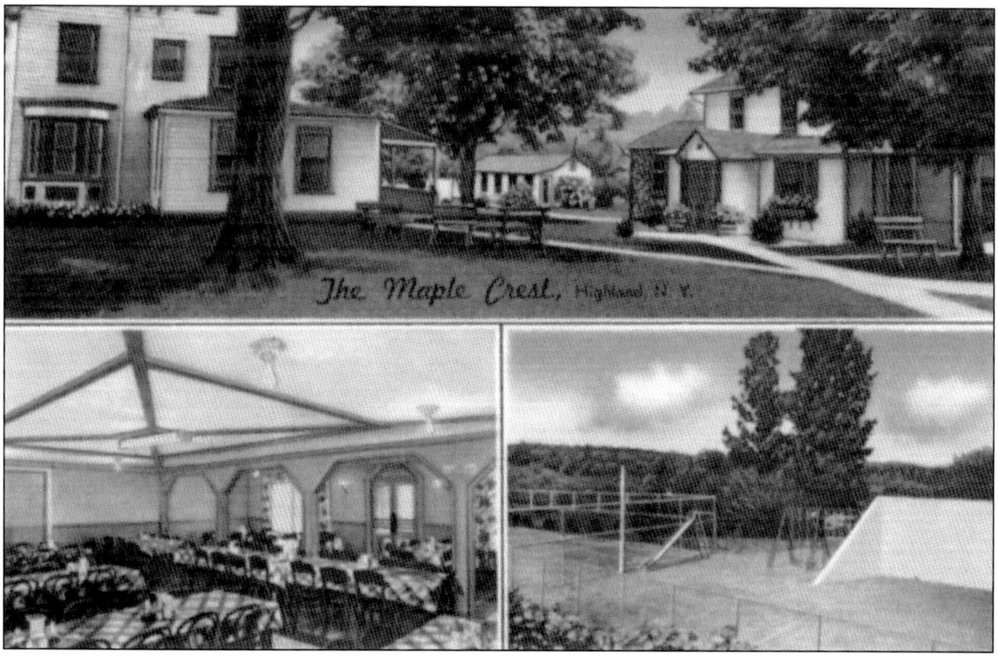

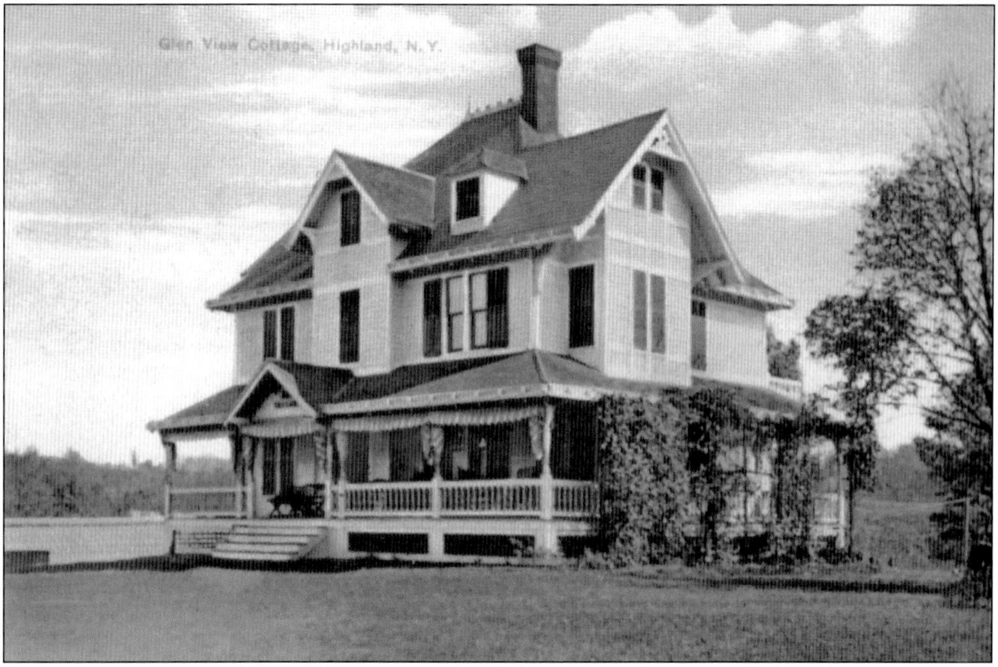

Two important tourist accommodations, Glen View Cottage and The Elms, were near the central business district of Highland. Glen View sits on a hill at the east end of Wilcox Avenue, which is off of lower Grand Street. The glen of Glen View is formed by the Twaalfskill Creek as it begins its steep descent toward the Hudson River at Highland Landing. Today, Glen View is a private residence. The Elms is on Main Street near the municipal parking lot and is an apartment house today. Across from it on Main Street is Torsone's Funeral Home, which occupies the former Elting home shown on page 32.

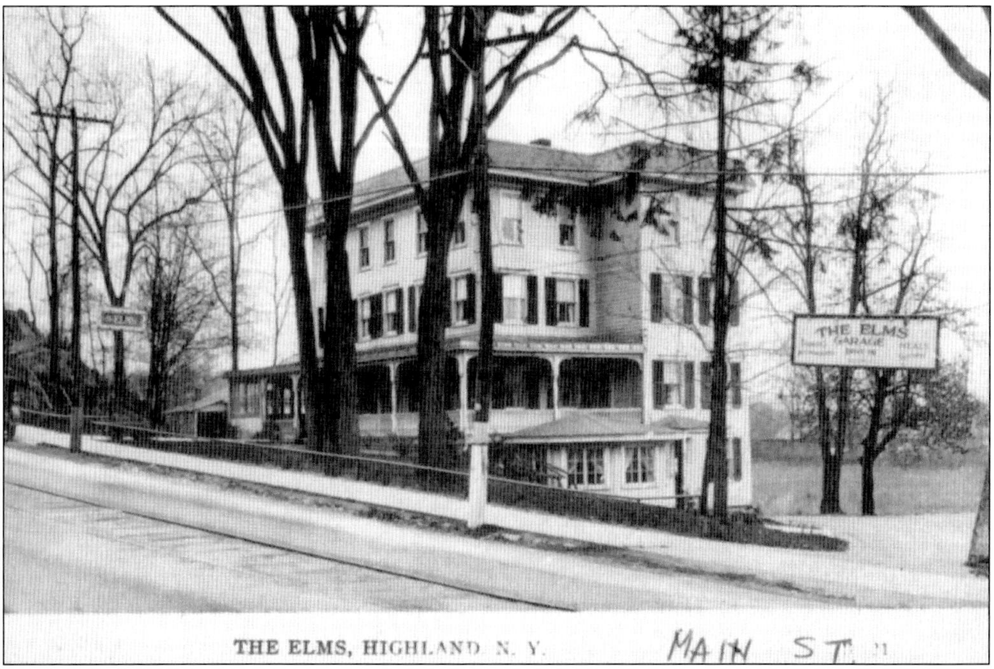

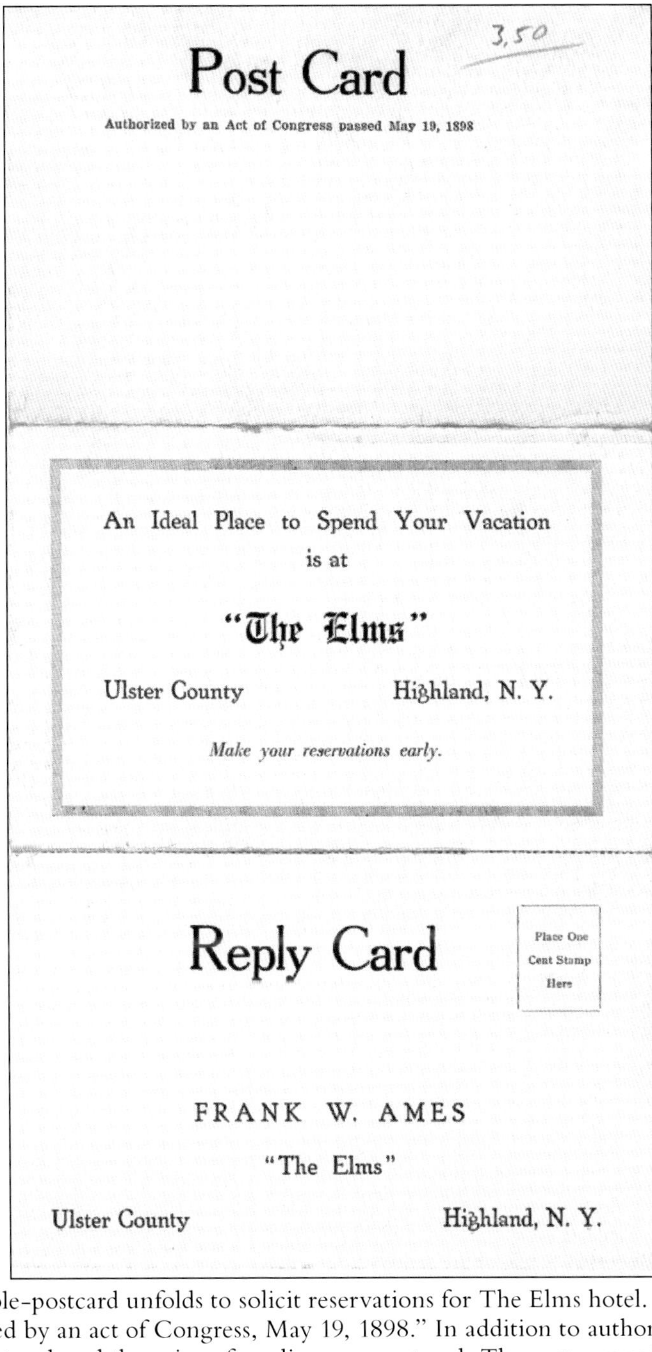
3,50

Post Card

Authorized by an Act of Congress passed May 19, 1898

An Ideal Place to Spend Your Vacation
is at

"The Elms"

Ulster County Highland, N. Y.

Make your reservations early.

Reply Card

Place One Cent Stamp Here

FRANK W. AMES

"The Elms"

Ulster County Highland, N. Y.

This folded triple-postcard unfolds to solicit reservations for The Elms hotel. Note the line on top: "Authorized by an act of Congress, May 19, 1898." In addition to authorizing the folding postcard, the act reduced the price of sending any postcard. The cost was reduced from 2¢ to 1¢. Although that does not seem to be very much today, it was probably a boon to what would become the ubiquitous and popular postcard. The bottom third of the card is a return card for the recipient's reservation. The reverse of the three sections contains information on the hotel, its location, and a photograph of it. It states that The Elms, which sits at an elevation of 280 feet, could accommodate 30 guests. The c. 1920 card announces, "Every room is light and airy." It also mentions that there are four churches nearby. (Courtesy of Gail Russell.)

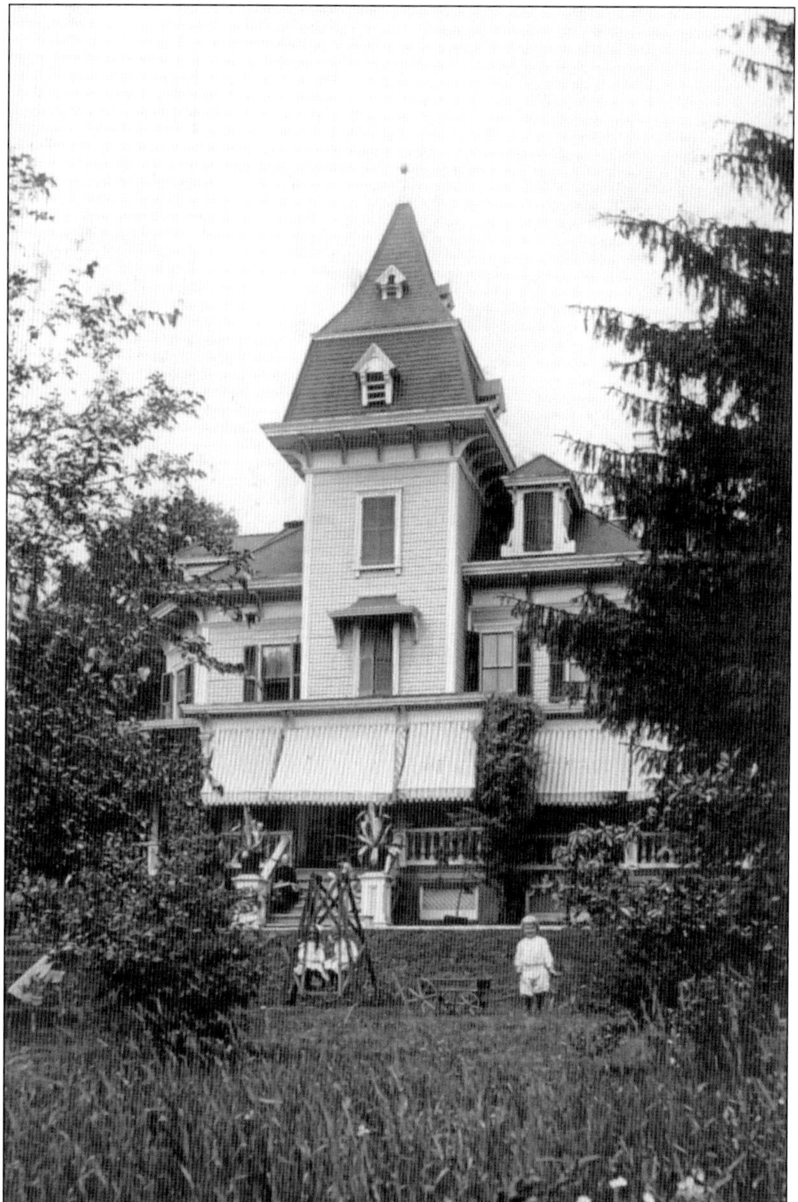

The Highland View House was constructed in 1868 as a residence for the family of wealthy investor and dentist Dr. Charles H. Roberts. About 20 years later, he built a grand estate not far from his first Highland home. This smaller home then became a hotel, welcoming guests to its lofty perch overlooking the future site of the Mid-Hudson Bridge. His estate was the subject of family arguments and litigation, which made good reading in the newspapers of the day. One of Dr. Roberts's daughters, Grace Roberts, ran a dairy farm of very high regard. The farm and its fabulous stone barns were razed to build the current Mid-Hudson Bridge approach. Much of Dr. Roberts's property is now contained within the Franny Reese Park and is open to the public for hiking and picnicking. Only ruins of the once-great mansions are visible. Franny Reese Park is off Mack's Lane, south of the Mid-Hudson Bridge.

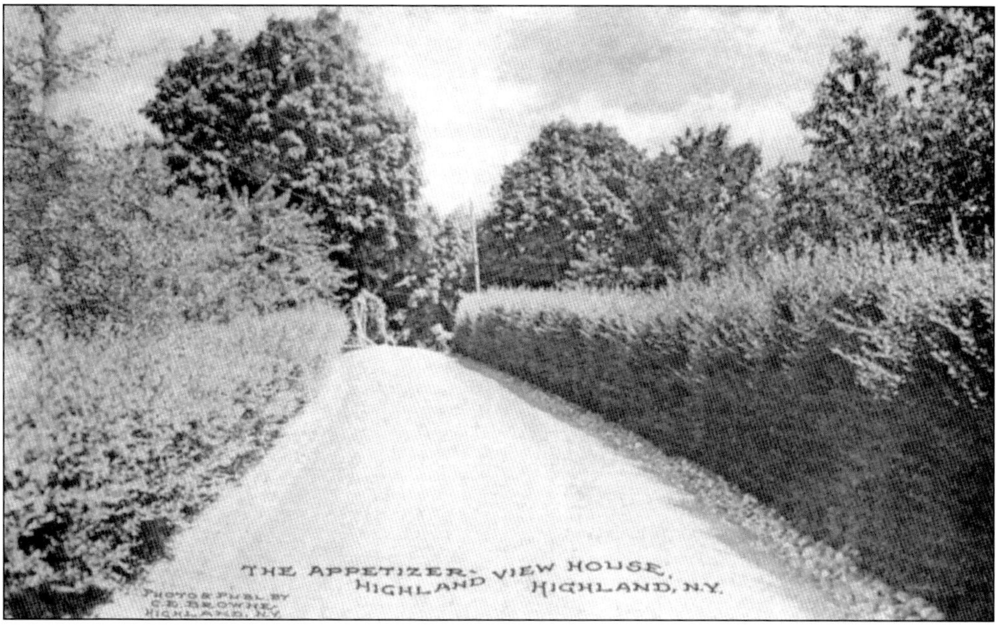

The Highland View House entrance road appears well maintained and probably was an appetizer for the beautiful hotel and grounds. Below, the barns, gardens, and housing for the hotel and farm help appear just as tidy as the approach to the hotel. Looking at these images, it is hard to imagine what must have transpired to bring the entire property to the few ruins that are visible in Franny Reese Park today. Another part of the Roberts family property was closer to Route 9W and included barns and the historic Reuben Deyo Halfway House, built in 1819. Deyo's inn got the name Halfway House because it was about halfway between New York City and Albany on the post road. Before the fight was lost to save historic buildings, newspaperwoman Mabel Abbott wrote *Biography of A House* about the Deyo inn.

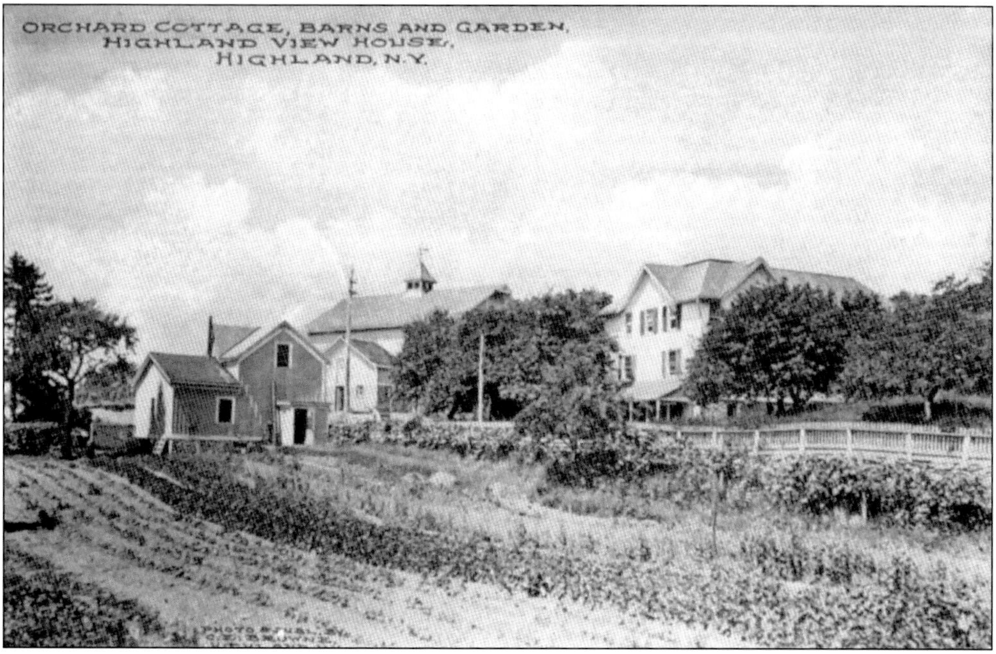

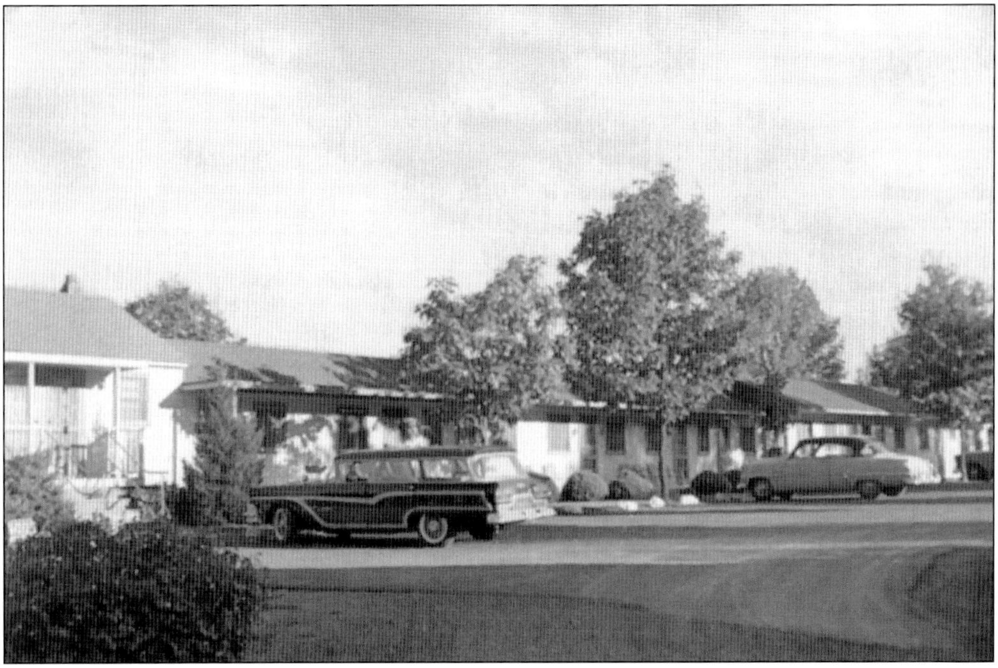

Small motel units popped up to accommodate a nation on the move. Whether for business or pleasure, places such as Galach's Motel (which was just a half mile north of the traffic circle shown on page 98) bragged about being the closest motel to the business center. The sender writes to his mom and dad that he has visited Franklin Roosevelt's home, grave, and museum, and that he is on his way to Niagara Falls. The above card is dated May 5, 1961. Pictured below, Schmidt's Motel was located "300 feet off highway" at the Mid-Hudson Bridge Circle. A. Northagel was the owner.

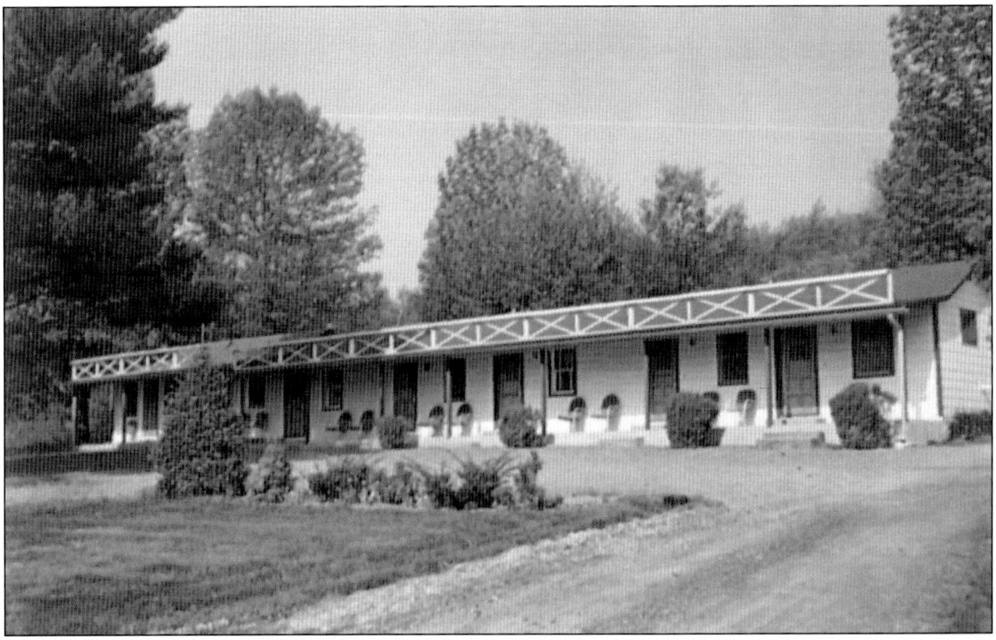

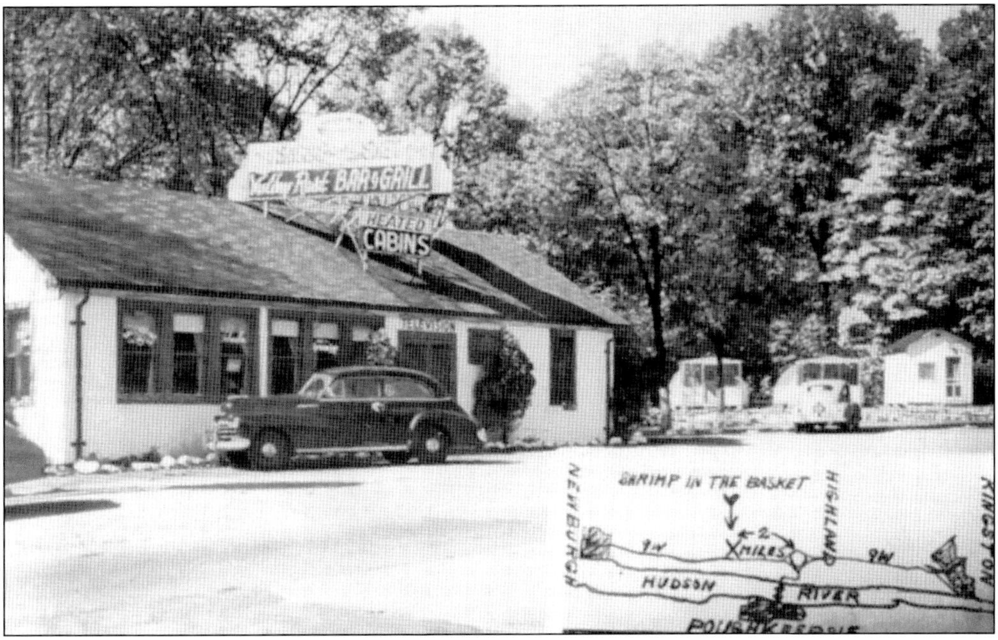

"Valley Rest—Where good friends meet," proclaims the text on the card's reverse (it probably meant in its restaurant and bar, not in its cabins). Valley Rest boasted "Fine foods. Shrimp in the basket. Heated cabins. Full liquor license." It was just two miles south of the bridge traffic circle (see page 98) on Route 9W. "Television" is advertised on the sign above the door.

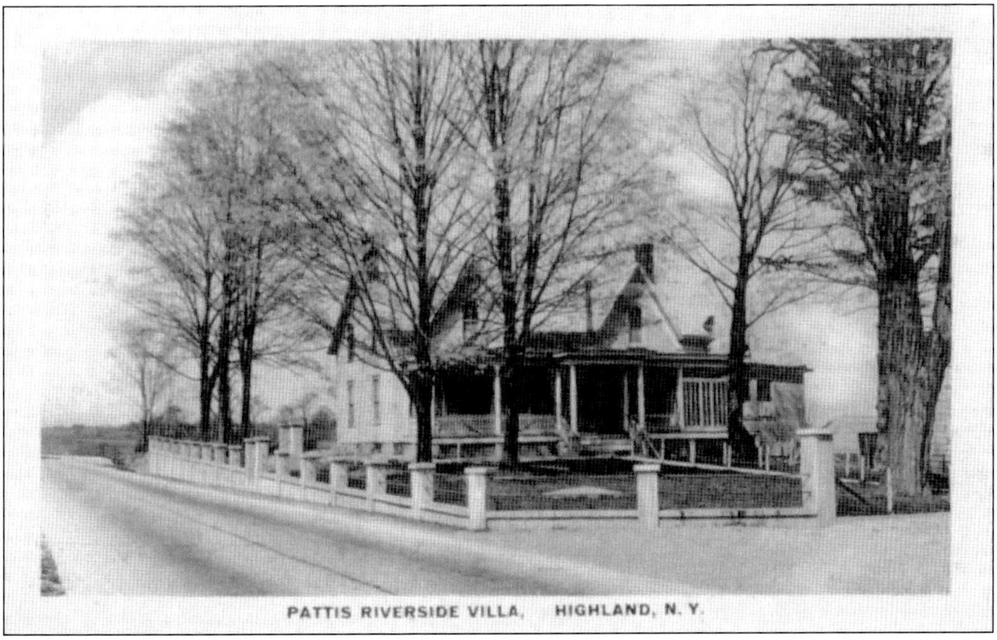

PATTIS RIVERSIDE VILLA, HIGHLAND, N. Y.

Pattis Riverside Villa was stretching credulity with the "riverside" in its name. The river is quite a distance east. Riverside was actually the name of the hamlet where this inn was located and did not mean that it was actually on a river. The villa building still stands on Cummings Lane off Route 9W, just north of the Route 299 intersection. Now a residence, the wall and many of the pillars are still easily seen from Cummings Lane. (Courtesy of Gail Russell.)

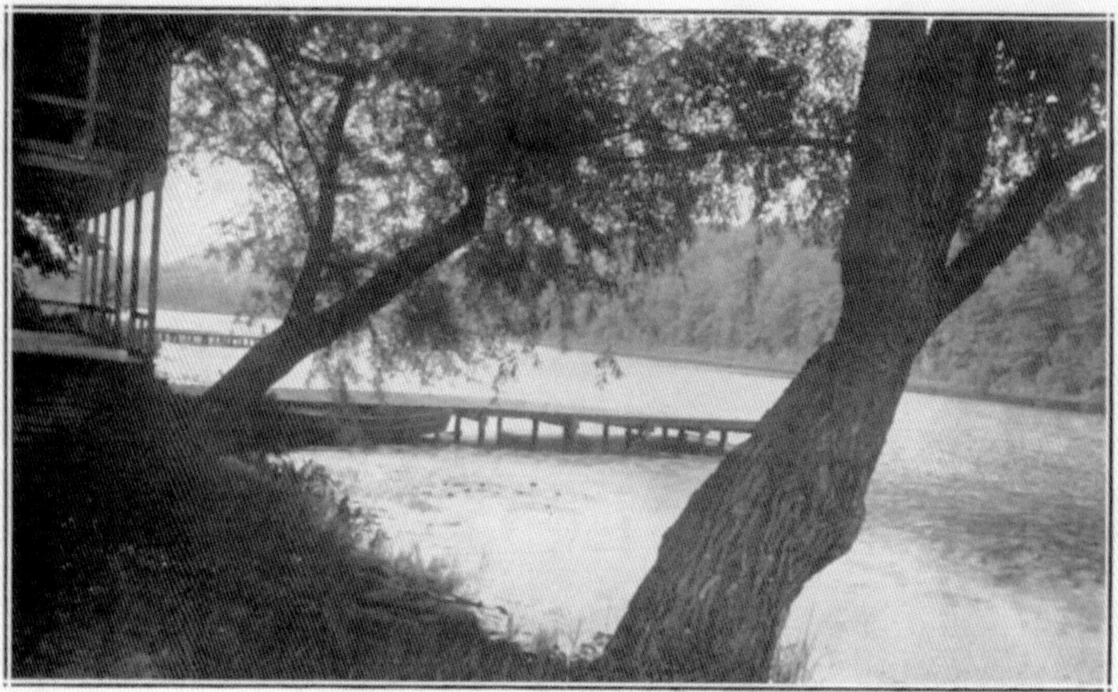

8-90 Westernaire Guest Ranch, Highland, N. Y.

One of the most colorful properties sporting a Highland address is actually in the adjoining township of Esopus. It is situated at the north end of Plutarch Road. The lake above is known as Auchmoody's Pond and was part of a large farm that spanned the line between Lloyd (Highland) and Esopus Townships. Originally, the lake was called the Passant Binnewater. In its early years, the land was a very large chicken farm. Sometime in the early 1930s, it became the Fresh Air Club, a nudist colony protected by large stone pillars and metal gates. Photographs of the club and its members are immortalized in the book *On Going Naked*, published in 1932. Later, the site became the Westernaire Guest Ranch, a dude ranch, and remained so until the late 1940s. The property has remained private since then. Auchmoody Pond empties into the Swarte Kill Creek, which runs north. The Swarte Kill Creek runs parallel to and between North Eltings Corners Road and Plutarch Road, to where Plutarch Road crosses over it just before the intersection with Swartekill Road.

Four

The Hudson River

Settlements in and around Highland primarily started at the Hudson River where the Twaalfskill Creek long ago eroded a break in the west shore escarpment. Long before that, in geologic time, glacial ice sheets up to a mile high smoothed out the mountains that had been pushed up even earlier by the movements of the tectonic plates that undergird our continents today.

From earliest times, water was a main transportation mode. The Hudson carried lumber, stone, pelts, ice, bricks, livestock, fish, meat, cement, and produce to the growing cities. Coming into the small towns and cities lining the river's shores were new settlers, manufactured goods such as tools and machinery, and, most importantly, new ideas.

When the Hudson froze, it became the life source for the hundreds of ice-harvesting businesses that flourished along its shores. The invention of refrigeration melted the ice-harvesting business in the dance of creative destruction—in this case, the obsolete being replaced with something cheaper, less dangerous, more reliable, more hygienic, and requiring less human muscle.

The river was not all work and no play. The Hudson River Intercollegiate Regatta brought thousands to both of its shores beginning in 1895. Until the regatta moved to another site in 1949, local hotels and boardinghouses—including the Whitley House, The Point, and Bellevue Villa—took in the young men who would delight the throngs on race days. The huge steamboats bringing thousands of visitors also added to the river's excitement. Whether headed to one of the vast amusement parks (at the site of the current Marist College or Kingston Point) or just for a round-trip on the Hudson without disembarking, the river provided many hours of delight for decades.

Barons of industry built their American castles along the Hudson, and many of those homes still reign from their perches. Fabulous yachts were things of wonder, gliding on the Hudson to berths in boathouses that rivaled most of the area's homes. Today, tugboats push and pull barges, and container ships run the Hudson's course. Most recently, modest tour boats entice residents and visitors to experience the Hudson River in a more intimate way.

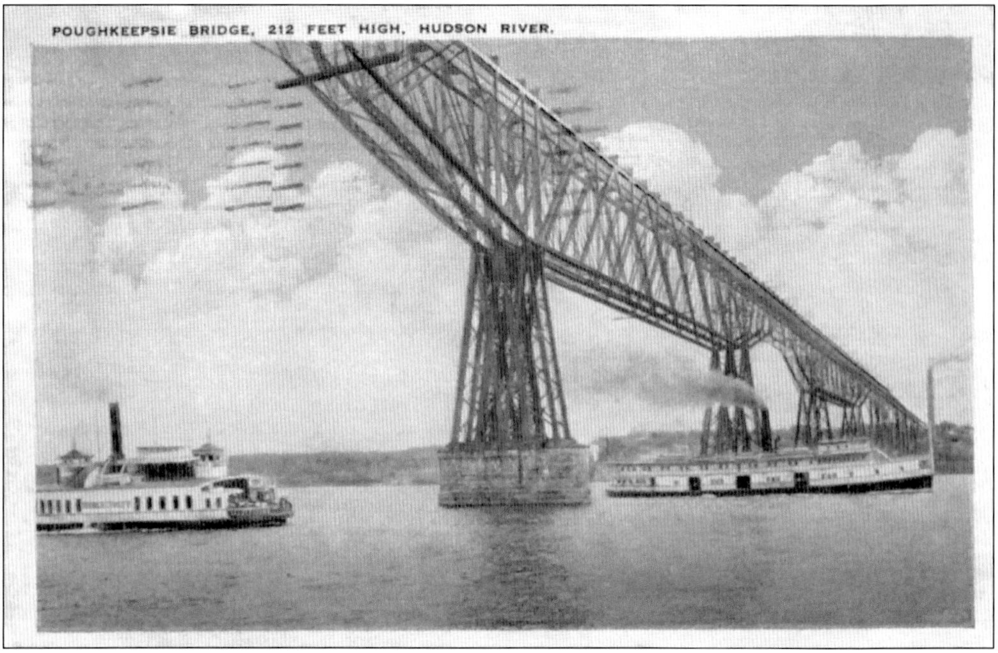

Highland's Hudson River port, called Highland Landing after 1865, had many earlier names, including Yelverton's Landing, Valentine Baker's Landing, and New Paltz Landing. Now rehabilitated as a public park, Highland Landing is again a deepwater port that can accommodate large ships. The park also boasts boat launches for smaller craft. The above and below photographs show the ferry *Brinckerhoff*, which docked not far from the new park. The *Brinckerhoff*, built in 1899, ran between Highland Landing and Poughkeepsie from 1922 to 1941, even surviving competition from the Mid-Hudson Bridge, which opened on August 25, 1930. The *Brinckerhoff* was a walking-beam-design vessel. When funds could not be raised to rehabilitate her, she was dismantled at Mystic, Connecticut. (Both, courtesy of Town of Lloyd Historian's Office.)

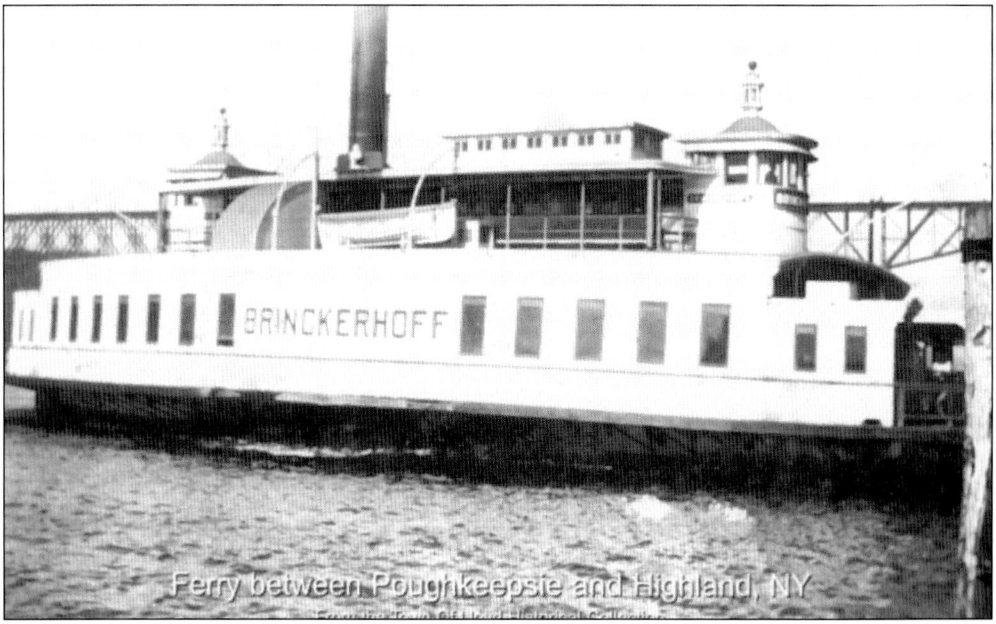

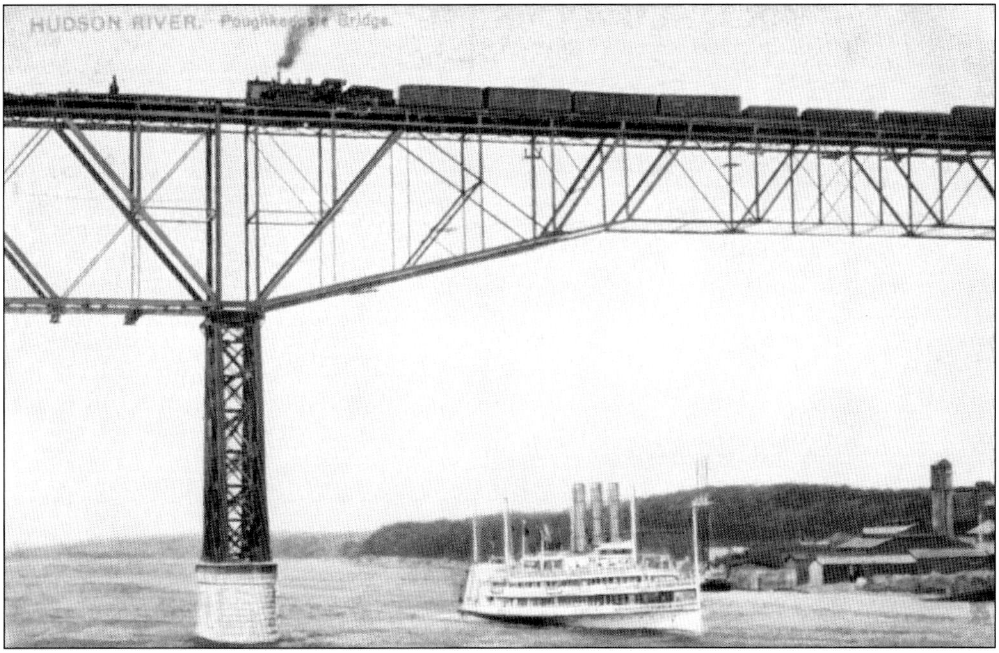

Passenger boats plied between Albany and New York with regularly scheduled stops at smaller ports. The Hudson River Day Line began in 1863 with the ships *Daniel Drew* and *Armenia*. They provided day-boat service between Albany and New York City with stops along the course to pick up and discharge passengers. (Courtesy of Town of Lloyd Historian's Office.)

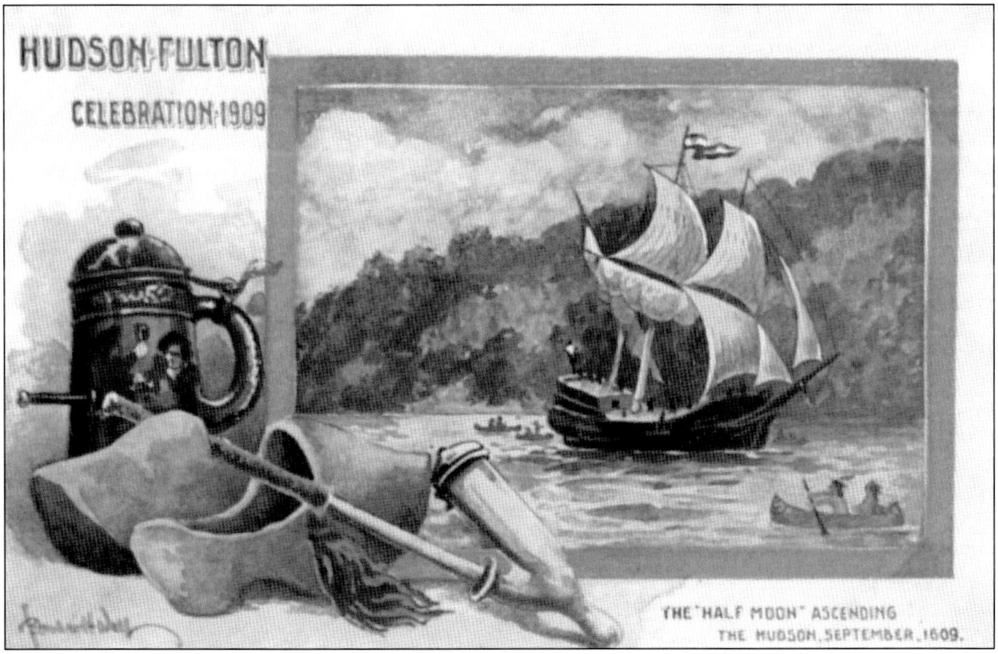

Today, the Hudson River accommodates tour boats, fuel tankers, international ships, tugboats and barges, pleasure craft, jet skis, and, on special occasions, replica ships, such as the two-masted schooner *Armistad* and Henry Hudson's *Half Moon*, pictured above in the 1909 Hudson-Fulton Celebration postcard.

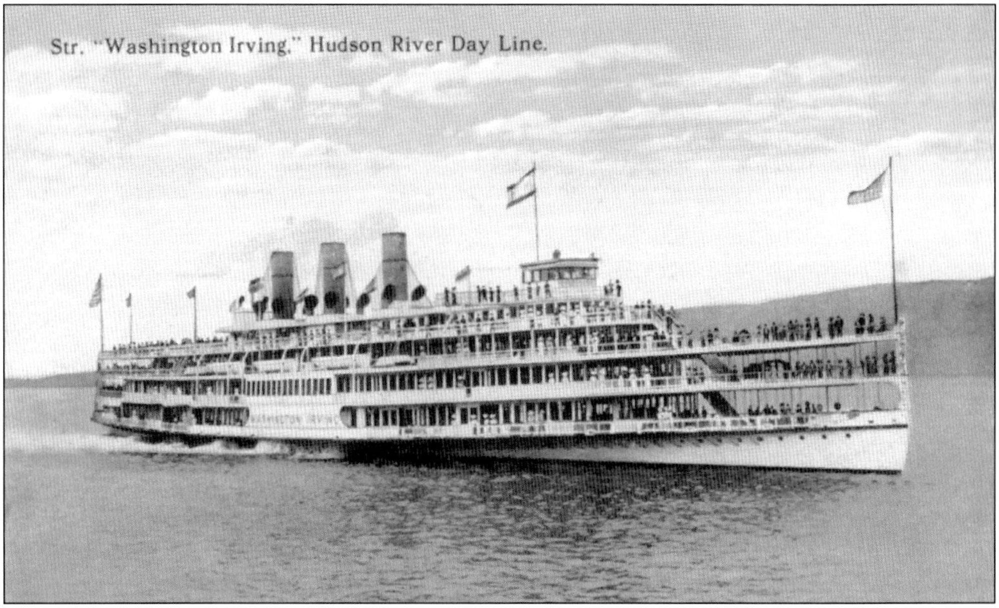

Elegance was the byword of the Hudson River Dayliners. The company advertised that it carried passengers only and no freight. With their beautiful salons and gorgeous views, the boat trips were mini-vacations that the growing middle class could afford, and they flocked aboard. Passengers bought tour books showing both shores and noting significant features along the entire trip from New York to Albany.

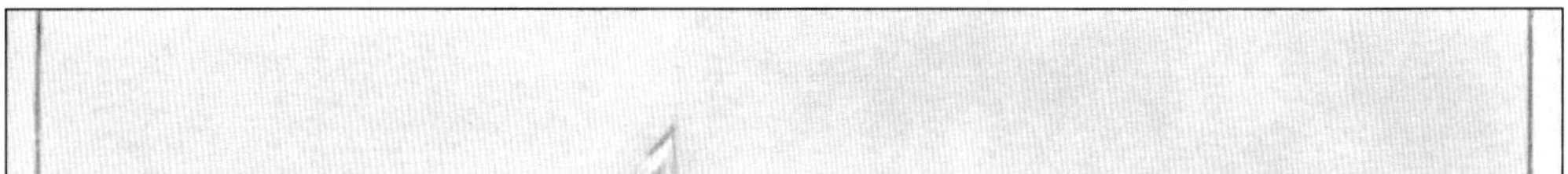

Built in 1927, the *Peter Stuyvesant* was the last Day Line boat built for the run between Albany and New York City. She featured the newer design of a single-screw propeller. She was named for the fourth and last governor of New Netherland, the Dutch colony that became New York. The ship served until the 1960s. She finished her days as a restaurant in Boston but floundered in the blizzard of 1978 and sank.

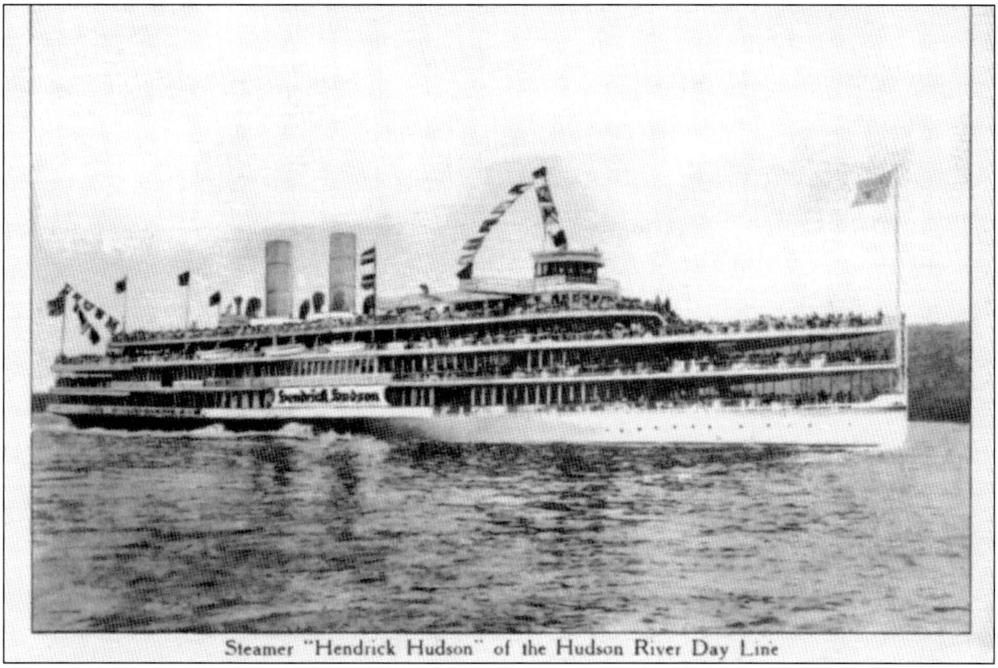

In 1906, the first million-dollar Day Line ship, the *Hendrick Hudson*, entered service on the Hudson (sharing it with the oldest steamboat in service, the *Norwich*, built in 1836). Built at Newburgh, New York, the *Hendrick Hudson* was scrapped in 1951. Considered a palace in her day, she carried more than 5,000 people.

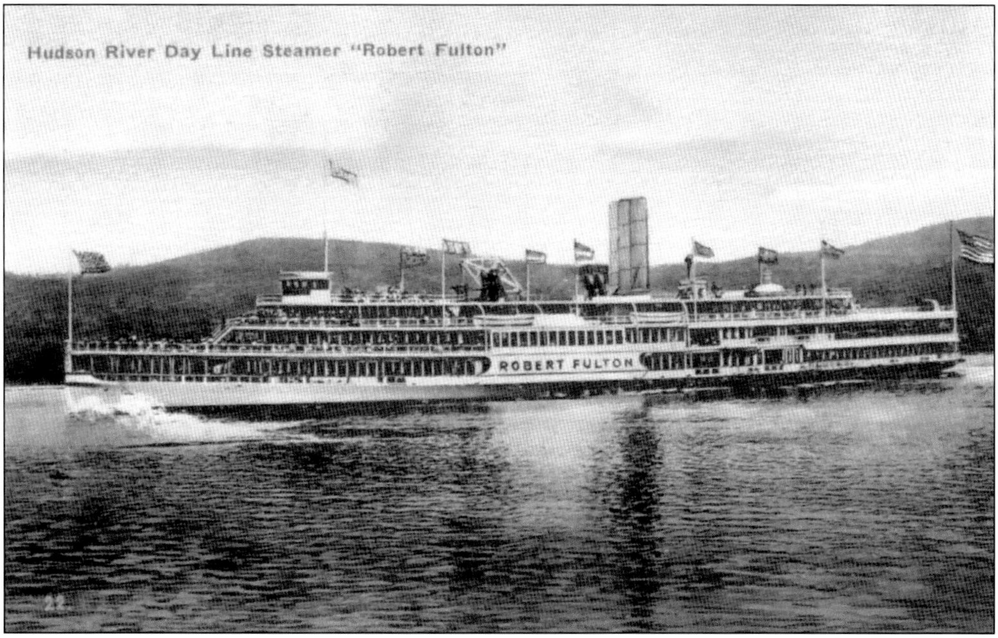

The *Robert Fulton* entered service on the Hudson in 1909, just as her 1807 forebear, the *North River* (also known as the *Clermont*), was being touted on the Hudson-Fulton Celebration postcards. The ship made her final run between New York City and Albany in 1948, signaling the end of regular passenger service on the Hudson between those two cities.

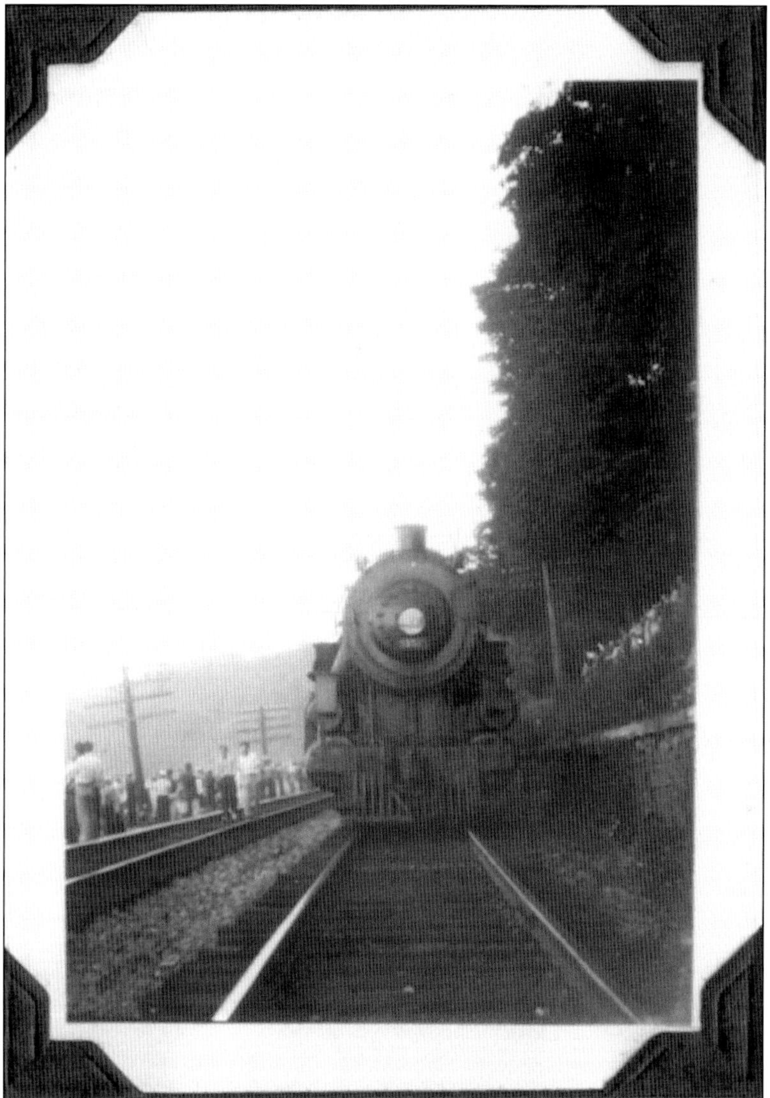

1936 Highland, NY. Crowd watching College Regatta on the Hudson River.
From the collection of Vivian Yess Wadlin

The river was also a source of sport. The hugely popular Hudson River Intercollegiate Regattas (1895–1948) featured crew races among 11 major rowing colleges—Cornell University, Syracuse University, the University of Pennsylvania, Columbia University, the University of Washington, the US Naval Academy, the University of Wisconsin, Princeton University, Rutgers University, the Massachusetts Institute of Technology, and the University of California. During the regattas, the West Shore Railroad converted flatcars into mobile bleachers. Spectators could ride along the racecourse as the crew teams struggled at the oars to become the next regatta celebrants. This postcard was produced from an original photograph taken during the 1936 regatta. Today, Marist College's rowing teams are out practicing at sunrise as soon as the ice is off the Hudson. The river is often calmest that time of day. Marist's teams compete with other colleges almost every weekend during the rowing season.

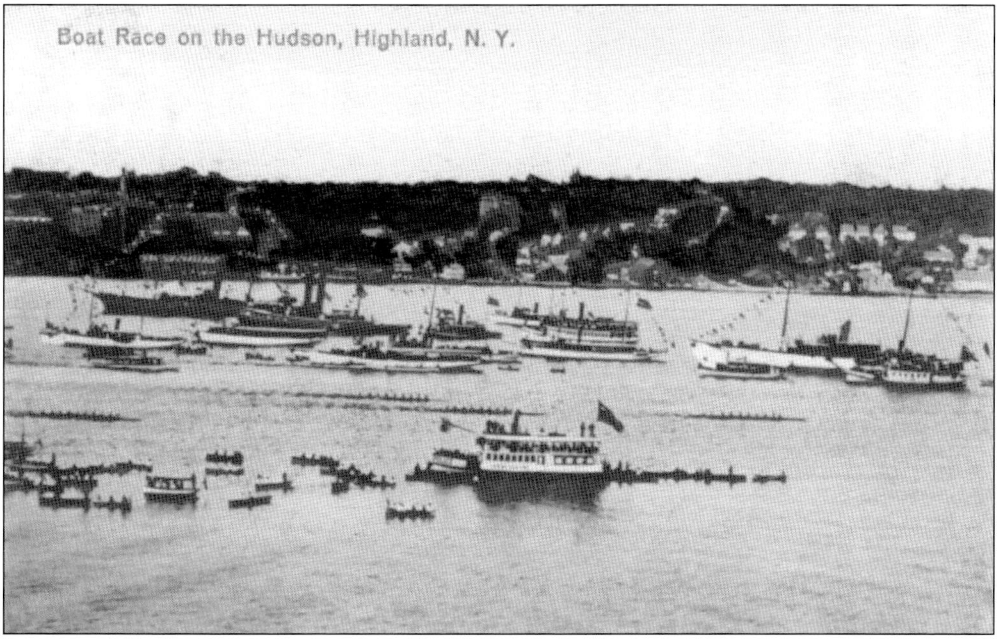

Graceful sloops and smoking steamers brought tourists from all over the nation on race day. Signal flags atop the Poughkeepsie-Highland railroad bridge told cheering crowds which college won each contest. Older Highland residents tell of cars being backed up along River Road and into the village on race days, and children would sell refreshments to regatta goers at the intersection of Grand Street and Vineyard Avenue.

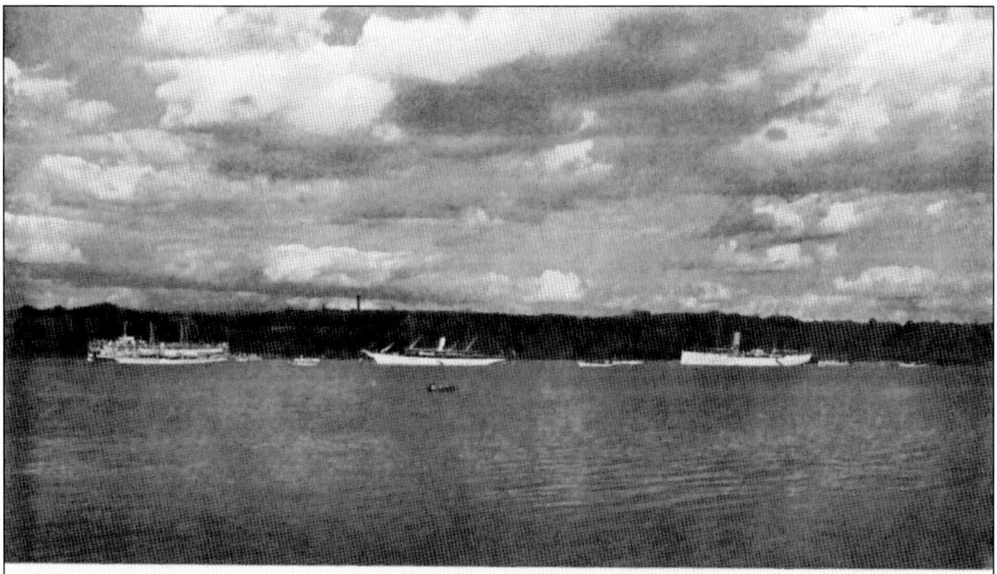

This pre-1906 postcard shows some of the private yachts that came for the Regatta Race Day. The yacht in the center appears to be Col. Oliver Hazard Payne's yacht, the *Aphrodite.* It was often seen in the Hudson on its way to and from the colonel's mansion in West Park. (Courtesy of Gail Russell.)

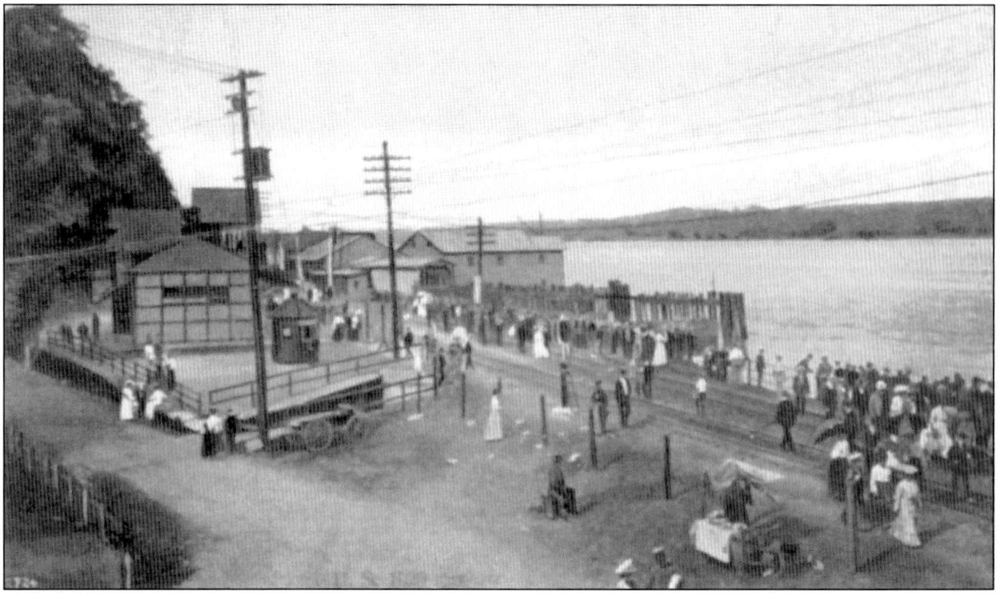

The West Shore Railroad began freight and passenger service in 1883. The postcard above, postmarked at Highland on March 14, 1910, shows the Highland station. The correspondent writes, "Don't forget the boat races near station (shown on this card) next summer." The station is now an apartment building.

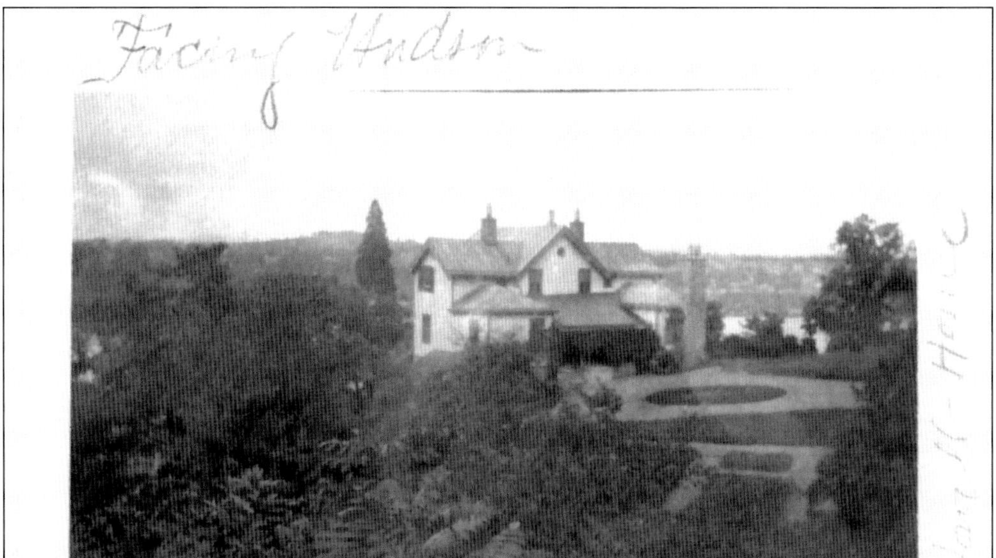

Crew teams stayed at various inns along the river. The Point hosted a team, while its neighbor to the north, Bellevue Villa, accommodated the University of Pennsylvania team in the late 1890s. The Point was razed in 2012 and replaced by a residence. (Courtesy of Town of Lloyd Historian's Office.)

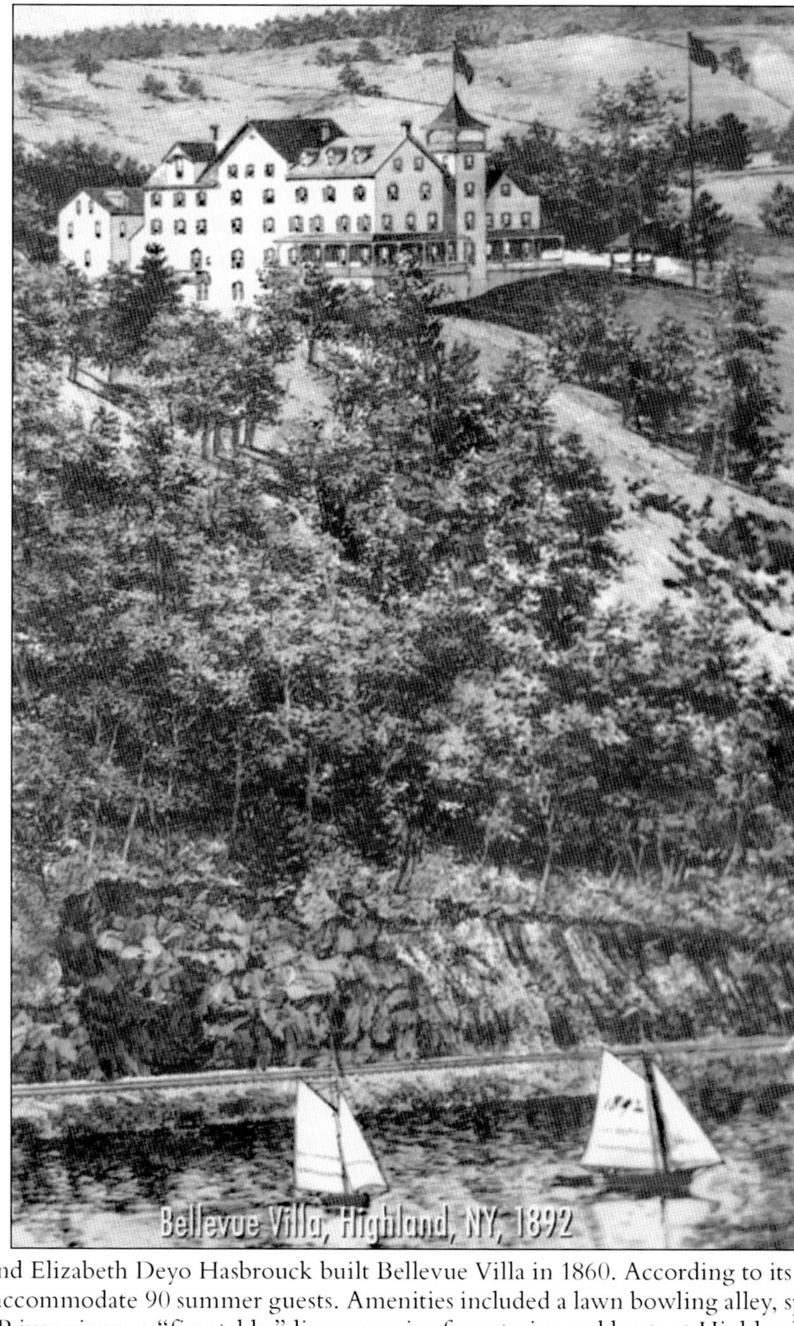

Abram and Elizabeth Deyo Hasbrouck built Bellevue Villa in 1860. According to its brochure, it could accommodate 90 summer guests. Amenities included a lawn bowling alley, spectacular Hudson River views, a "fine table," livery service from trains and boats at Highland Landing, and fresh water that was supplied by an aboveground aqueduct from the nearby Illinois Mountain. The access from the landing was by a dug road up the face of the escarpment. Bellevue Villa Hotel housed the Pennsylvania crew team when they were in town for the regattas each year. Dr. C.H. Ganse purchased the hotel for $14,250 on November 1, 1904, but less than two months later, Bellevue Villa burned to the ground on December 22, 1904. The aqueduct was not used in the winter because it would freeze, so there was no water available to fight the fire. The Town of Lloyd Historical Preservation Society used this hand-colored etching for a postcard.

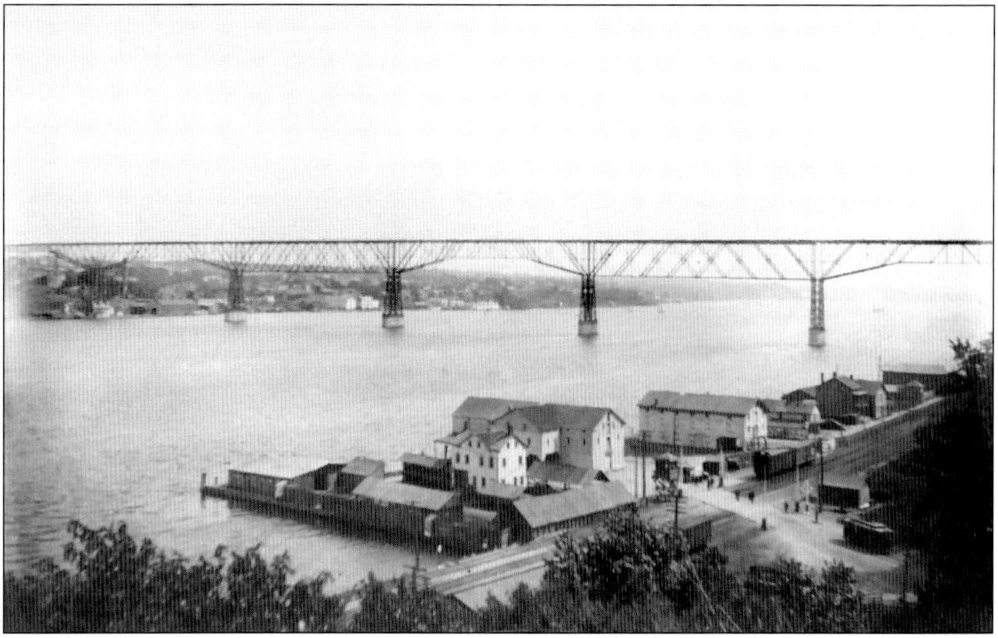

Some of the businesses that were along the Hudson River in 1912 included warehouses, icehouses, docking facilities, and foundries. Highland Landing was a very busy place. Barges, cargo ships, steamships, and ferries came by water, and railcars and trolleys met them. (Courtesy of Town of Lloyd Historian's Office.)

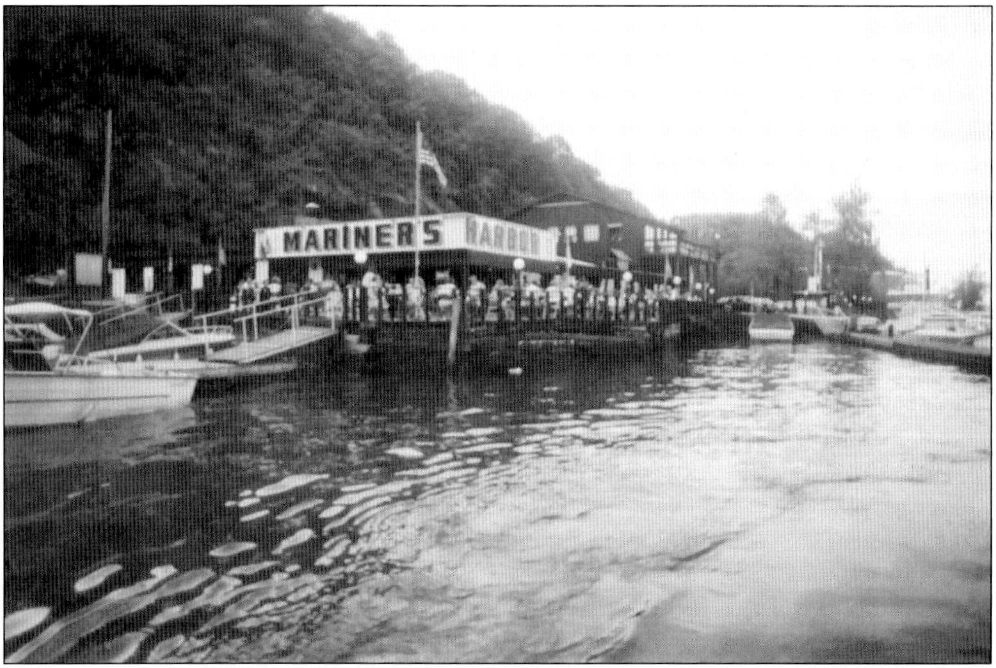

Mariner's Restaurant is the one business that has survived at the river. In spite of severe hurricane damage from Irene (2011) and Sandy (2012), the restaurant came back both times, better and more cherished by Highland residents and visitors. Today, it is the only business on this once-busy waterfront.

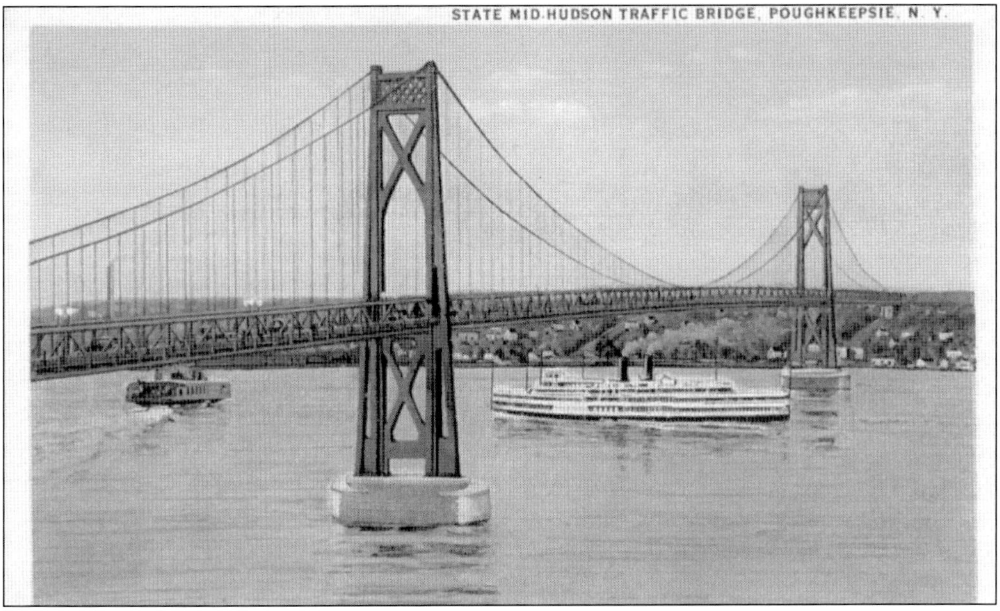

The Mid-Hudson Bridge opened on August 25, 1930, with a large celebration in Highland that was attended by Gov. Franklin D. Roosevelt. Building the bridge cost $5.89 million, and Roosevelt promised that "it will be operated as a toll bridge until the state collects the cost of its erection." The bridge spans 3,000 feet, and at its highest point, the roadway is 135 feet above the Hudson.

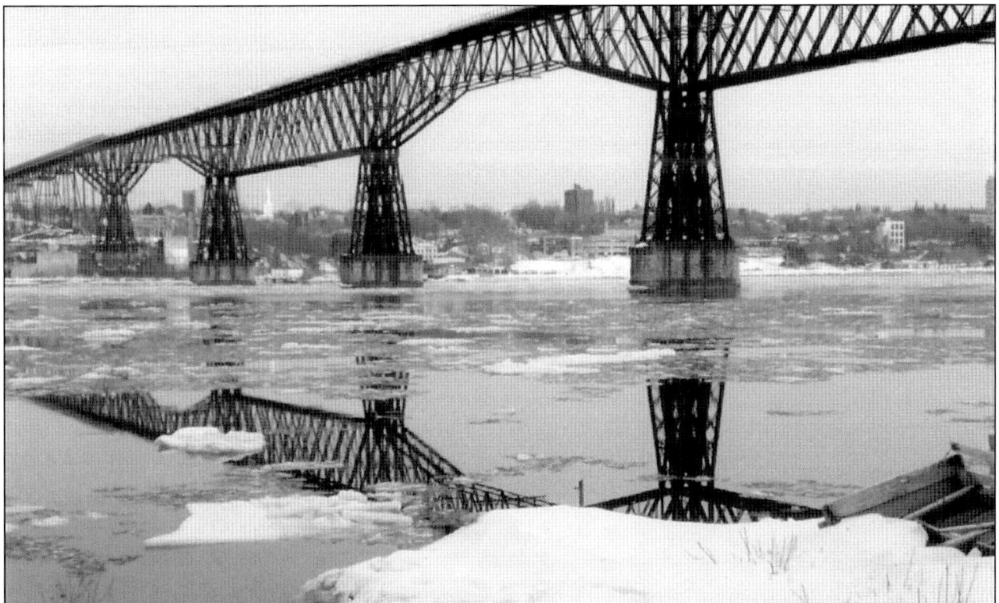

The largest tourist attraction today in the Mid-Hudson region is the former railroad bridge between Highland and Poughkeepsie, now the Walkway Over the Hudson State Park. Niagara Falls is the only state park that gets more visitors annually. The walkway is 212 feet above the river and 1.28 miles long. This modern postcard shows a view from the Highland side of the river in the winter of 2012.

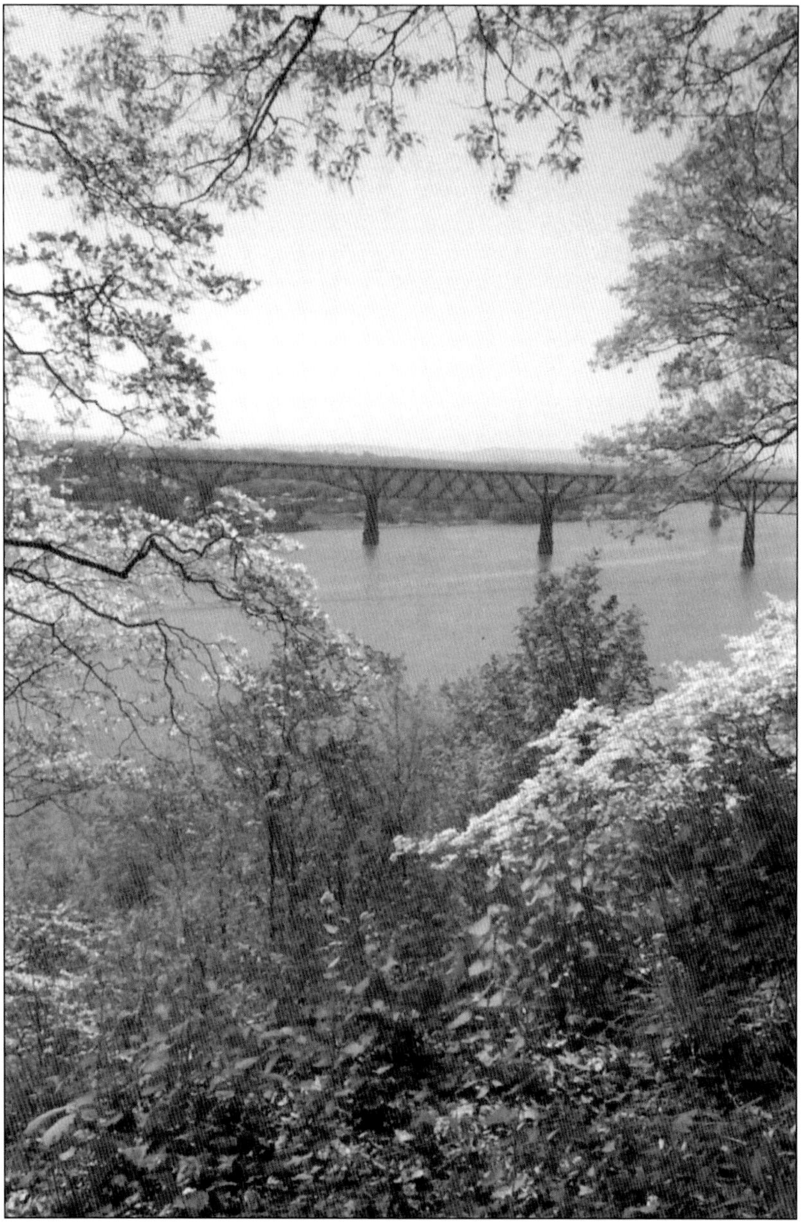

Although fall gets the most points for Hudson Valley beauty, spring along the Hudson has a fascination all its own. With the yellow-green of just leafing trees, the red of maple buds, the pink of fruit tree blossoms, and the white of wild dogwood, the beauty of spring is fast becoming a tourist draw. This card shows the view through dogwoods from the site of Bellevue Villa, which burned down in 1904. In addition to dogwood, some of the trees visible from the site include chestnut oak, red oak, maple, sassafras, hop hornbeam, white mulberry, and witch hazel. The site now houses a private residence. Although not visible in the card, Marist College is just to the left of this view. Marist's crew teams, fireworks, celebrations, and beautiful buildings make the view somewhat different from the one enjoyed by guests of Bellevue Villa. In the postcard, Walkway Over the Hudson is visible in the distance, behind that is Poughkeepsie, and beyond that is a range of mountains in Connecticut.

Five

Inland Transportation

The road from Highland Landing to New Paltz was blazed in 1766, but most parts of it could only be traveled on foot or horseback. A private New Paltz Turnpike Company was organized in 1807 and completed a turnpike, or toll road, along the route in 1832. It used the tolls to maintain the road and to pay a return to investors who provided the capital. Another toll road in Highland was built by the Highland and Modena Turnpike Road Company, organized in 1866. It is the present route of Vineyard Avenue.

On other roads, highway maintenance was a communal affair, using a system that went back to colonial times. Every able-bodied man had been required by law to do roadwork for six days each year between April and August. Any man who did not report for roadwork would be assessed a substantial penalty, although there was also an option of sending a servant or slave as a substitute. This work would be under the direction of road commissioners, who were first appointed by the New York Colonial Assembly in 1729. When the Town of Lloyd was organized in 1845, three commissioners were appointed; subsequent commissioners were elected annually.

In 1898, the state legislature enacted a statute for the improvement of public highways and began using state funds to pave main routes, usually with macadam. The post road from Newburgh through Highland to Kingston (the predecessor of Route 9W) was one road that got paved under the 1898 statute, although the job was not entirely completed until 1908.

An even bigger boon to inland transportation occurred in 1897, when an electric trolley line began operating through Highland. Investors bought the route of the old New Paltz Turnpike, and tracks were laid from the steamboat and railroad depots at Highland Landing to the Wallkill Valley Railroad in New Paltz. However, as automobiles improved, more travelers chose to drive instead of taking the trolley line, which made its final run in 1925.

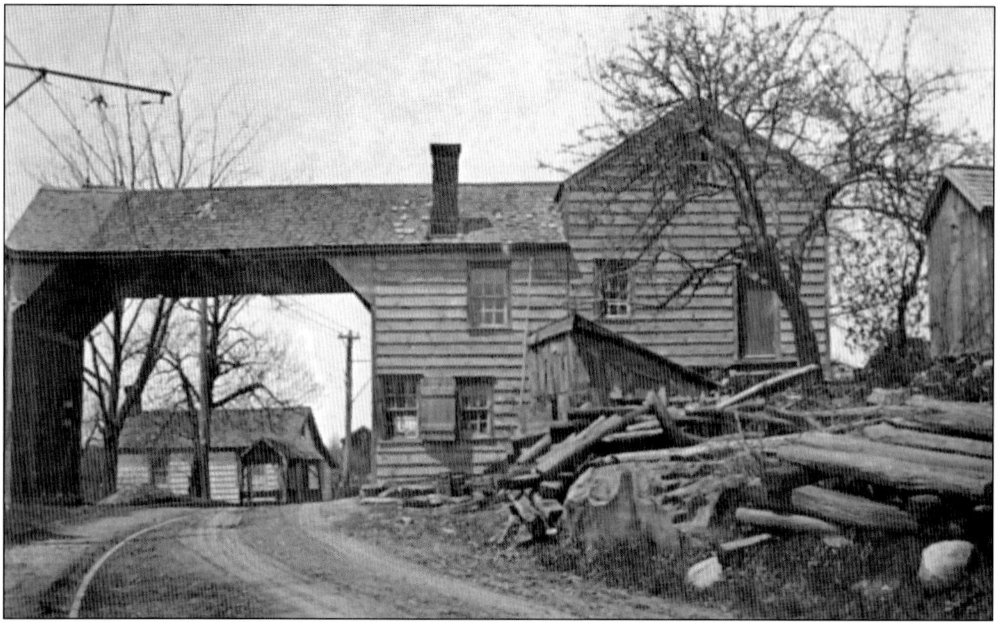

While most roads in the 19th century were haphazardly maintained using conscripted labor, the New Paltz Turnpike Company used toll revenues to maintain its road. This was one of the tollhouses. The route was bought by investors, who laid tracks and started running an east–west electric trolley in 1897. Note the tracks and overhead trolley wires on the left. (Courtesy of Gail Russell.)

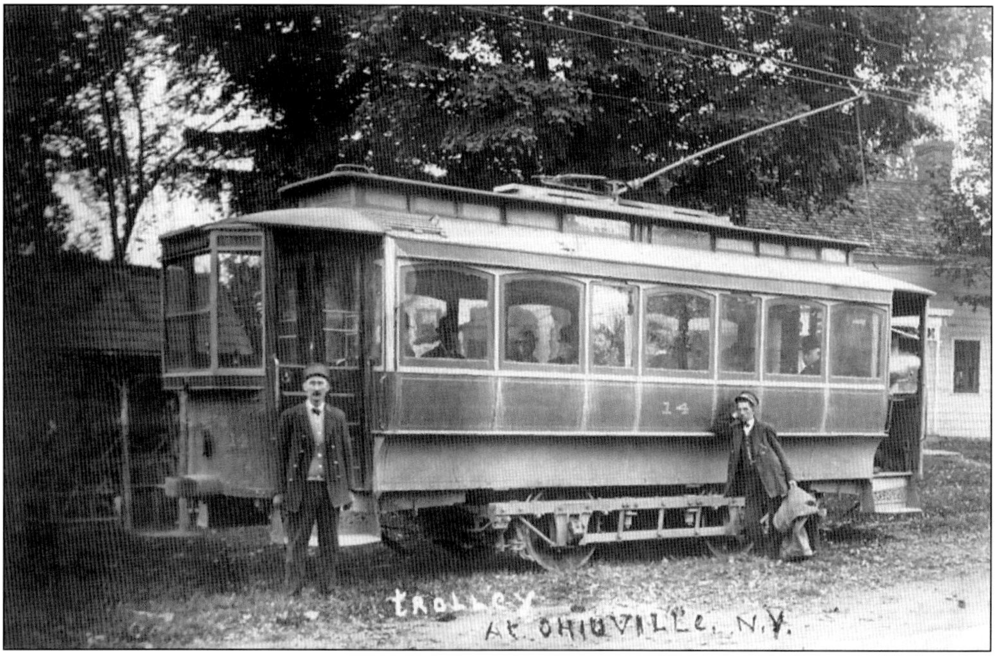

The motorman and conductor of trolley car No. 14 pause for a stop at Ohioville on the route from Highland to New Paltz. Trolleys operated mostly in larger cities, and this was the only trolley line in Ulster County to go between two villages. The route was nine miles long, and with numerous stops along the way, the trip from one end to the other took 45 minutes.

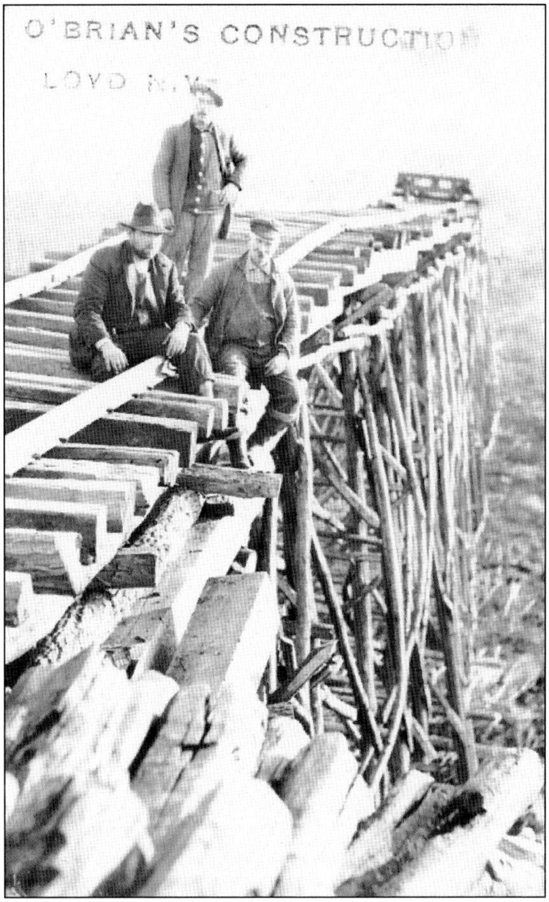

The company that built the railroad bridge from Highland to Poughkeepsie did not own any railroad lines on either side of the bridge. The Hudson Connecting Railroad Co. laid out tracks west from the bridge through Highland and as far as Campbell Hall. However, others had larger plans and organized the Central New England Railway, which bought out many small connecting lines on both sides of the railroad bridge to make a single railroad through New York and Connecticut. Wooden trestles such as this one were later replaced using stone, concrete, or steel to carry the tracks. The railroad was often a good neighbor, and it appears from the postcard below that part of its bridge structure was used to support a plank-decked surface for wagons.

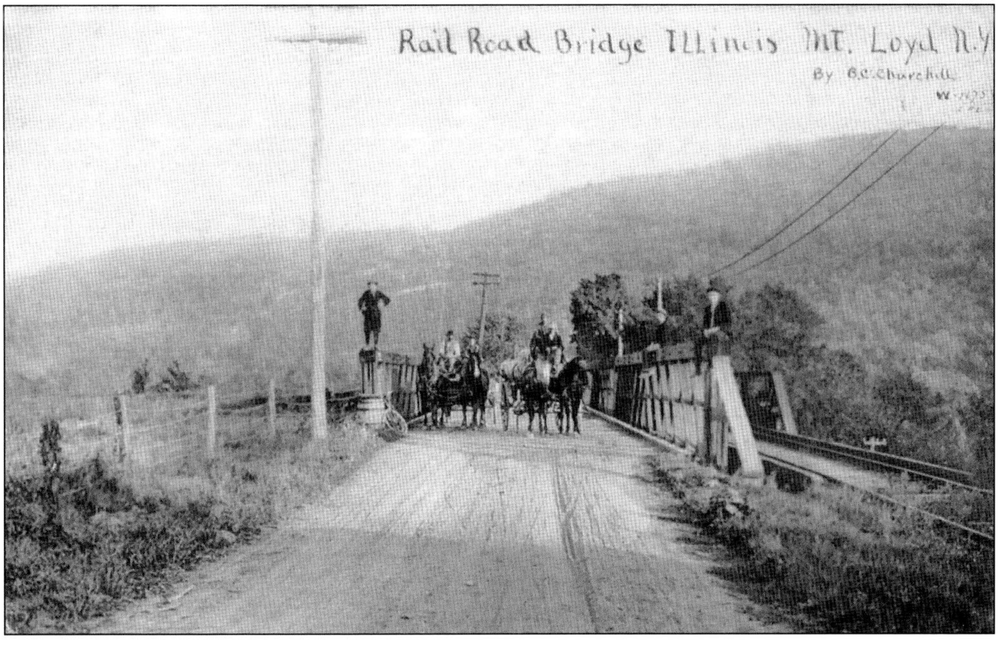

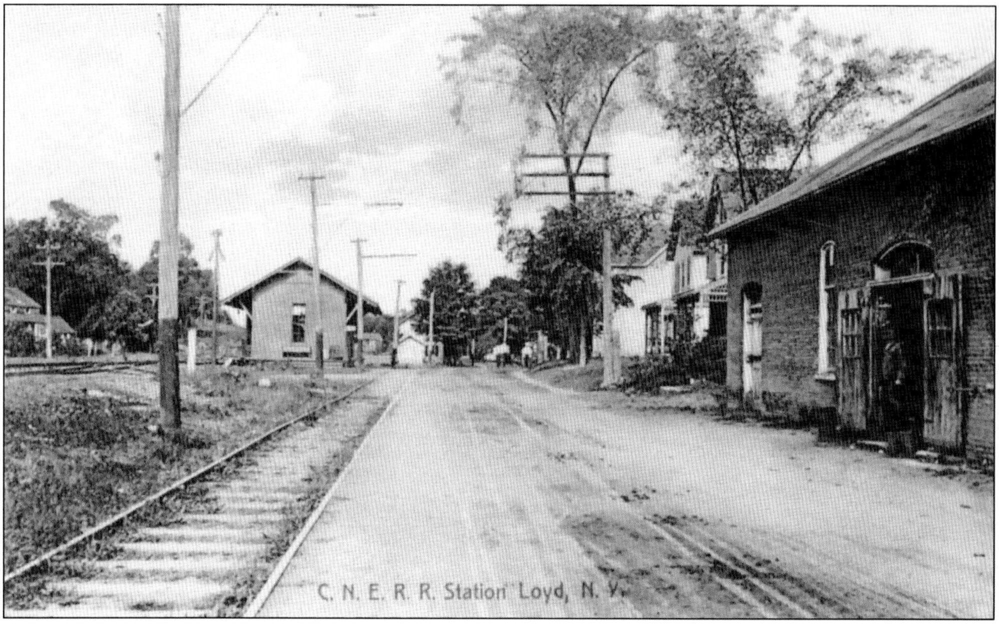

The now-vanished village of Loyd was a point where travelers could transfer between the railroad and the trolley line. In the postcard above, the trolley tracks are in the foreground. The building on the right was the powerhouse that generated electricity for the trolley by burning coal. Still standing today, it is now the Highland Hose Company's Fire Station No. 2. Because the electricity was direct current, which does not transmit efficiently over long distances, it was advantageous to generate it at a point about midway in the trolley line. To the left of the trolley tracks at a distance is the railroad station, and on the left side of the station are the railroad tracks. The postcard below shows the trestle at Brooks Crossing, which carried the trolley over the railroad tracks.

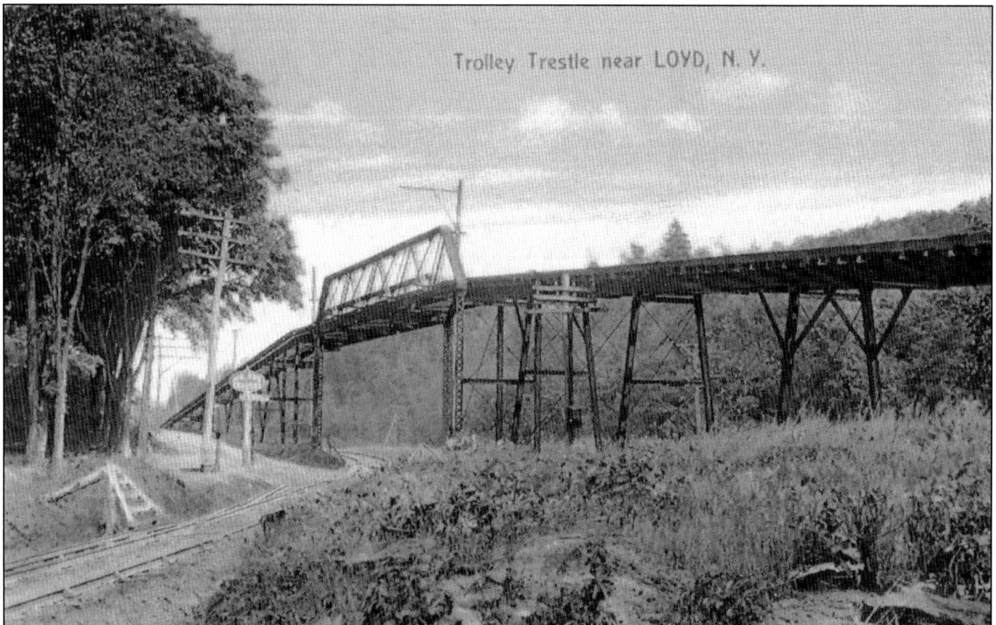

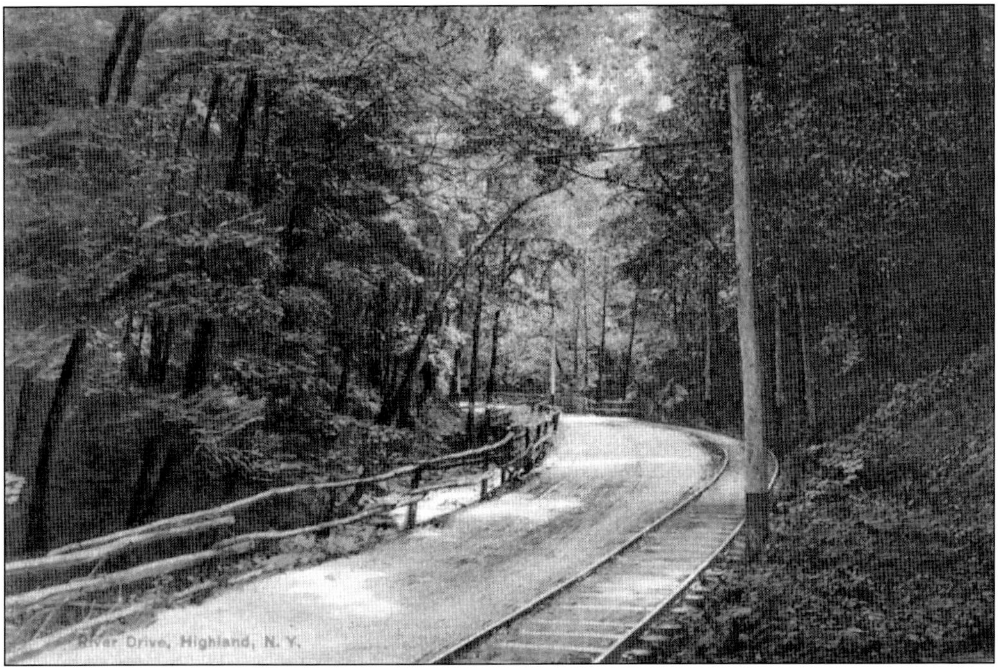

River Road is seen before and after being paved. The roadway was built in 1897 to accommodate the new electric railway. The original road to the river, now Maple Avenue, was considered too steep for the trolleys. In the postcard above, the ruts and sharp curves of the unpaved road presented a challenge for carriages and automobiles. Only a rickety rail fence served to protect drivers from plunging into the Twaalfskill Creek. Below, one can see the rebuilt roadway after the state paved it and erected concrete and iron guardrails. The opening of the new road prompted a huge celebration in Highland (see the photograph on the bottom of page 12).

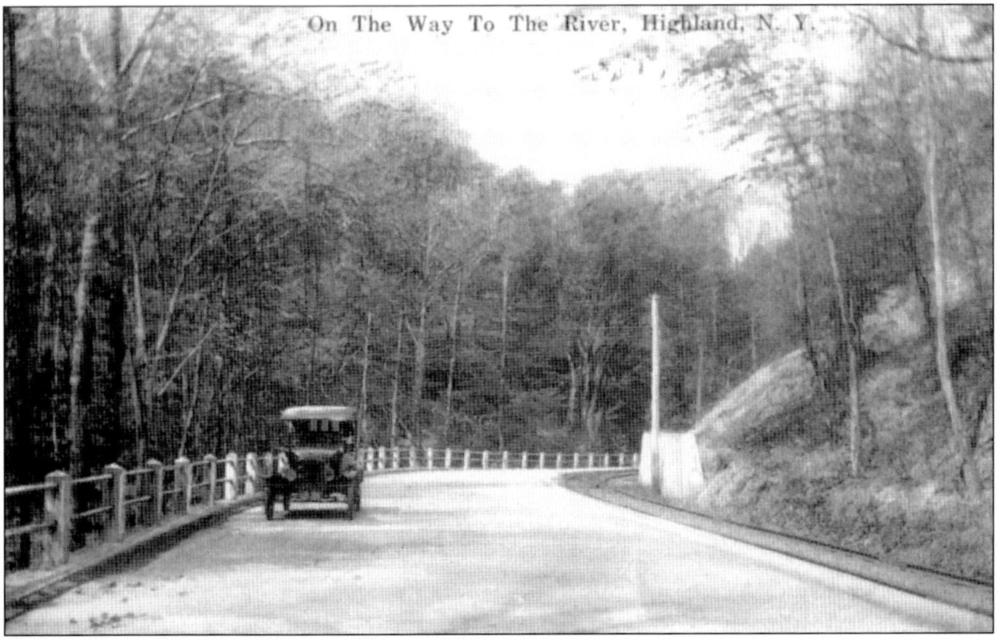

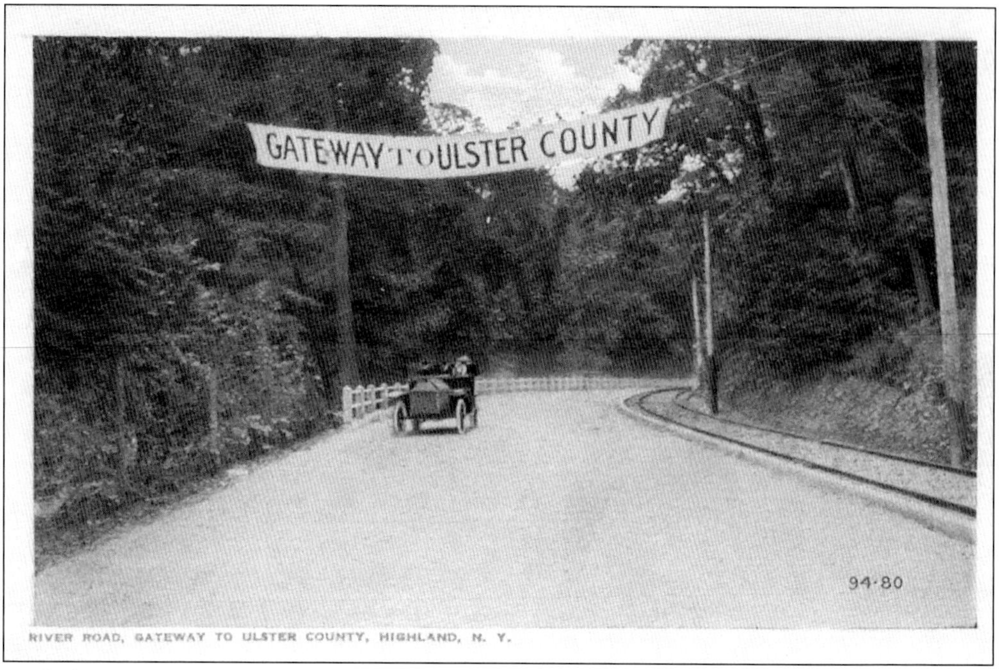

With the opening of the new state road to the river in 1915, Highland proudly proclaimed itself as the "Gateway to Ulster County." This was not an idle boast, because many people did arrive by steamboat and train at Highland Landing, where they then took the trolley or were driven up River Road to the village.

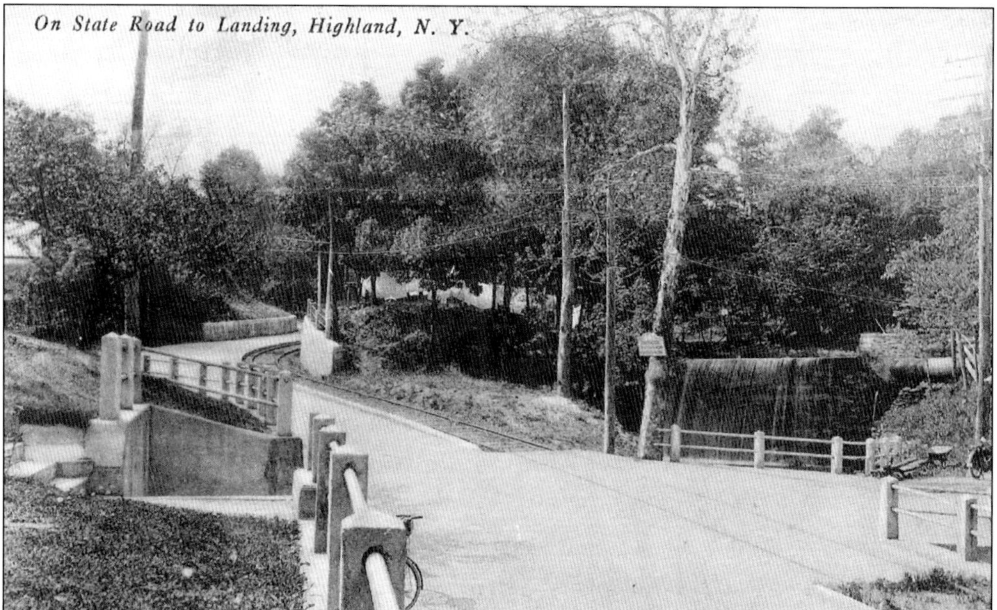

Another view of the new state road is shown here around 1915. On the right is Bellevue Road, and behind the railing, a waterfall flows over Shantz's dam on the Twaalfskill. To the right of the waterfall is a large pipe, which carried the water to turn the waterwheel in Schantz's mill.

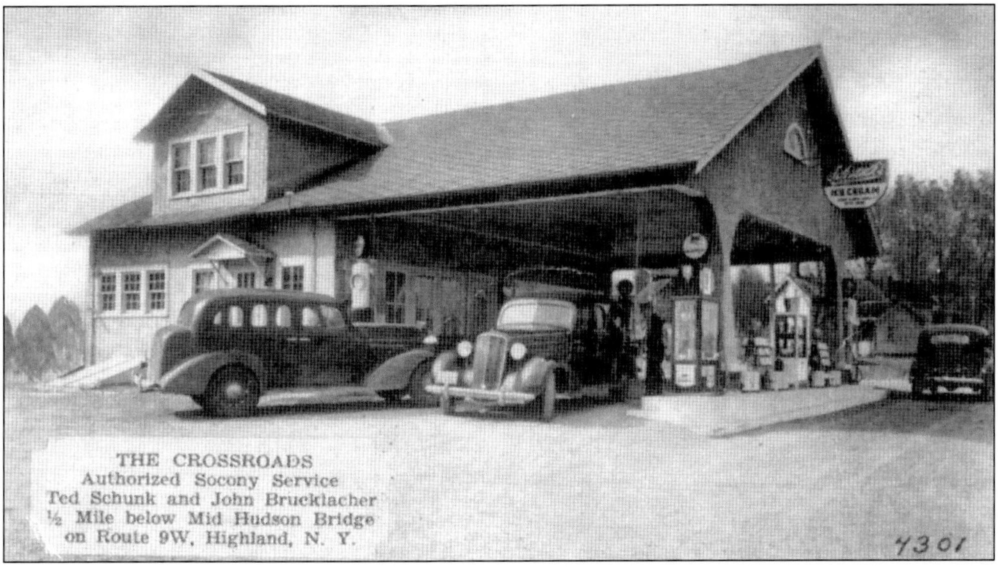

The advent of the automobile spawned new needs, and service stations, often called garages, sprang up along the highways to meet them. The Crossroads establishment was located at the intersection of Route 9W and Chapel Hill Road. This place also sold snacks and other non-automotive merchandise, making it a forerunner of today's convenience mart. (Courtesy of Gail Russell.)

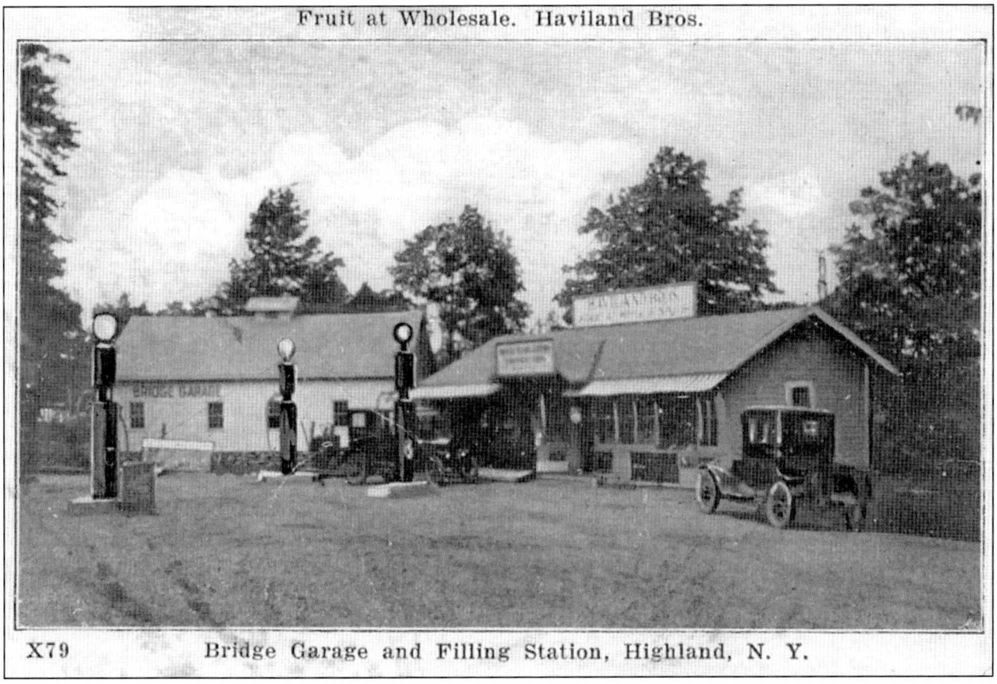

The Haviland brothers had a fruit store on the corner of Haviland Road and the post road, now Route 9W. When the Mid-Hudson Bridge opened in 1930, Haviland Road became the route to the new bridge. Located on this strategic corner, the Havilands put gasoline pumps out front and added other automotive services, calling their establishment the Bridge Garage. A new Sunoco gas station is now on this corner.

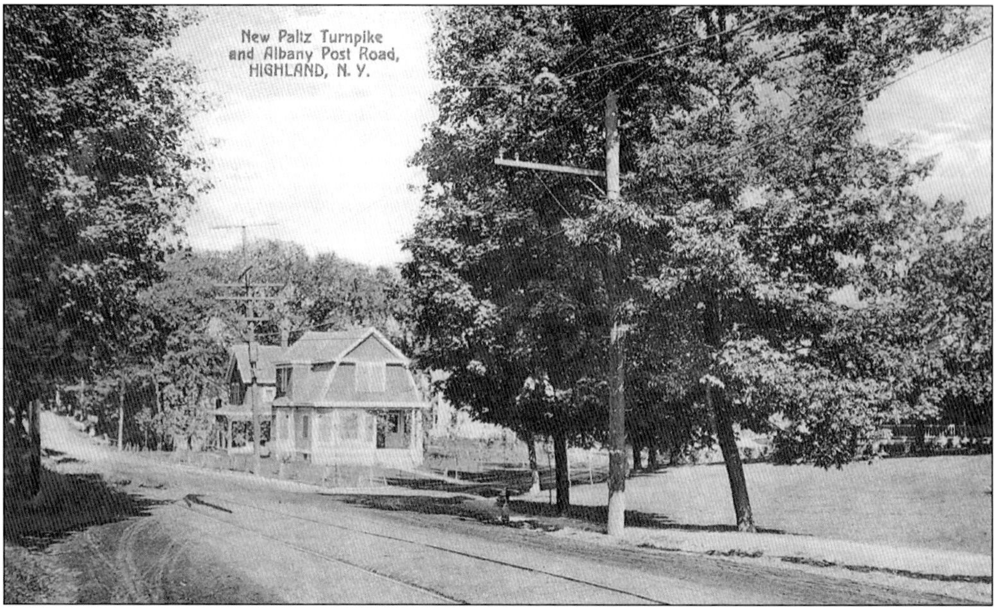

This c. 1930 postcard shows a familiar intersection in Highland—the corner of what is now New Paltz Road and North Road, which leads to the present Highland post office, located one and a quarter miles north of the village. The Albany Post Road was the main north–south route between Newburgh and Kingston. Before the Route 9W bypass was built, all traffic was routed through downtown Highland.

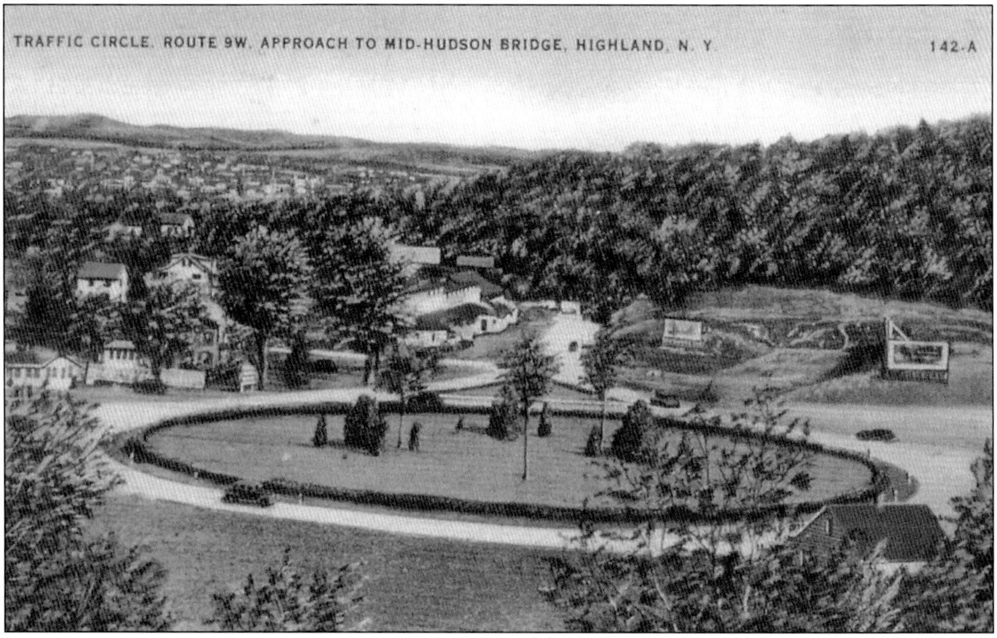

A traffic circle, known as the Bridge Circle, was at the intersection of Route 9W, Haviland Road, and Tillson Avenue. Around 1920, the state began building traffic circles to speed up vehicles at busy intersections. Hundreds of them were built throughout New York, but later studies showed that accident rates at traffic circles were more than three times higher than at square intersections. The state then spent millions of dollars to remove most of the traffic circles.

Six

Nearby Places

The Township of New Paltz once stretched from its present western border to the Hudson, including what is now Highland and the entire Town of Lloyd. Highland's early settlement and its road, rail, and river connections made it a hub for inland farms and communities to reach the outside world. Highland was surrounded by small hamlets at crossroads that provided necessities for the rural population.

West of the town center of Highland, usually at roads crossing the New Paltz Turnpike, were hamlets with a store and post office and names such as Loyd, Centerville, and Plutarch. An important early community that survives is Ohioville. It had a school, church, stores, hotels, gas stations, a trolley stop, and a restaurant.

South of Highland on the post road (Route 9W) was the hamlet of Milton, and west on the Modena Turnpike (Route 44/55) were Clintondale, Ardonia, Modena, and Gardiner. At the Modena intersection with Route 32, some of the original buildings survive.

North of Highland along the post road (Route 9W) in the Town of Esopus were the hamlets of Esopus, West Park, Ulster Park, and Port Ewen. Some of the 19th century's rich and famous, including such notables as Col. Oliver Hazard Payne and naturalist John Burroughs, made their homes in Esopus. Burroughs's cabin in the woods, named Slabsides, and his chestnut study are in the National Register of Historic Places. Judge Alton B. Parker's home in Esopus became the focal point in the 1904 presidential race. Democrat Parker campaigned from his porch but was defeated by the traveling campaigner Teddy Roosevelt. Mansions such as Aberdeen and the Smith House were many things at different times in their histories.

Northwest of Highland were other hamlets, including Eddyville, Dashville, and Rifton. Dashville Falls provided waterpower for huge mills, creating jobs and manufacturing a variety of products, such as woolens, rugs, foodstuff, and blankets for the Union army during the Civil War.

East of Highland is the mighty and majestic Hudson. Though not the heart of Highland, it is certainly one of its major arteries.

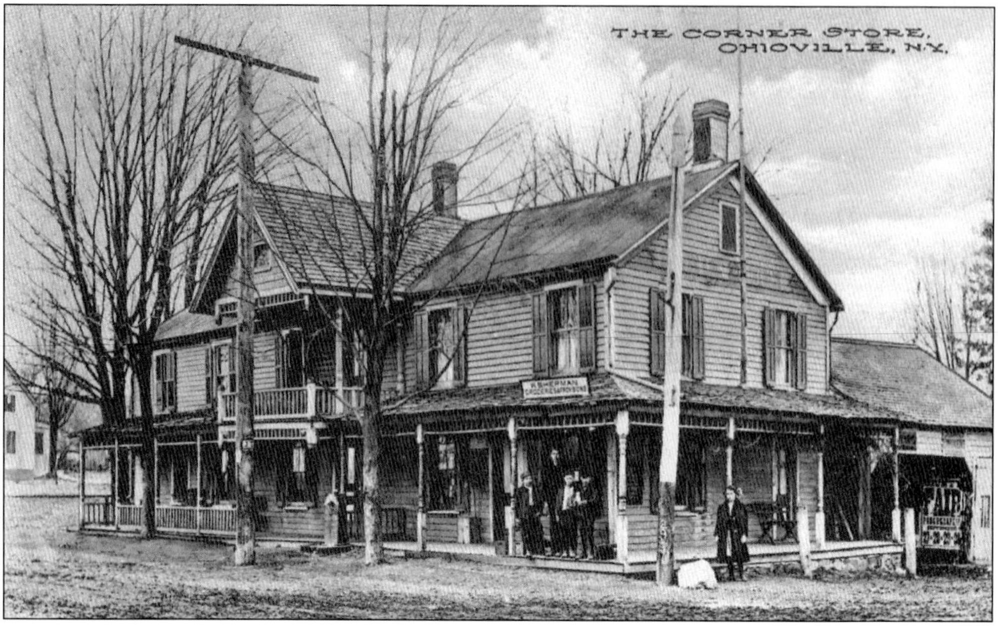

Ohioville lies to the east of the New York State Thruway Exit 18 on Route 299. North Ohioville and South Ohioville Roads make up the crossroads. The thruway is only the latest development to create change in Ohioville. Known to early settlers as Helltown, it was dignified to Ohioville in 1850. With its own store, post office, hotel, restaurant, livery stable, school, and church, it was worthy of its new name. In 1897, the Highland–New Paltz Trolley rolled into town, and suddenly the world was passing by. Travelers were going to the casino, the normal school, the theater in New Paltz, the mountain hotels, to work in the fields, or to the sewing and knitting mills in Highland. This building is on the northwest corner of Ohioville Road and today is the Village Restaurant.

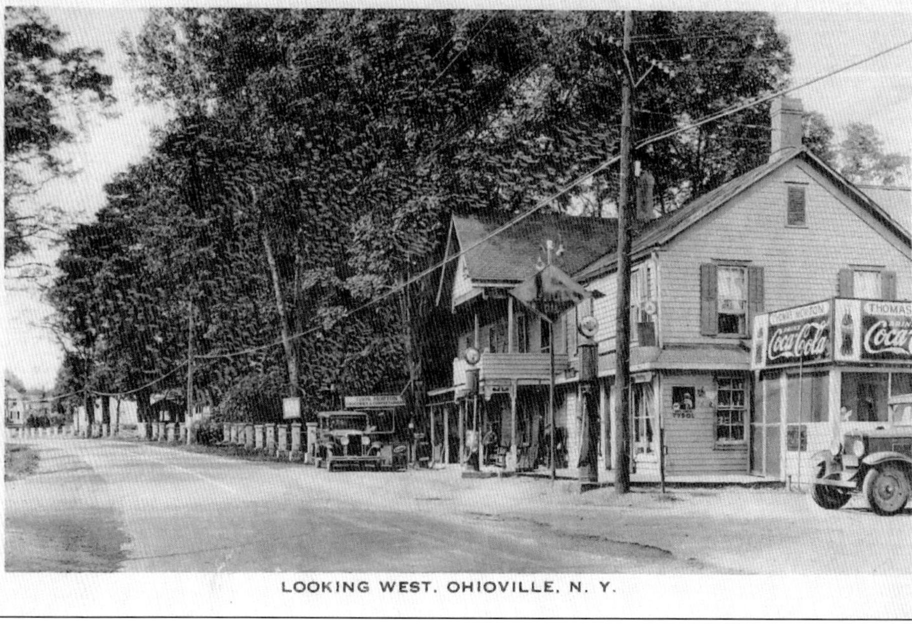

LOOKING WEST. OHIOVILLE, N. Y.

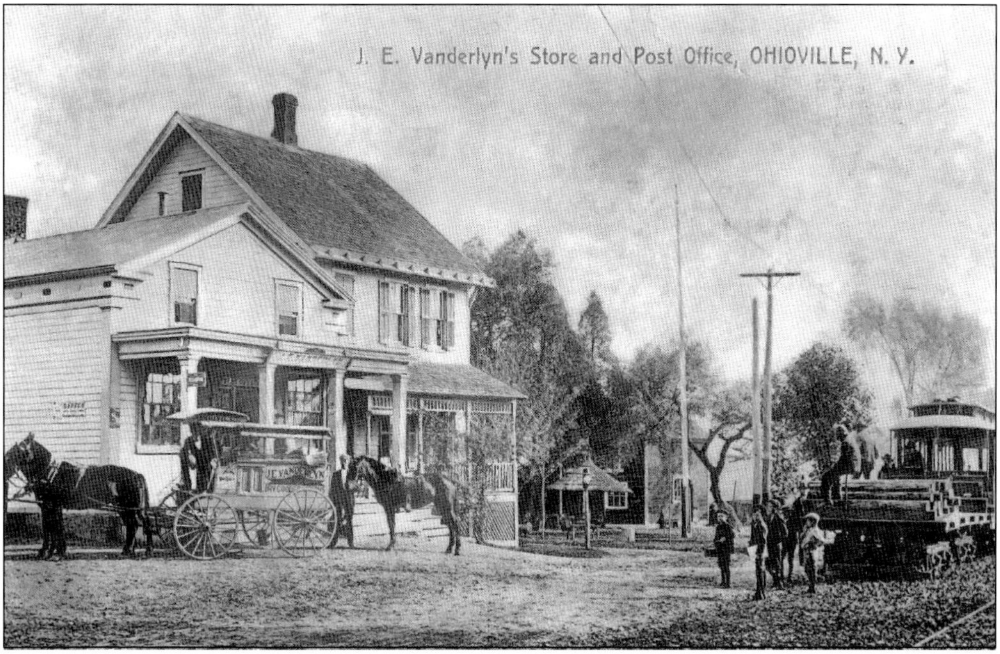

John Vanderlyn's store and post office was on the northeast corner of the Ohioville corners. The Joe Tantillo family ran a grocery store there, and today their grandson has a consignment shop in the same building. Joe Tantillo's brother Sal ran a gas station on the southwest corner for more than 50 years. Below is Vanderlyn's livery stable. His granddaughter Jean Vanderlyn, of New Paltz, was a trick rider in large circuses and traveled with Roy Rodgers and Gene Autry. As a child, her trick riding was featured in a newsreel that was shown in movie theaters.

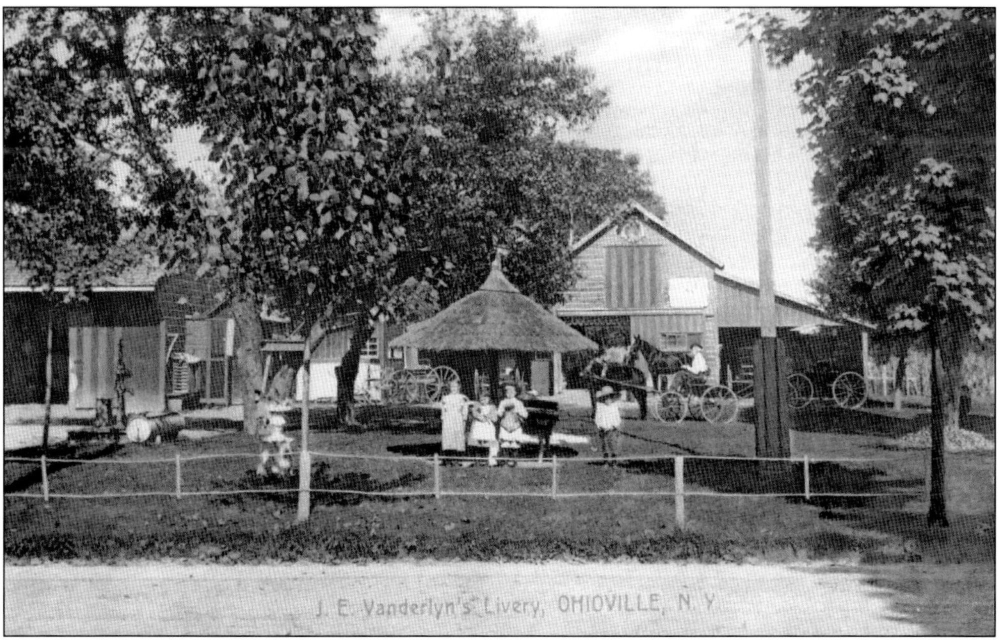

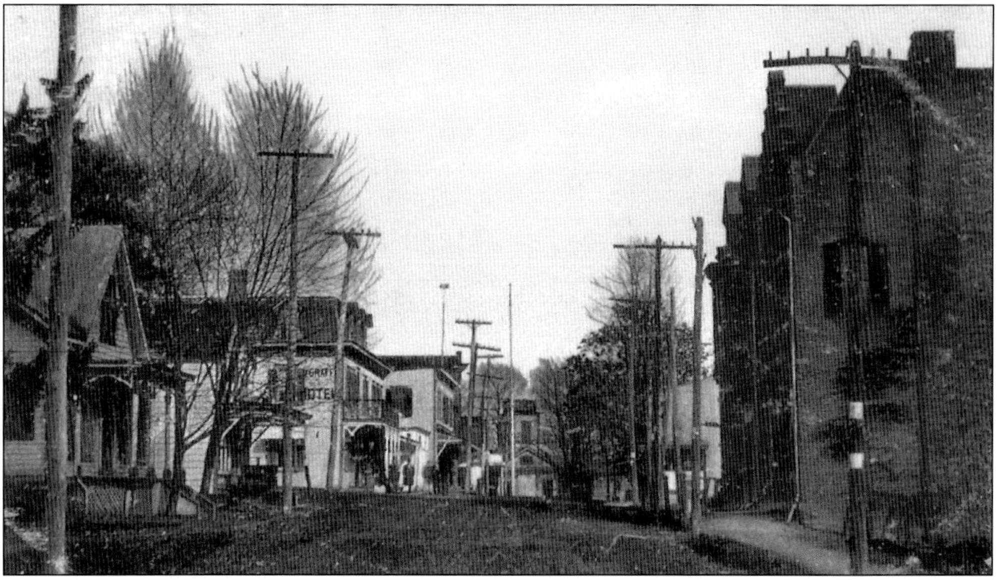

The hamlet of Milton was bypassed when Route 9W was upgraded. Once an important place because of its harbor and surrounding farms, it is a lovely, quiet village today. Its fame was sparked when scenes from *The Fugitive Kind* starring Marlon Brando were filmed on its main street in 1959. The card above was postmarked in 1908.

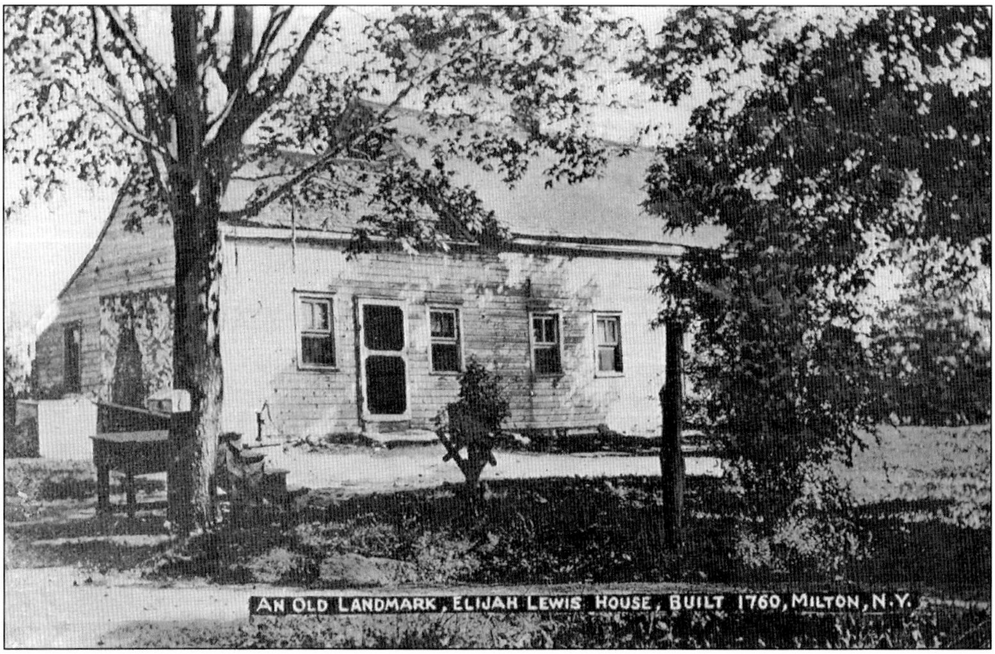

Though changed considerably, the 1760 Elijah Lewis homestead still stands at the corner of Old Indian Road and South Road in Milton. It is believed that George Washington stopped there three times. An addition to the house was built in 1950s. This postcard was postmarked in 1914. The sender simply noted, "Saw this house."

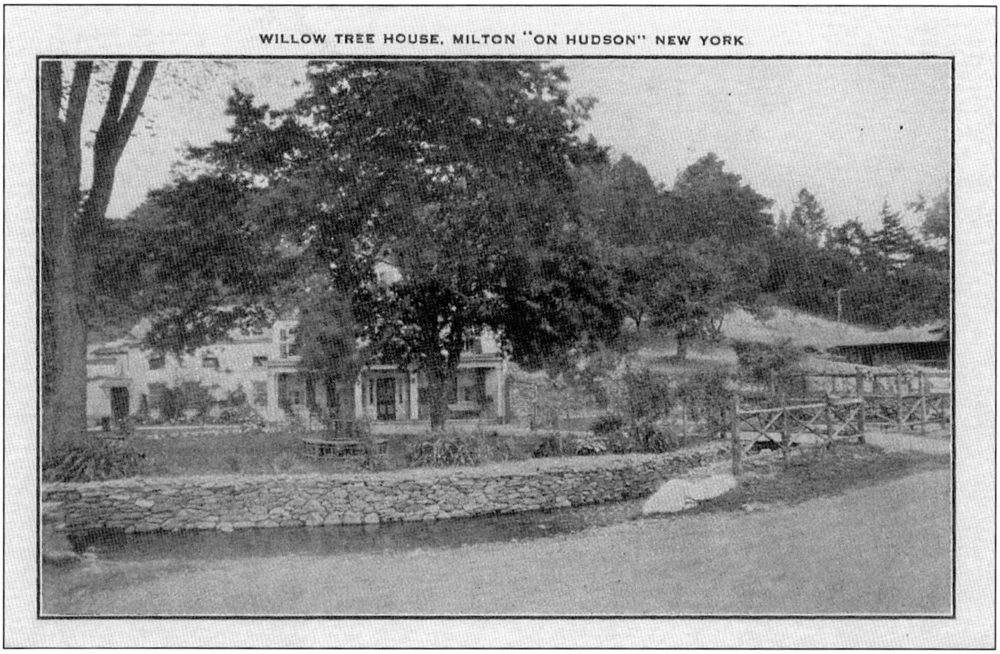

People came to Milton for many reasons. Some just visited places such as the Willow Tree House for a meal. Artists came for the company of other artists. The Elverhoj Art Colony housed musicians, designers, and performing and fine artists. It held musical concerts and put on theatrical productions for a paying public. The ads for its presentations ran in many local papers. *Elverhoj*, which means "elves' hill" in Danish, is a Danish comedy whose overture is often heard in concert. Later, the colony's location became one of the many Ulster County properties of the followers of the black charismatic leader Father Divine. His other properties included Krum Elbow, which overlooks the Hudson on Red Top Road.

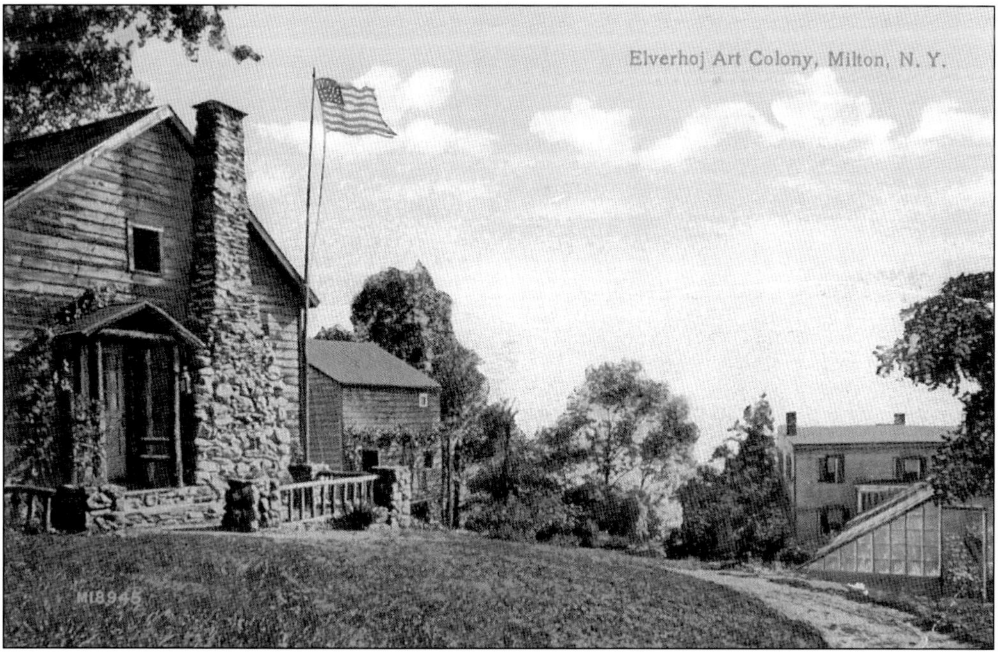

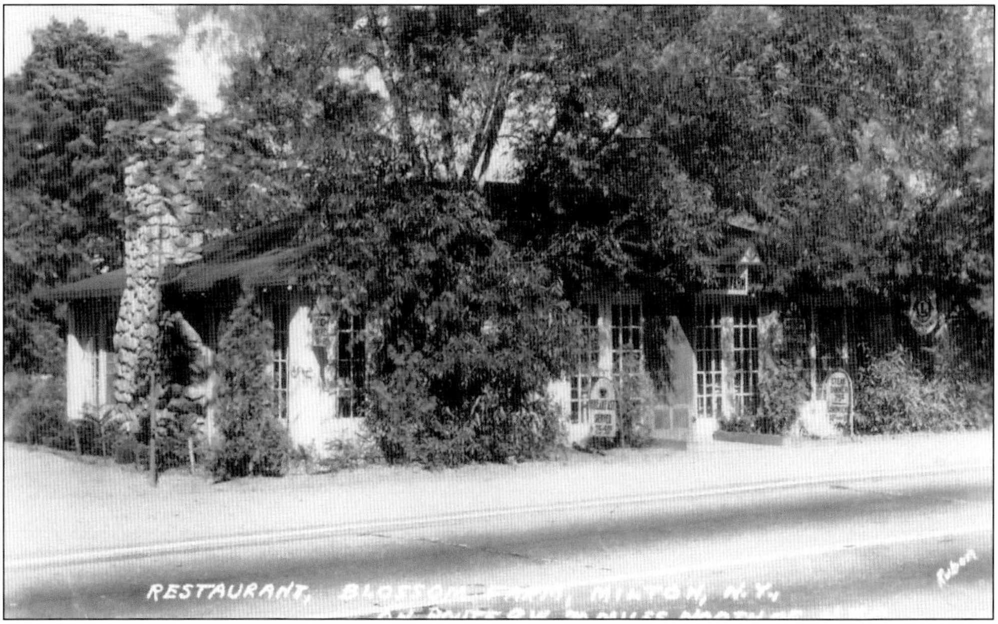

Many roadhouses and rest stops opened for business along Route 9W, each seeking to slake the thirst and sate the hunger of the passing throng. The two signs by the doors advertise that breakfast was 25–50¢ and that a steak dinner was 75¢. South of Highland, Milton had many such establishments. It seems that it was important to give a potential stop's mileage from New York City, or another well-known city, so that travelers could plan their stops. The above image indicates that Blossom Farm is 70 miles north of New York City. The below postcard for Hickory Tree Lodge states on the back that it is 84 miles from New York City and 12 miles from Newburgh.

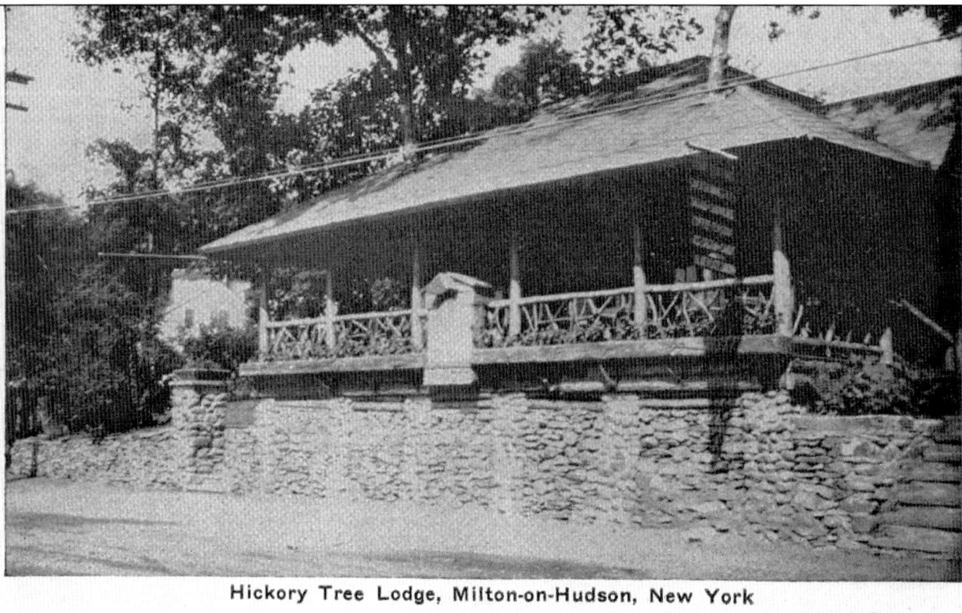

Hickory Tree Lodge, Milton-on-Hudson, New York

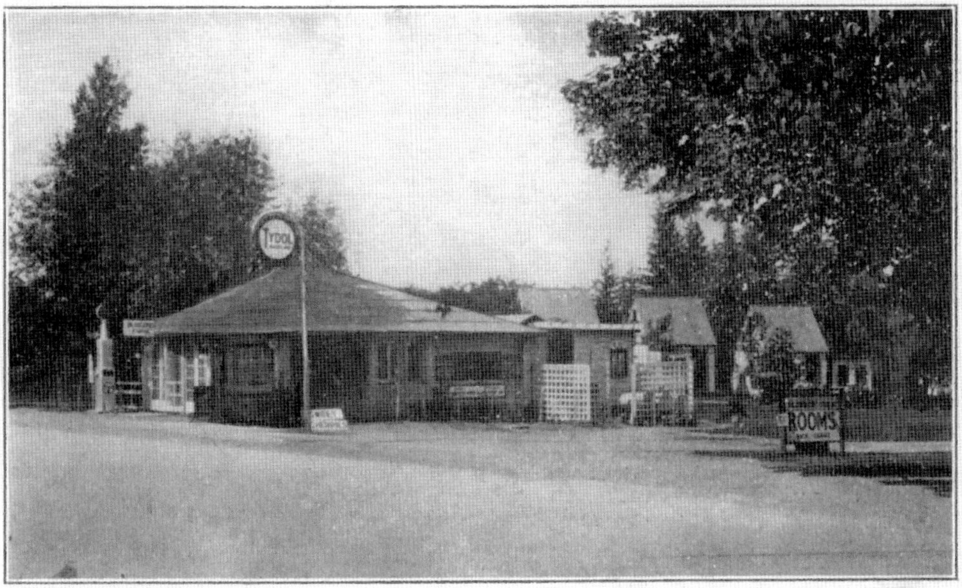

86 Restaurant and Overnight Cottages, Blossom Farm, Milton, N. Y., on Route 9W

Tydol gasoline and other products were available at Blossom Farm's filling station. The farm also had a restaurant and provided overnight cottage rentals (cottages served as precursors to motels). The tiny cottages are visible on the right side of the card. The sign at the base of the Tydol signpost says "Sweet Cherries." At the top of the previous page is a later picture of the same building. The affordability of automobiles, more leisure time, and more disposable income created the "See the USA in Your Chevrolet" ads that became classic in the 1950s. The card below features the inviting cobblestone-fireplace seating, with Adirondack-style chairs and intimate tables, of Blossom Farm's restaurant.

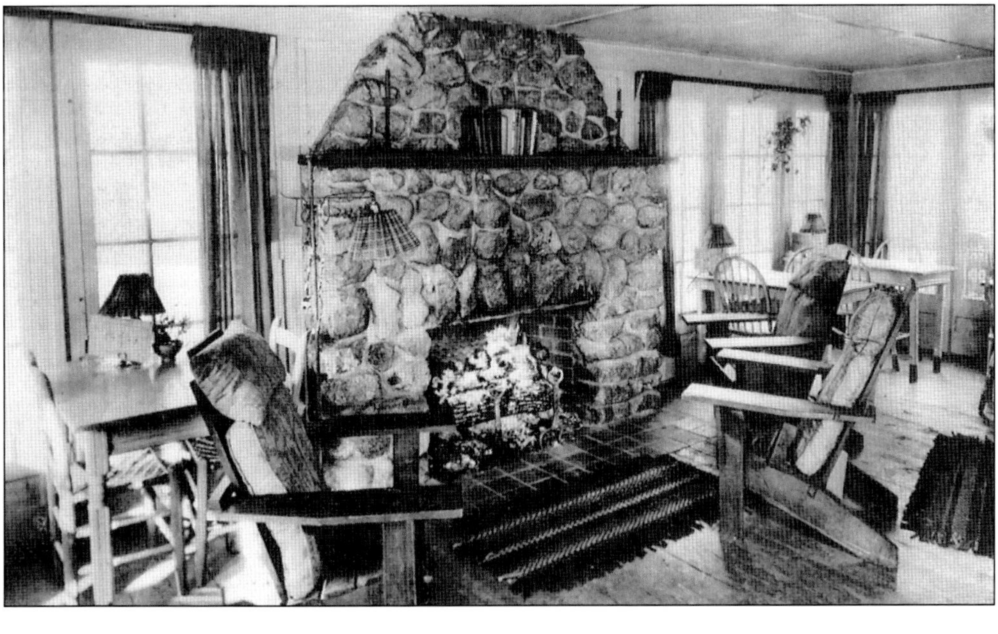

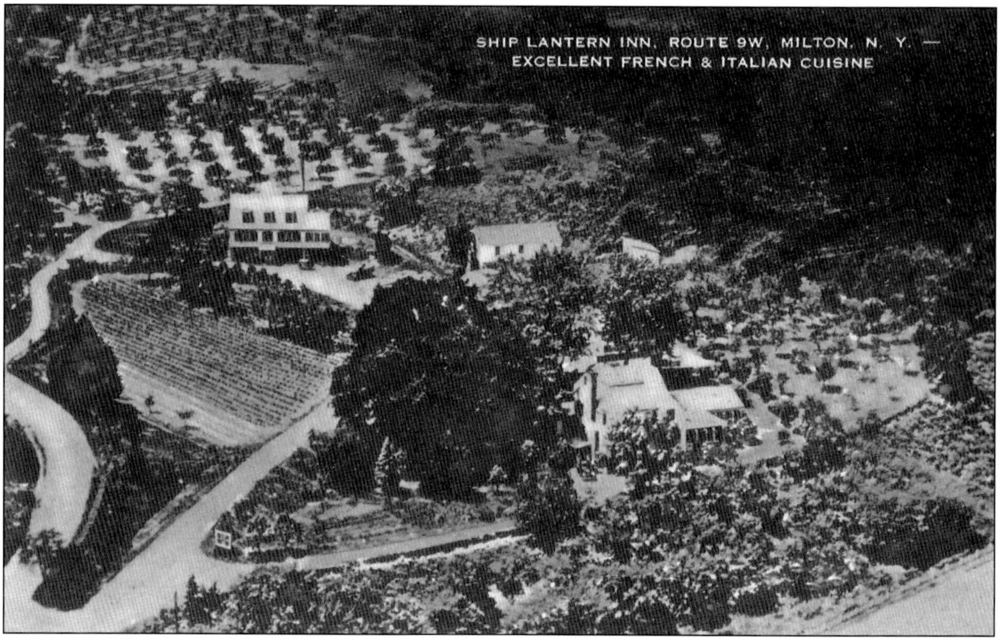

Route 9W was the most popular route traveled between Albany and New York prior to the New York State Thruway opening. The 9W corridor had gas stations, overnight accommodations, and restaurants that have disappeared for the most part. However, the Ship Lantern Inn has stood the test of time. The surrounding lands have changed greatly.

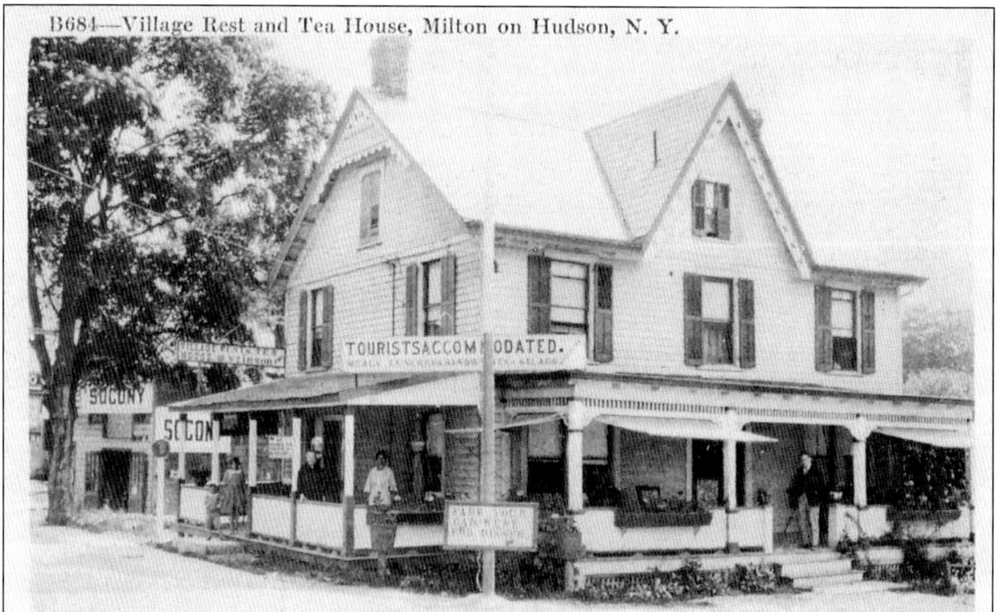

Signs abound at the Village Rest and Tea House. In addition to two Socony signs, there is another sign that reads, "Village Rest and Tea House, W. Stinton." A sign in the foreground states, "Tourists Accommodated. Meals, Lunches & Sandwiches & Salads." The sign to the right of the little girl on the porch says, "No horse or truck parking." On the pole at the center of the card, one is advised to "park your car here for dinner."

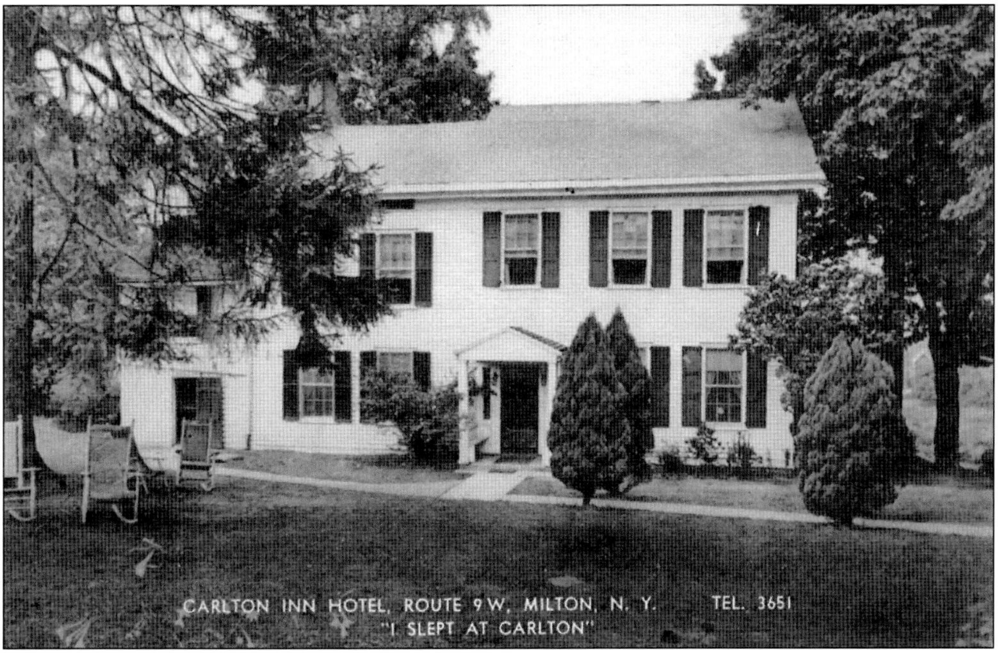

The Carlton Inn in Milton was located about 11 miles north of Newburgh. Eventually, the Carlton Inn added cabins and called itself the Carlton Hotel. It had another postcard printed that showed the cabins in full color, surrounded by mature trees, and touted its steam heat and coffee shop. The telephone number remained 3651.

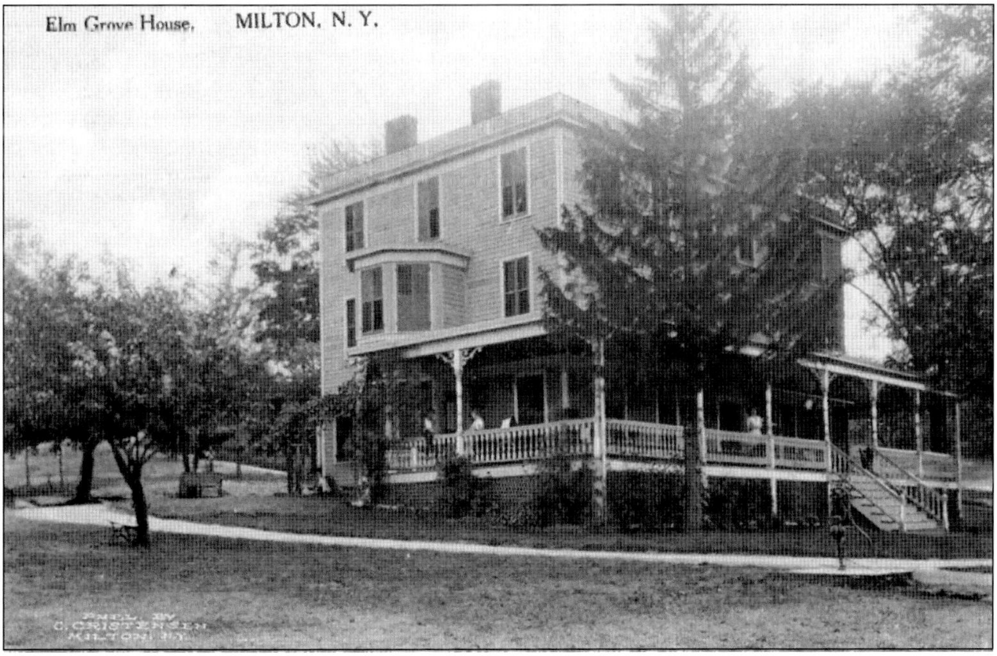

The Elm Grove House took guests for a longer stay. This postcard was sent in August 1912 from Milton to a New Jersey address, with the message that the sender "may come on Sunday afternoon with papa." Elm trees, once very numerous, were for the most part wiped out by Dutch elm disease. Their popularity lives on in the number of places with "elm" in their names.

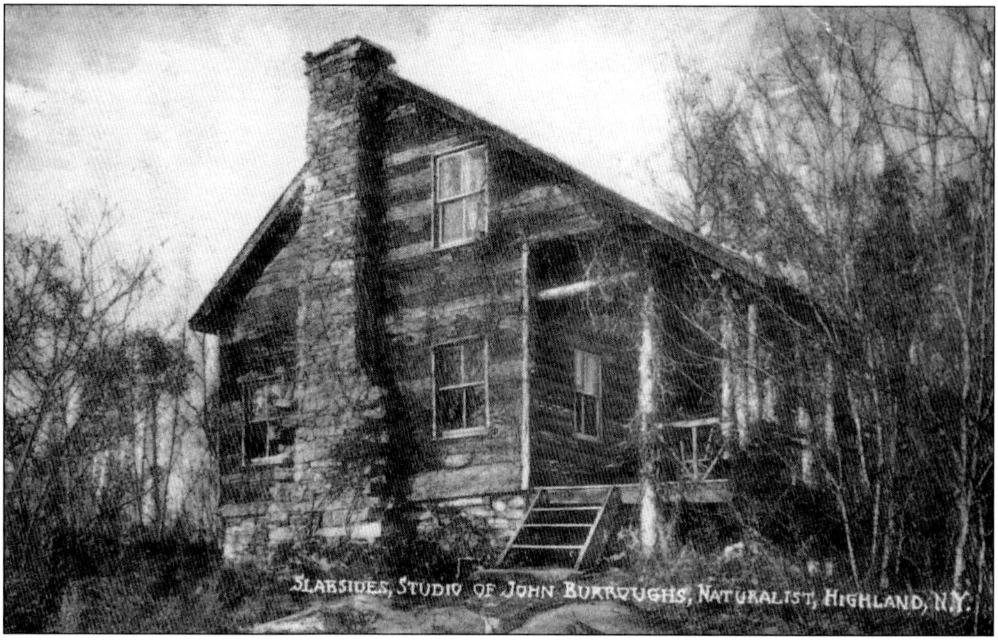

The Slabsides cabin of John Burroughs was not in Highland as this card would have one believe. It is located north of Highland in West Park. Burroughs (1837–1921) was visited at this site by Pres. Teddy Roosevelt, authors Walt Whitman and Theodore Dreiser, industrialists Harvey Firestone and Henry Ford, naturalist John Muir, and thousands of other admirers. The writings of author and naturalist Burroughs brought a love of nature to the multitudes. His books and articles were must-reads in school and at home. One can visit the site anytime and hike its extensive trail system on more than 200 acres. The cabin is open for tours twice a year (consult www.JohnBurroughsAssociation.org for details). Below is Burroughs's other study near Riverby, his home on the Hudson in West Park.

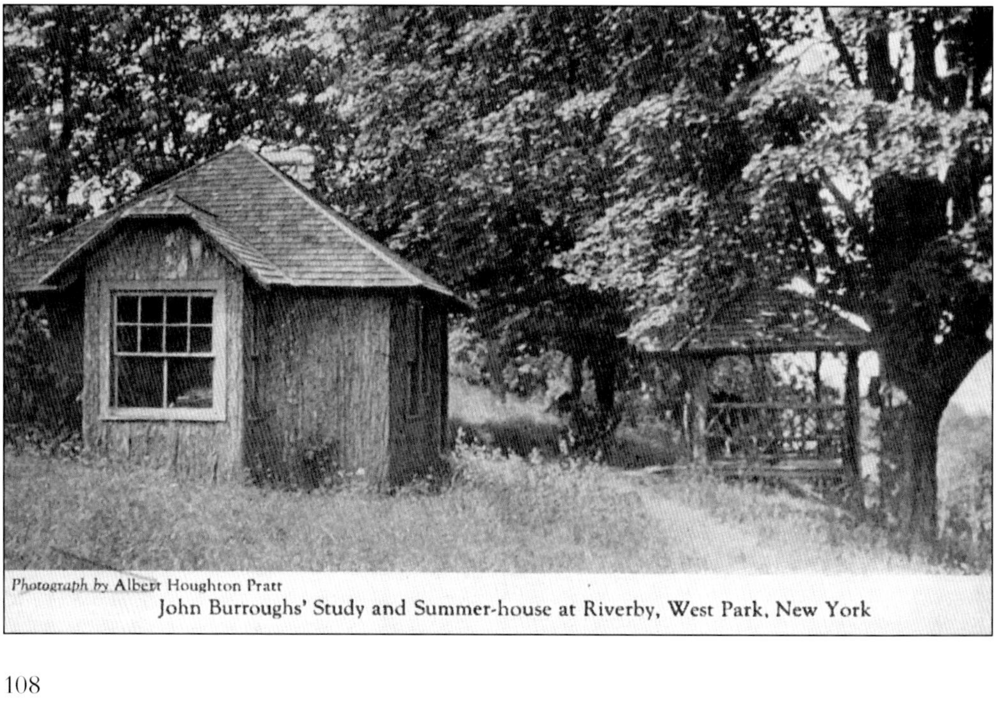

Photograph by Albert Houghton Pratt

John Burroughs' Study and Summer-house at Riverby, West Park, New York

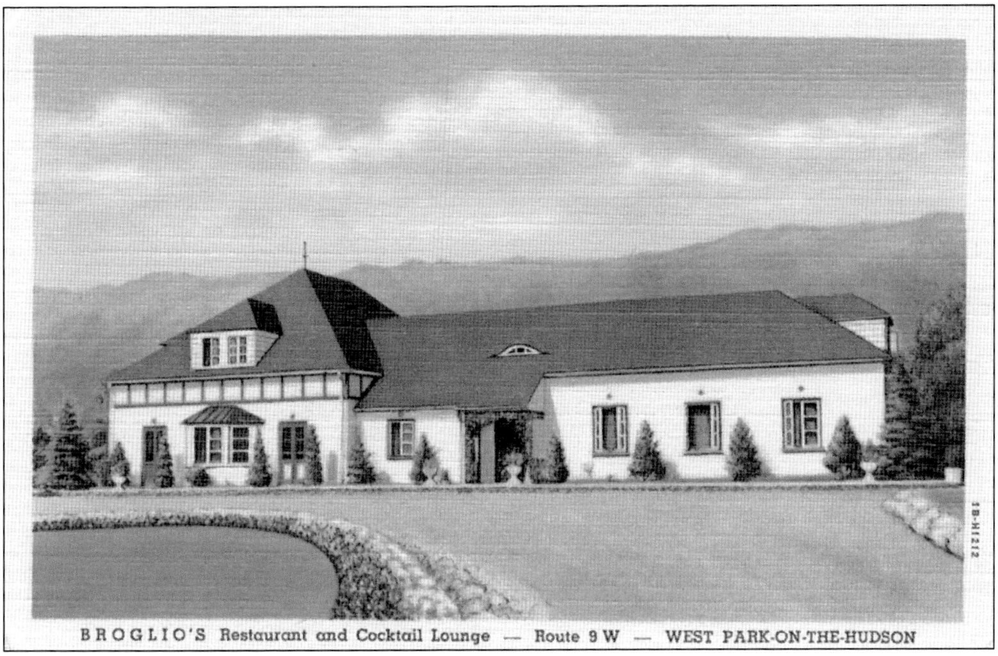

The Broglio family had a restaurant in Long Island and this one in West Park. In 1955, Lee Broglio and partners bought the establishment from the widow of founder Aldo Broglio. The new owners planned and redecorated the terrace room and dining room. Today, this restaurant and catering business is called Stonehedge for the stone walls that mark its drive.

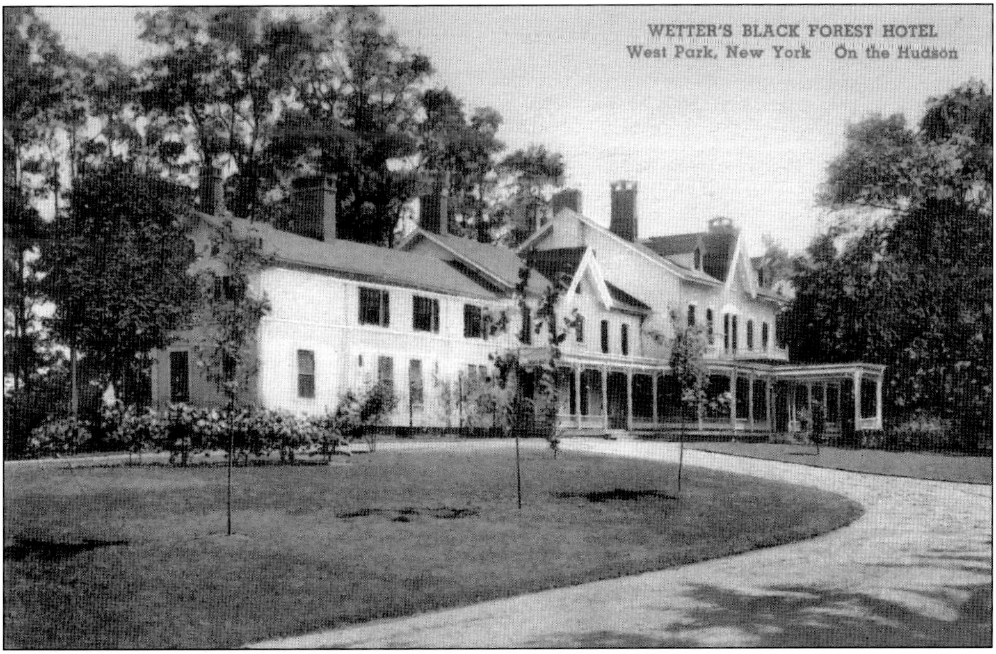

A fire destroyed the central section of Wetter's Black Forest Hotel, and it was never replaced. Now a private estate, the property has a view of the Hudson that is unobstructed by the CSX freight line, which runs inland just south of it. The train track comes between the Hudson and all properties south of this point.

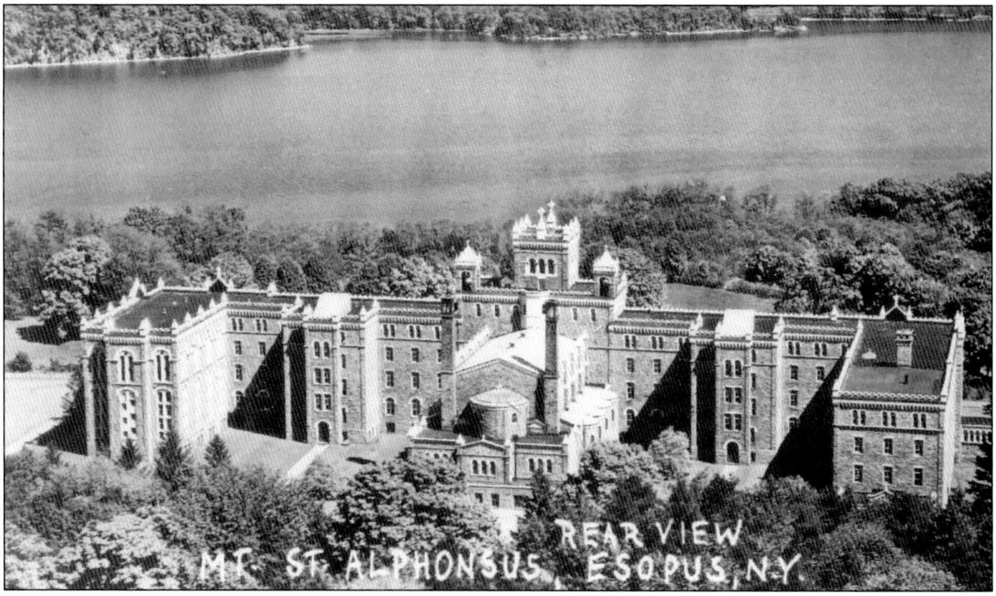

Mount St. Alphonsus on the Hudson is unexpected and spectacular. Built between 1904 and 1907 as a seminary for the Redemptorist Congregation, it is located in Esopus, north of the Town of Lloyd line. It ceased use as a seminary and became a retreat center in 1985. The Rifton-based Church Communities Foundation, known locally as the "Bruderhof," leased it in 2011 and then purchased it for $21.5 million. Today, it serves as a private high school, housing, and a farm and is now called The Mount. In the card below, Route 9W runs across the top. The Mount is approximately 400 acres of prime Hudson River shoreline land, and many speculated it would become a golf course because of its rolling hills and scenic beauty. A site not far from it was once considered for the location of the United Nations. A large collection of documents on that proposal is in the Klyne Esopus Museum in Ulster Park.

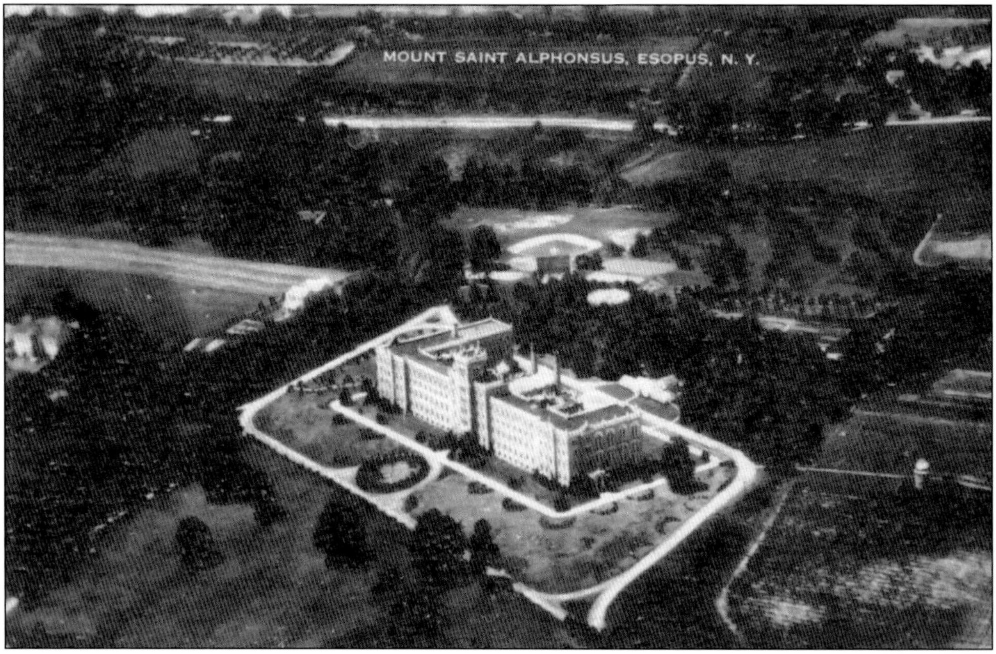

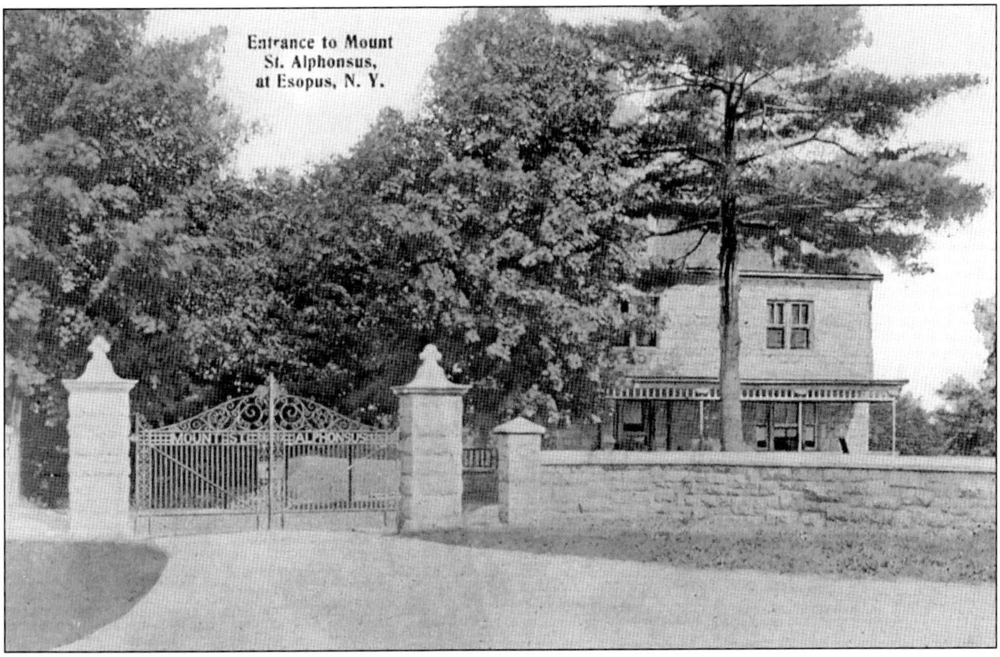

Today, the original Mount St. Alphonsus (now named The Mount) gate pillars and gatehouse are all one can see of the site's buildings from Route 9W in Esopus. A private high school for the Bruderhof community, outsiders are not allowed to visit without permission. However, from Route 9W one can see the beautiful rolling fields north of the gate that are part of the site. The Mount's new owners are farming the land and have greatly renewed the entire property.

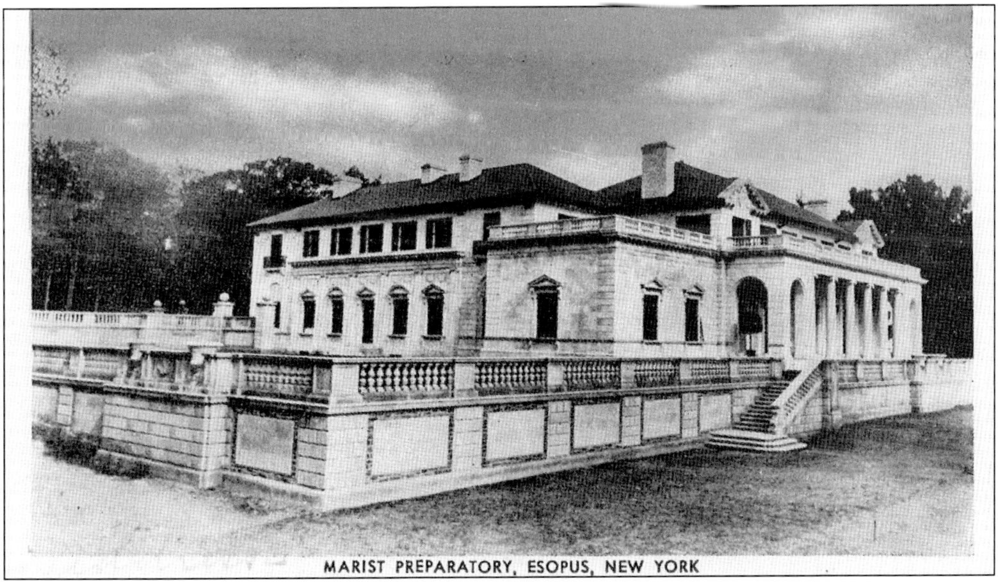

This was the Col. Oliver Hazard Payne home—42,000 square feet of the best that money could buy in 1905. It later became part of the Marist Brothers holdings and then went into private hands. Most recently, it was bequeathed to Marist College by Raymond A. Rich. The 60-acre Hudson River estate was valued at $65 million. Raymond Rich left another $10 million for a leadership institute in his very appropriate name.

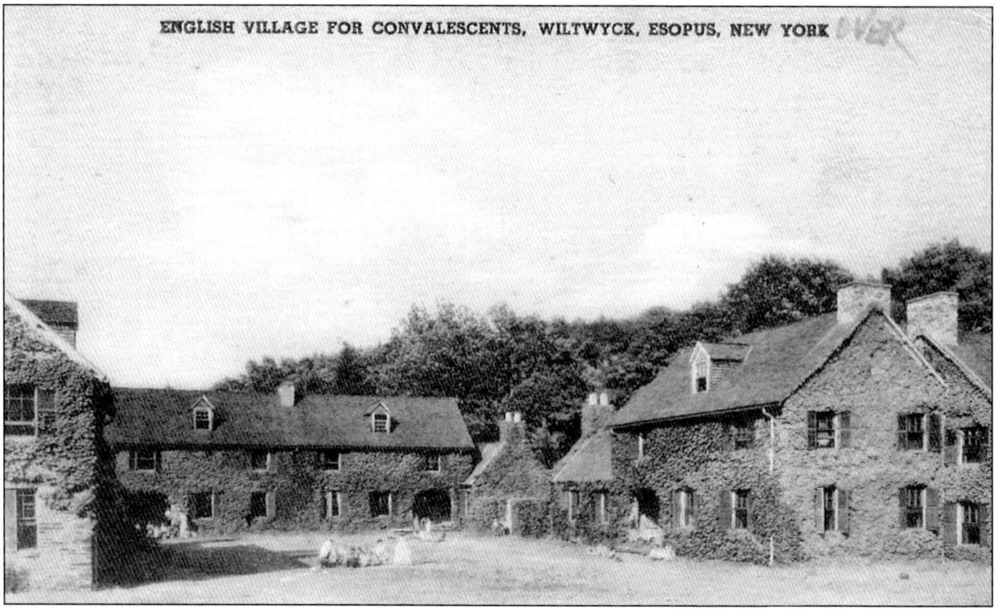

Colonel Payne's estate included the above cottages for workers and the barns below, which were designed by Julien Burroughs. Today, the cottages are rentals and the barns are awaiting their next iteration, which may be a luxury day spa and hotel. Former incarnations of the barns were the Wiltwyck School (for juvenile delinquents) in the 1940s and the Wiltwyck Village in the 1970s. Both complexes are on the west side of Route 9W, but the barns are a bit difficult to see, even though they are very close to 9W. The late boxer Floyd Patterson was remanded to the Wiltwyck School until 1947. He said the school changed his life from one of trouble to the path that led him to become an Olympic middleweight champion in 1952 and, later, the youngest heavyweight champion of the world. He eventually settled outside of New Paltz, where he lived until his death in May 2006.

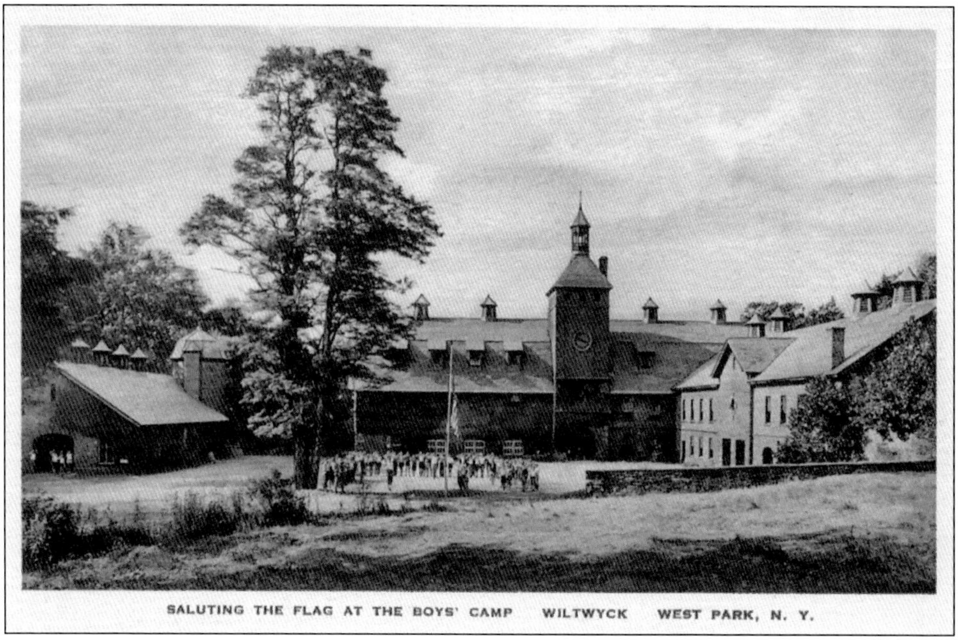

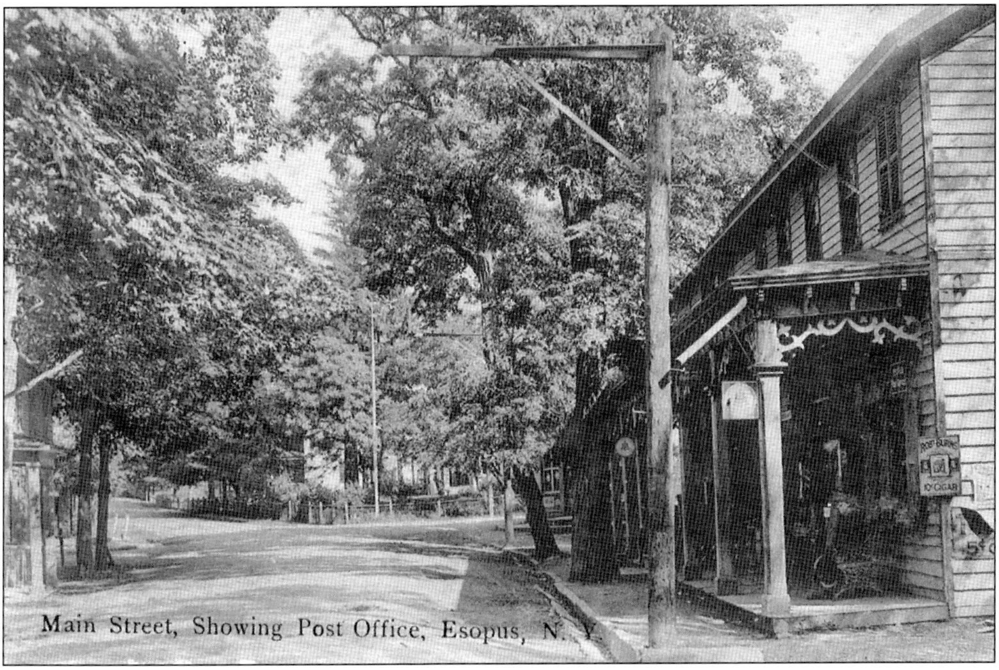

During the 1904 US presidential contest between Theodore Roosevelt and Alton B. Parker, this little post office corner was awash with reporters from around the world hoping for a word from Parker, who lived just east of it. The media came to Parker because Parker thought it unseemly for a candidate to go about making speeches. Parker lost.

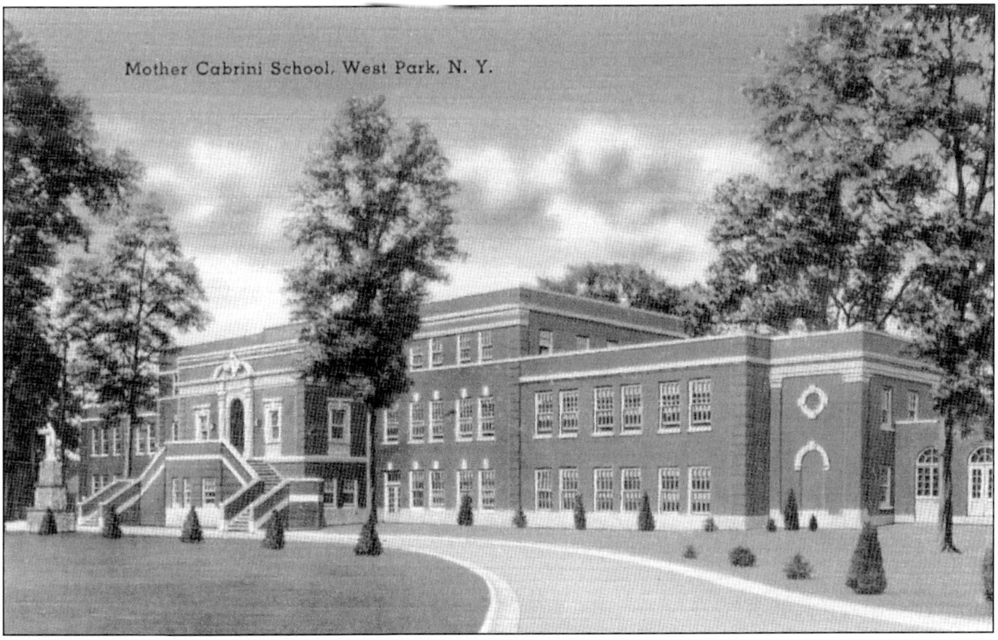

Born in 1850, the woman who became Mother Cabrini had immigrated to America from Italy. By the time she died in 1917, she had created 67 missions around the world to care for those less fortunate. Her mission in West Park began as an orphanage for Italian girls. Now closed, it is currently awaiting its next use.

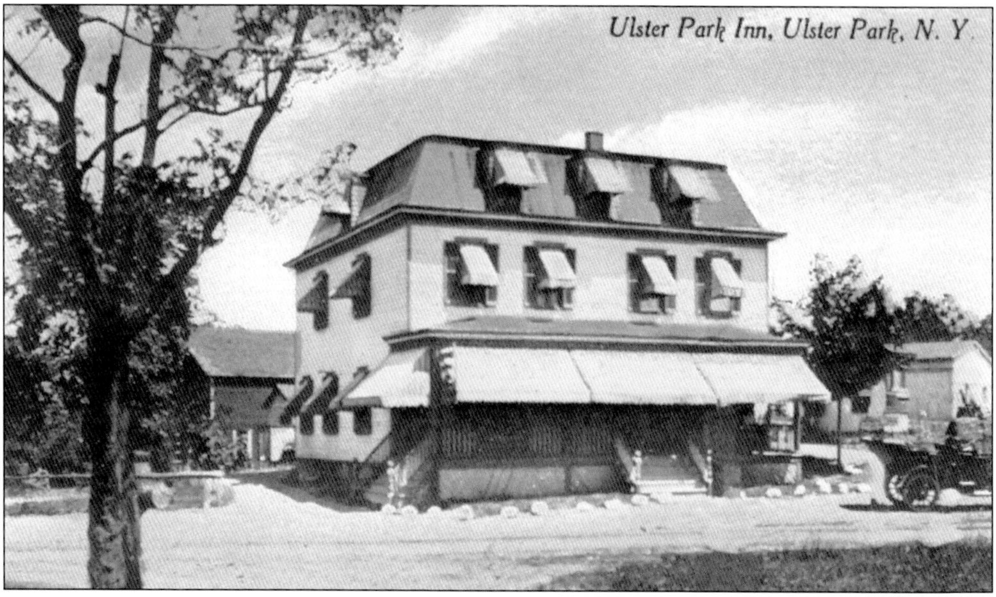

This building has seen many businesses come and go. Originally an inn and restaurant, the second floor was later the owner's residence. The card below is the bar, which had not changed drastically as of the 1990s. Some of the names it has borne are 9W Hofbrau (which was owned by Willy Harms), The Place, Lucille's, and Mr. B's, which it is called today. The postcard above is from about 1905, and the one below dates to around 1930. South of this location, at the intersection with Esopus Avenue, is the hamlet of Esopus. Its post office still operates, though there is another post office on Route 9W at its intersection with Floyd Ackert Road in West Park. Yet another post office serves the people of Ulster Park. In the early days of rural areas before telephones, having a convenient post office was central to communication with the outside world. Of course bars, such as the one below, aided communication, too.

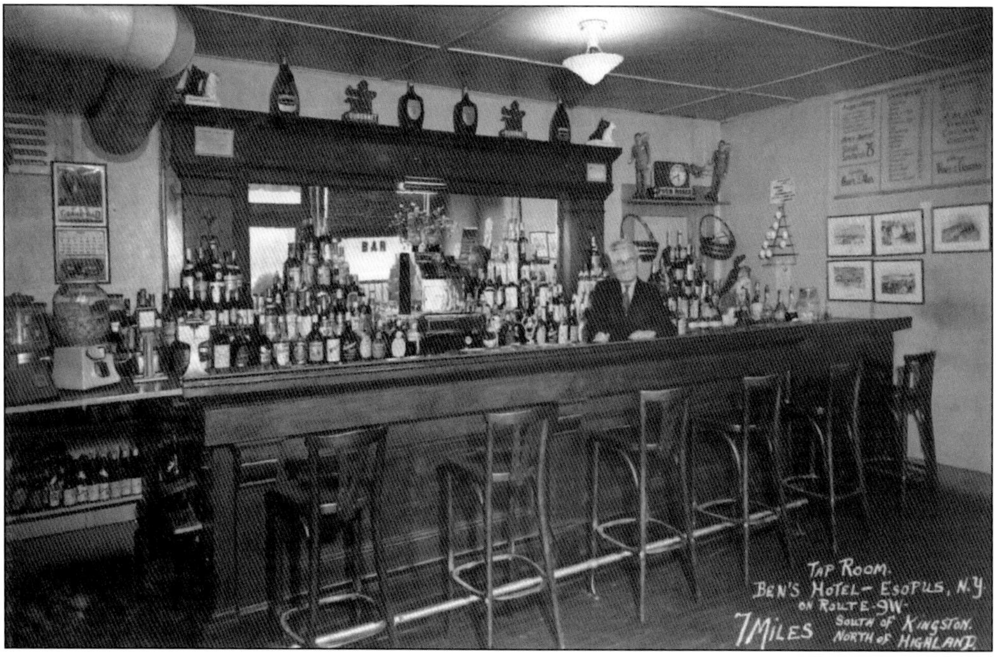

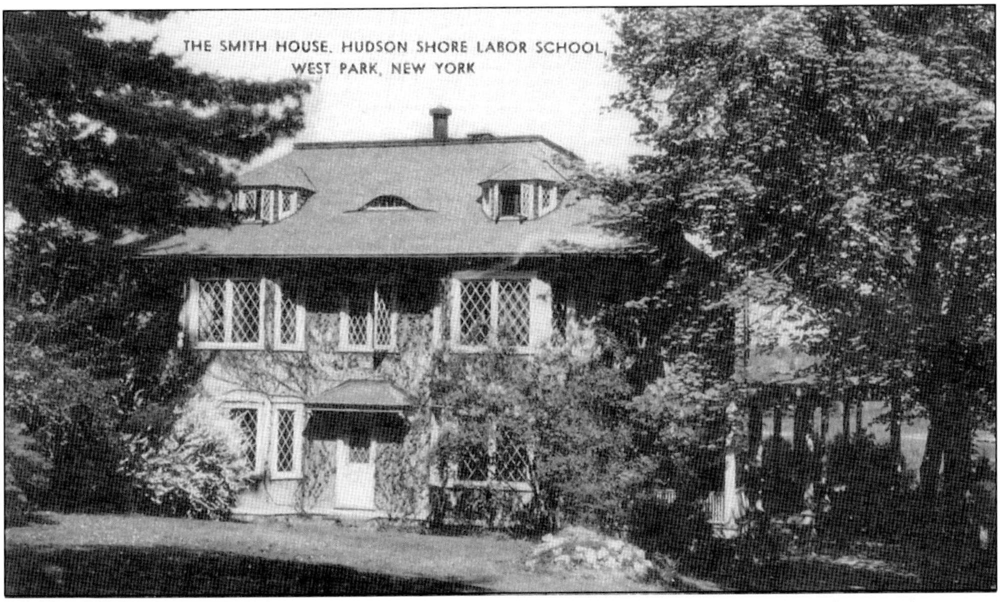

Esopus was a mecca for all kinds of spiritual retreats, schools, and monasteries. The Smith House (above) and Aberdeen (below) were at different times home to the West Shore Labor School. The school's mission favored unions and the labor movement. Eleanor Roosevelt was a speaker at Labor School events. According to the Bryn Mawr College website, Aberdeen was "the new home of the college's Summer School On the West Shore Railroad and Highway 9-W between New York and Albany. Available for conferences, institutes, and other educational or cultural activities. Rates on request." From the 1950s through most of the 1990s, the Johnson family lived there. Mr. Johnson commuted daily to the Poughkeepsie railroad station for his further commute to New York City. After housing schools for massage therapy and aesthetics, Aberdeen is for sale again.

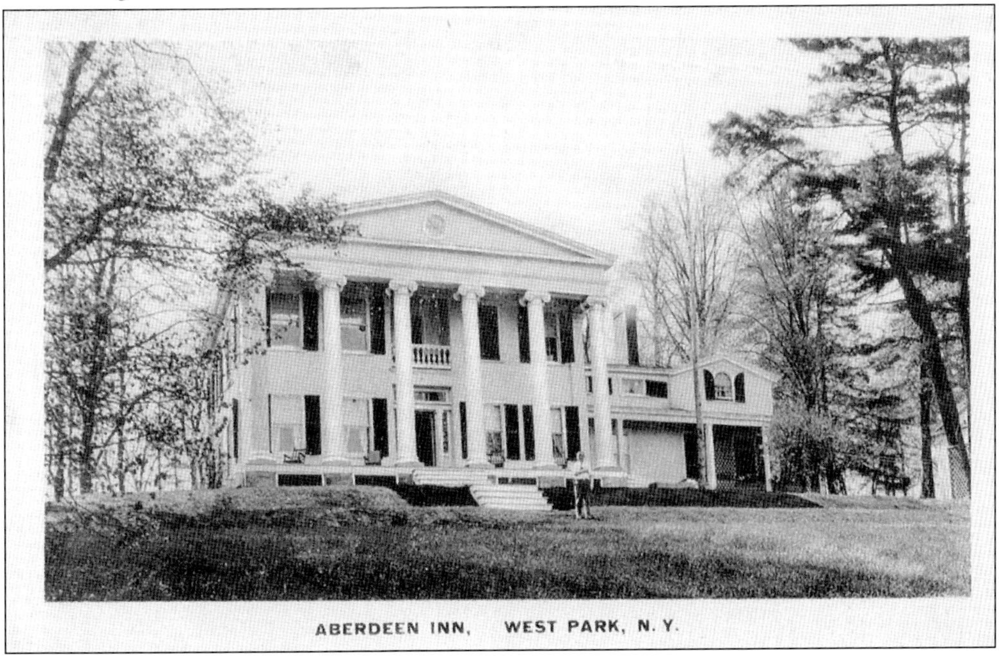

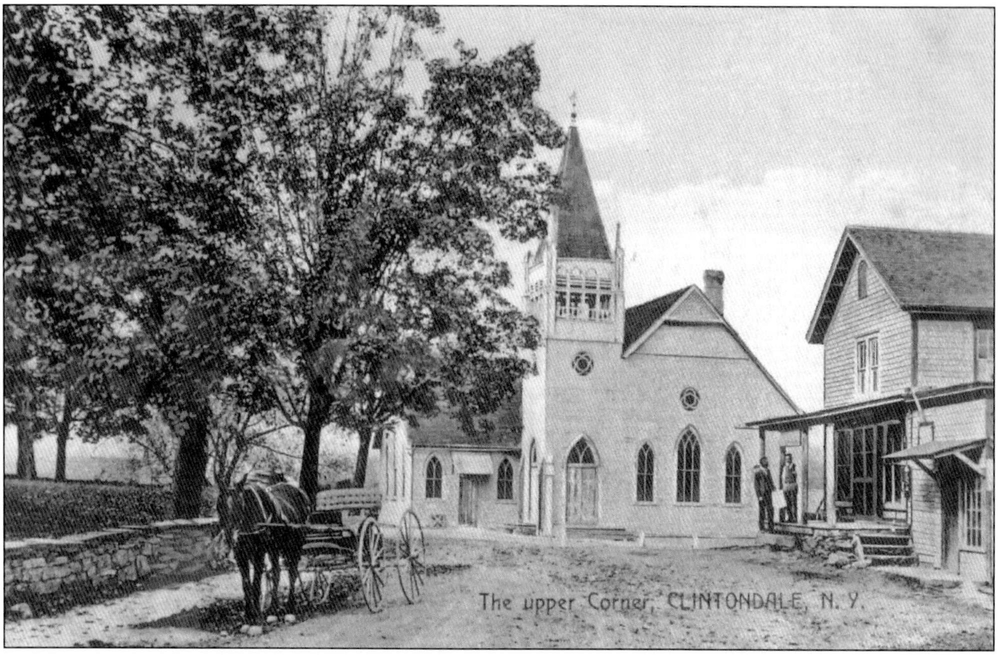

Clintondale is at the intersection of Route 44/55, Hull Avenue, and Maple Avenue. This postcard from the early 1900s shows the Methodist Episcopal church. The beautiful church steeple is gone now, but the remaining church building continues in use as a storage facility for a plumbing company. To the right is the same store that is featured in the card below: Charles Garrison General Merchandise. On the card below, the smaller sign above the porch indicates it was also the post office. The shop to the right, marked by a sign that reads "Lucas," was also owned by Garrison. The card below was postmarked 1910. There is still a small family-owned grocery store in Clintondale, not shown in these cards.

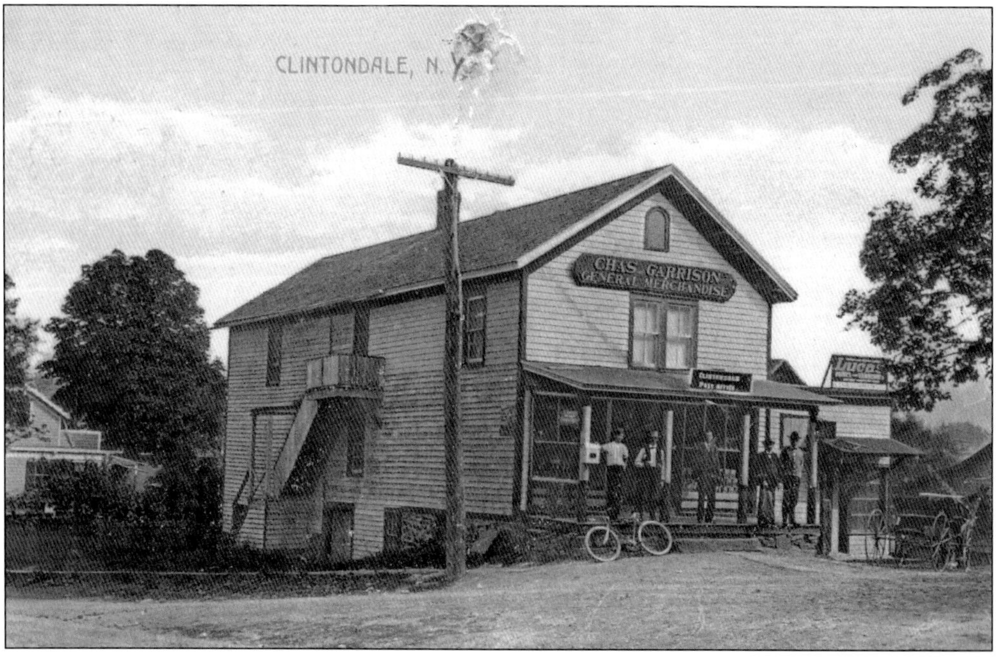

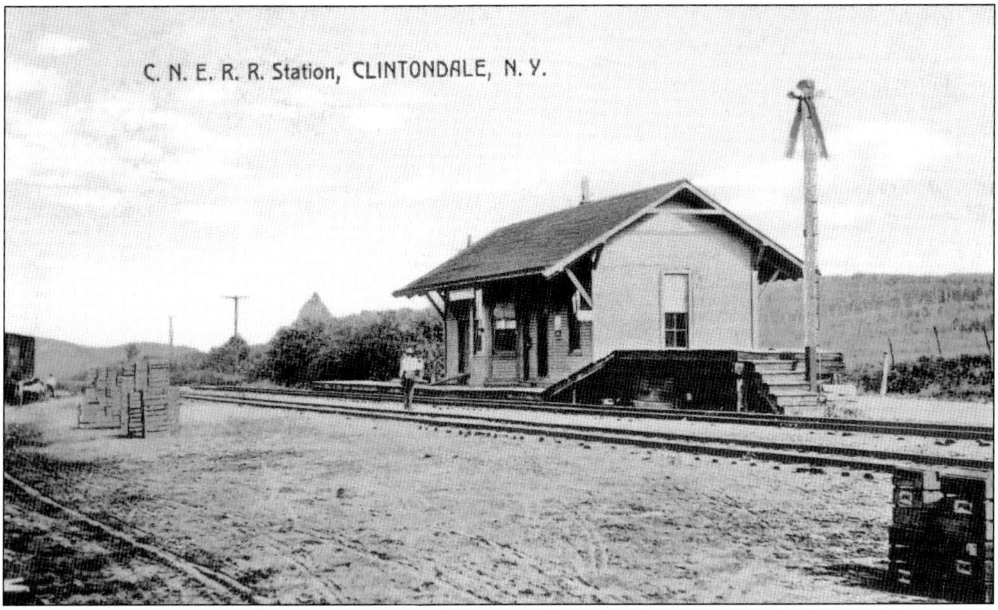

The Central New England Railway went west from the Poughkeepsie-Highland Railroad Bridge with stations or stops at Highland, Loyd, Clintondale, Elting, Mowbray, and Modena, and then went on to Maybrook and Campbell Hall. There were other "milk stops" along the way that were not regularly scheduled. The Clintondale Station was located on the north side of Station Road. It burned down in 1965. (Courtesy of Shirley V. Anson.)

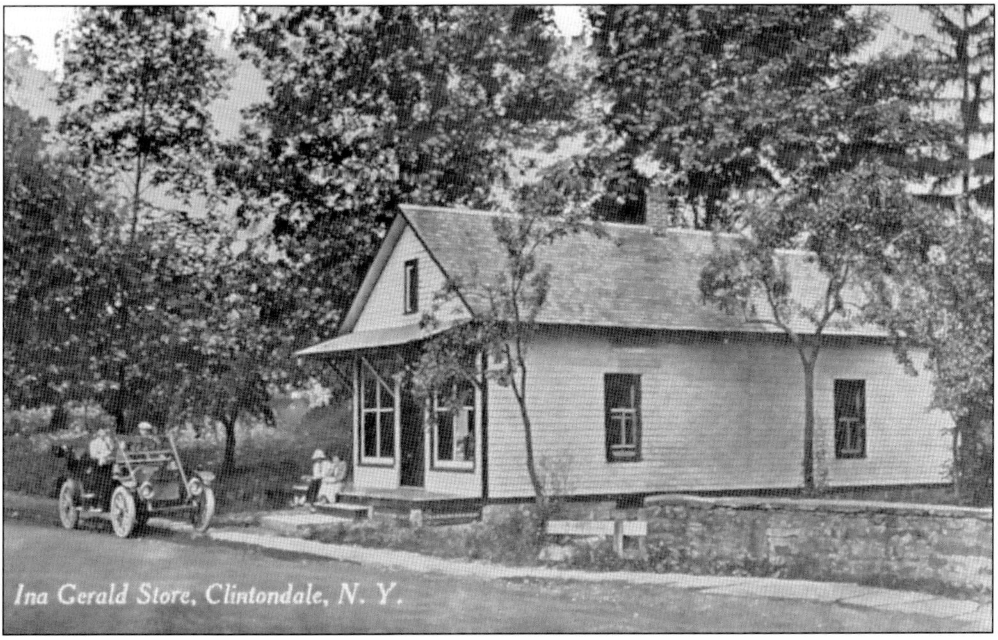

"How do you like the looks of the store? There are two others about the same size. We are greatly pleased with our pretty country home and are enjoying every moment of our stay." This card was sent on August 1916 from Clintondale to Watch Hill, Rhode Island. Clintondale is located in the middle of huge apple orchards, and the hamlet was an important center for many different businesses.

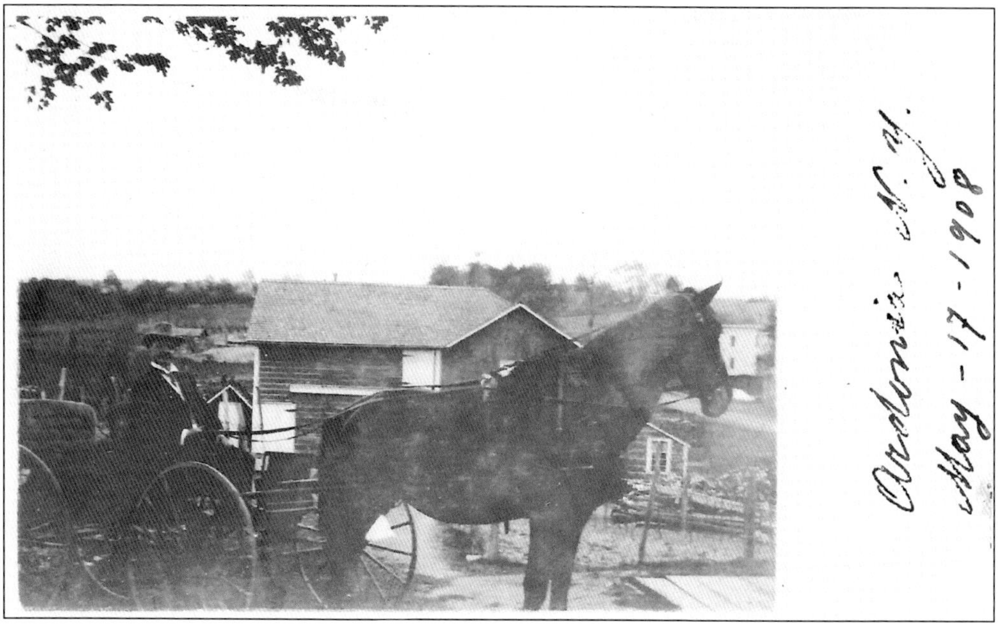

An unidentified wagon driver at Ardonia, New York, is pictured above. Ardonia is one of five hamlets in the Town of Plattekill. The other four hamlets are Clintondale, Modena, New Hurley, and Plattekill. Ardonia today has a long-serving bar and restaurant called Primo's and a grocery store. A lady's clothing shop was also in business until the 1990s.

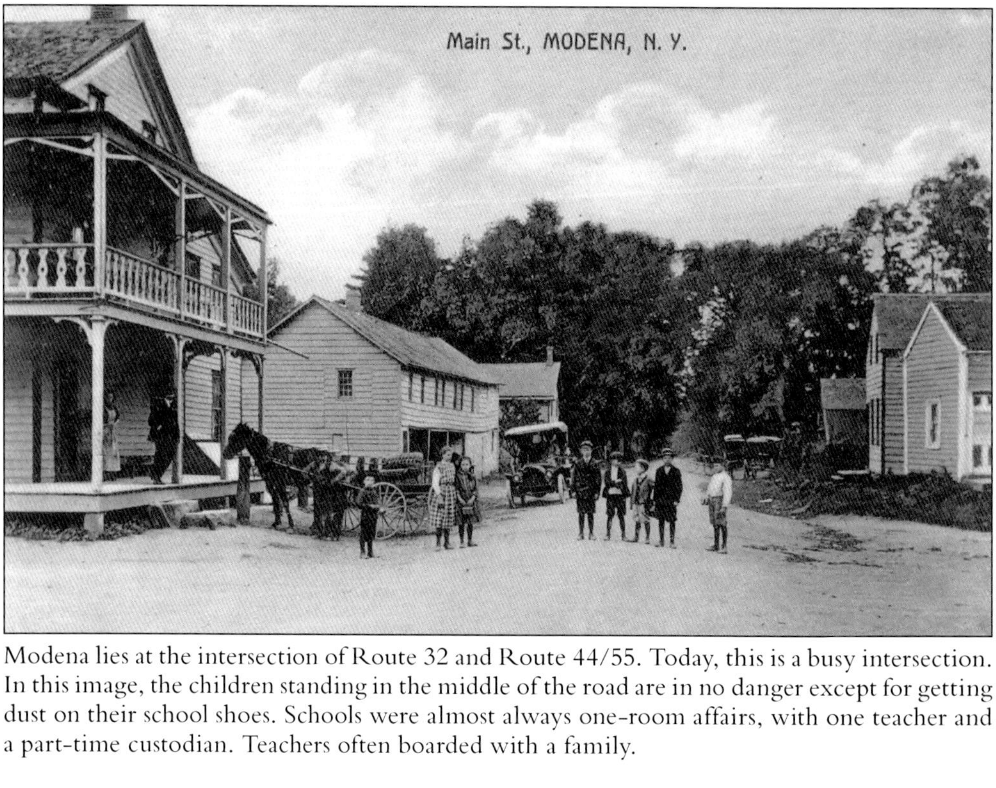

Modena lies at the intersection of Route 32 and Route 44/55. Today, this is a busy intersection. In this image, the children standing in the middle of the road are in no danger except for getting dust on their school shoes. Schools were almost always one-room affairs, with one teacher and a part-time custodian. Teachers often boarded with a family.

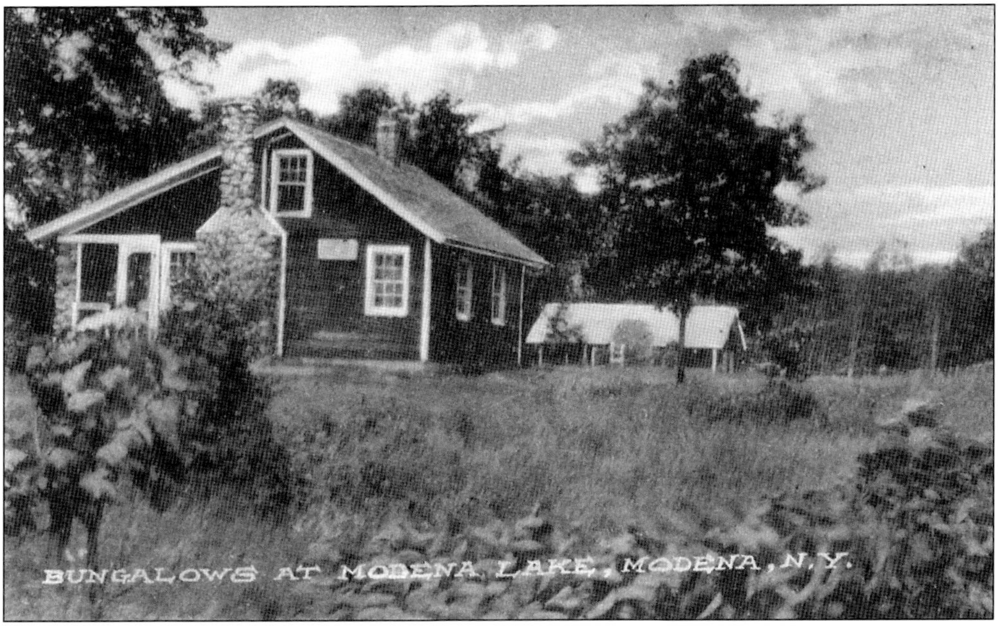

This inviting little bungalow is unmistakable today, as it looks essentially the same. It is situated on the north side of Route 44/55 by Modena Lake, also called Lembo Lake. The card was not mailed, so dating it is difficult, but it is from the early 1900s. The cabin is dark brown with white trim, just as it appears today.

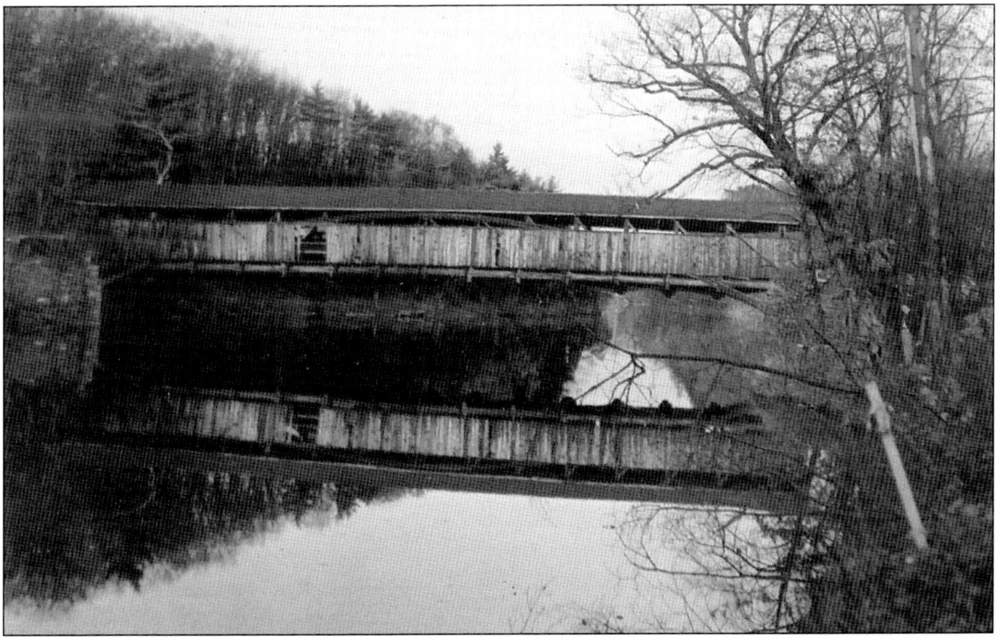

The 1844 Perrine's Bridge is New York's second-oldest covered bridge and the only one using Burr arch truss construction. It was built by Benjamin Wood. Located on Route 213 in the Town of Esopus, next to bridges for Route 32 and the New York State Thruway, it spans the Wallkill River. Perrine's Bridge was listed in the National Register of Historic Places in 1973. It has been repaired since this photo postcard by Kingston Candy Co.

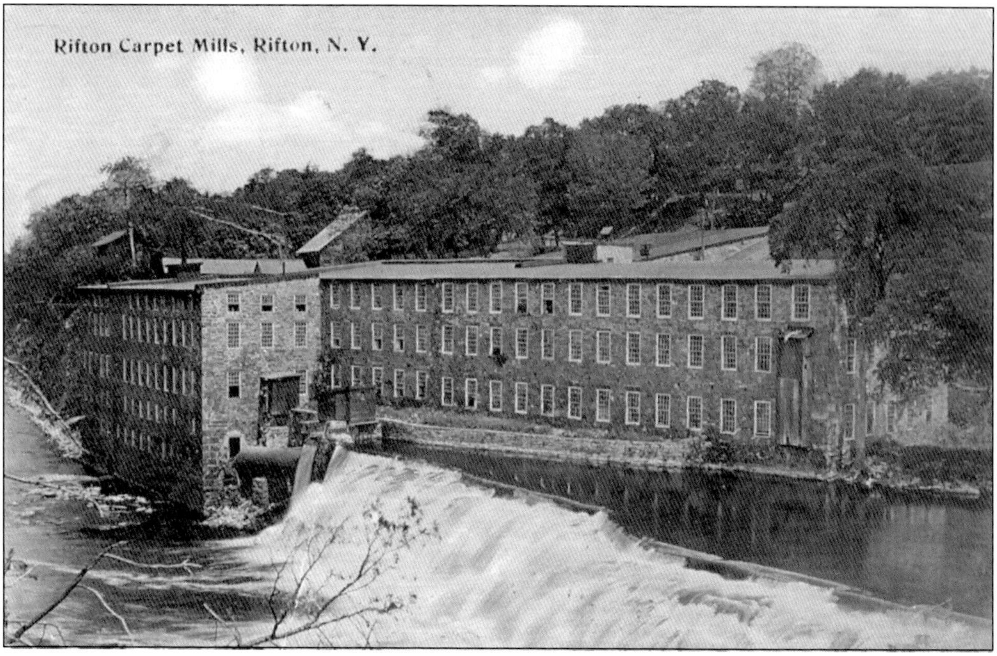

The Dashville Falls on the Wallkill River were a source of waterpower from the early 1800s through today. Ezekiel Elting built several mills here around 1825. Eventually, Jeremiah Dimick (also spelled Dimmick) ran the mill above in Arnoldton. Today, there is an electrical generating station (see below) on another part of the falls not far from Perrine's Bridge. Some ruins can still be seen of the Dimick Mill. Rifton was incorporated as a village in 1901 and at that point also included Dashville, Rifton Glen, and several other hamlets. In 1919, the New York State Legislature dissolved Rifton, because the mills were gone and there was no real purpose to the village remaining.

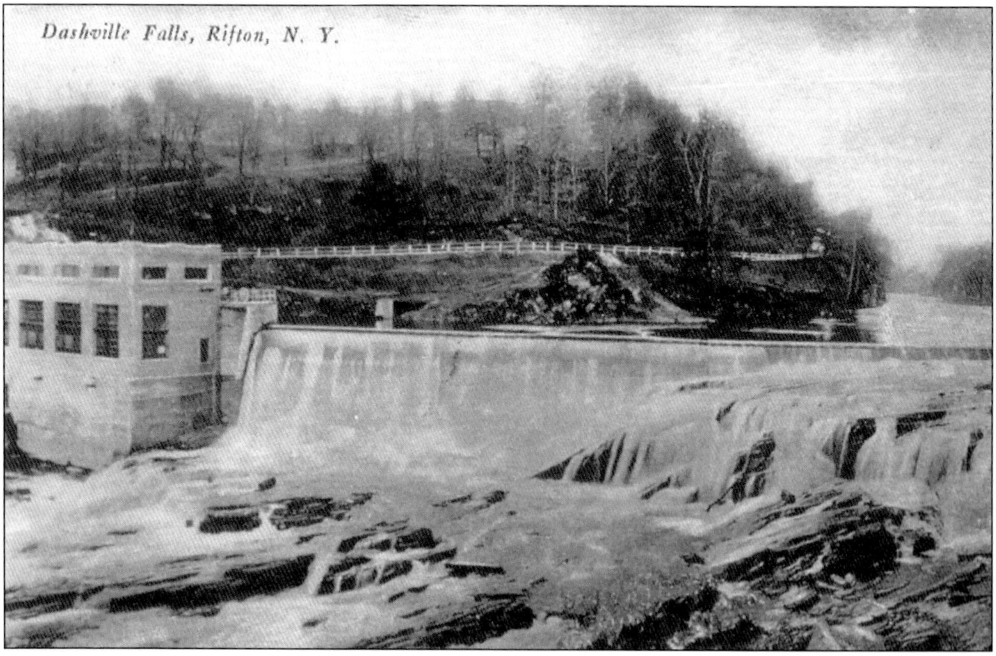

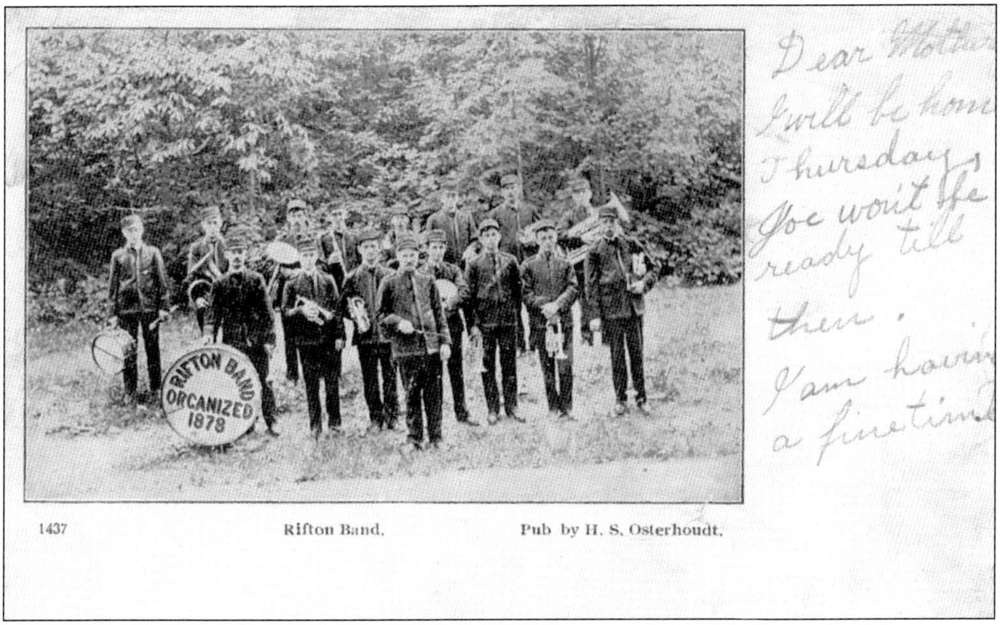

St. Remy is at the intersection of Main Street, Route 213, and New Salem Road. This card reads, "Dear Mother, I will be home Thursday. Joe won't be ready till then. I am having a fine time." The card was sent in August 1907 from Rifton to Mrs. D. Maloney in Kingston. The Rifton Band seems to be a marching band of young men.

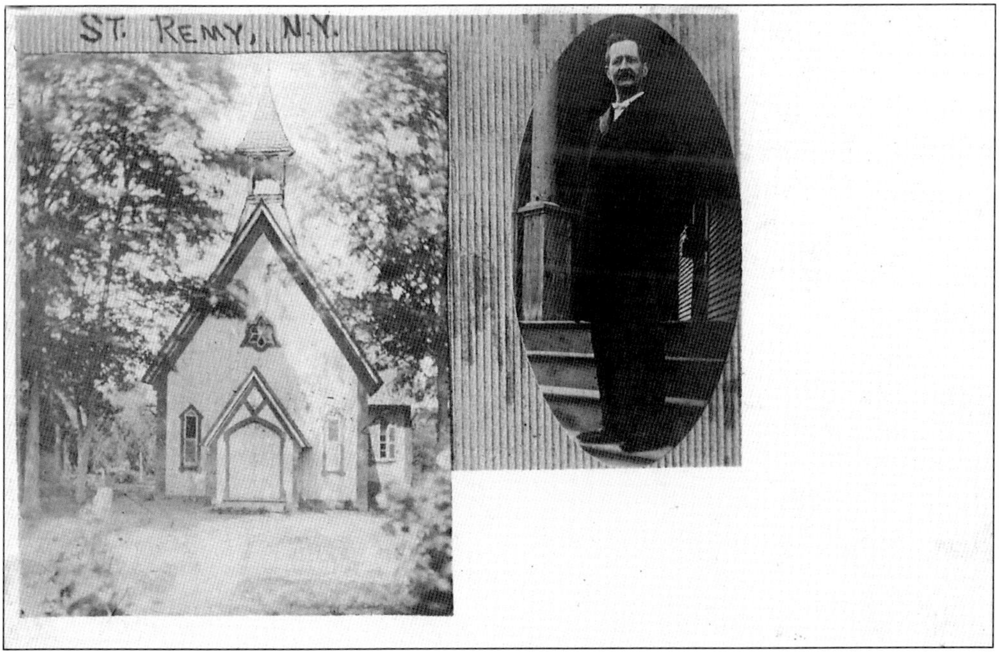

The minister of every small outlying church seems to have jumped on the postcard bandwagon with postcards to keep parishioners abreast of the spiritual doings of their group. These cards exist locally for churches in Clintondale, Plutarch, and other places. During the 1940s, another series of cards in Milton and Marlboro encouraged parishioners to attend special events. These were in color and featured a well-dressed family in a car headed to church.

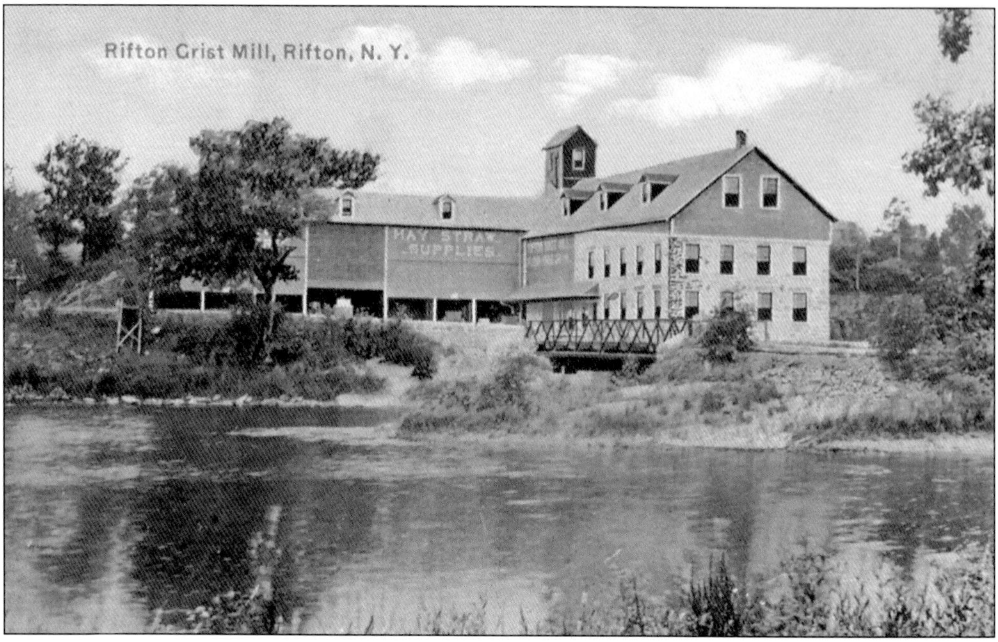

Grinding corn, wheat, and other grains into palatable flour kept gristmills busy. Using waterpower to turn stones weighing several tons was the common method. A gristmill ran until 2006 near Gardiner. The Rifton Grist Mill, shown here, was built to service the farms surrounding it. Grain milled was often paid for by the miller keeping a small percent of the flour. This card is postmarked 1914.

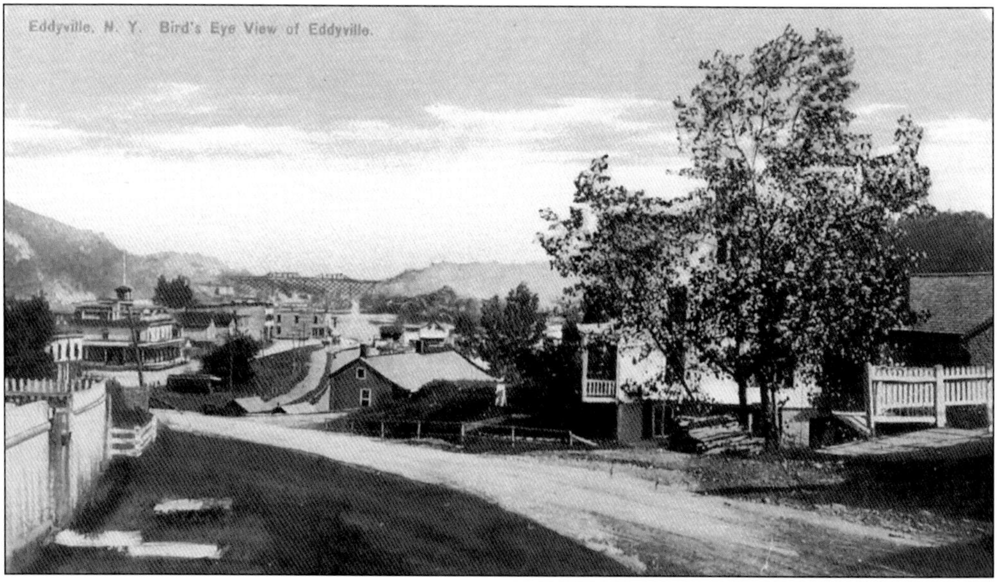

Eddyville is on Route 213 in Esopus. This postcard, looking toward the Rondout Creek, shows Schumann's Hotel on the left side. Schumann's is gone, but another nearby building is now the Anchorage bar and restaurant. In the far distance, the Jopphenbergh railroad bridge crosses the Rondout Creek in Rosendale. Today, that bridge is part of the Wallkill Valley Rail Trail, which allows pedestrian and bicycle travel from Gardiner to Kingston.

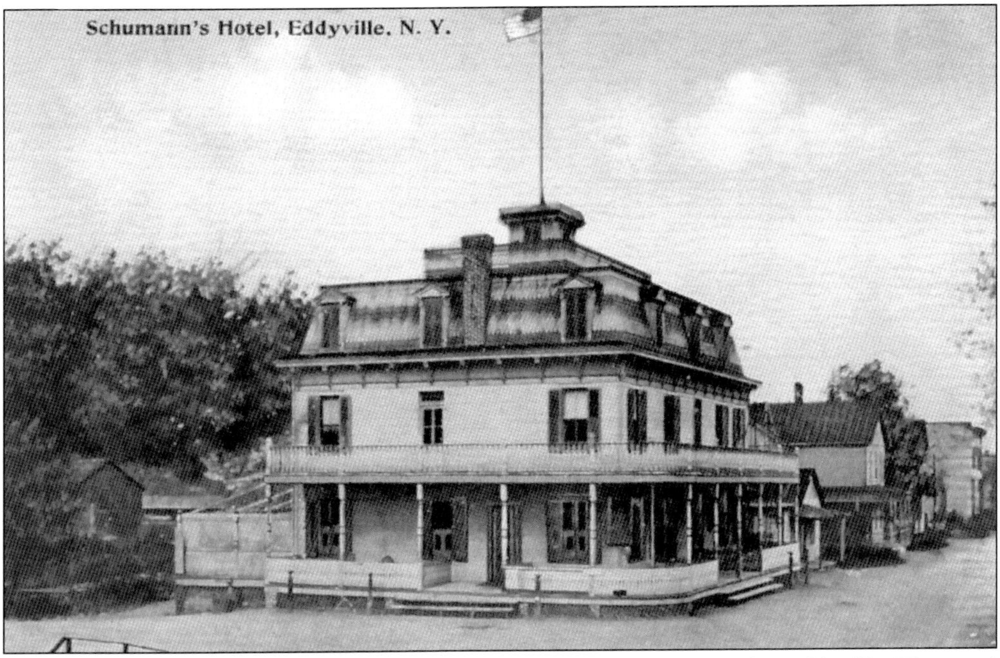

Schumann's Hotel was on the towpath of the Delaware and Hudson Canal in Eddyville. The canal ran from Honesdale, Pennsylvania, to Kingston, New York. The towpath is where the mules and their drivers walked to pull the canal barges. During the excavation of the canal in 1825, natural cement was discovered in Rosendale. That discovery started a huge business of mining and the construction of cement kilns. Some of them may still be seen on Binnewater Road.

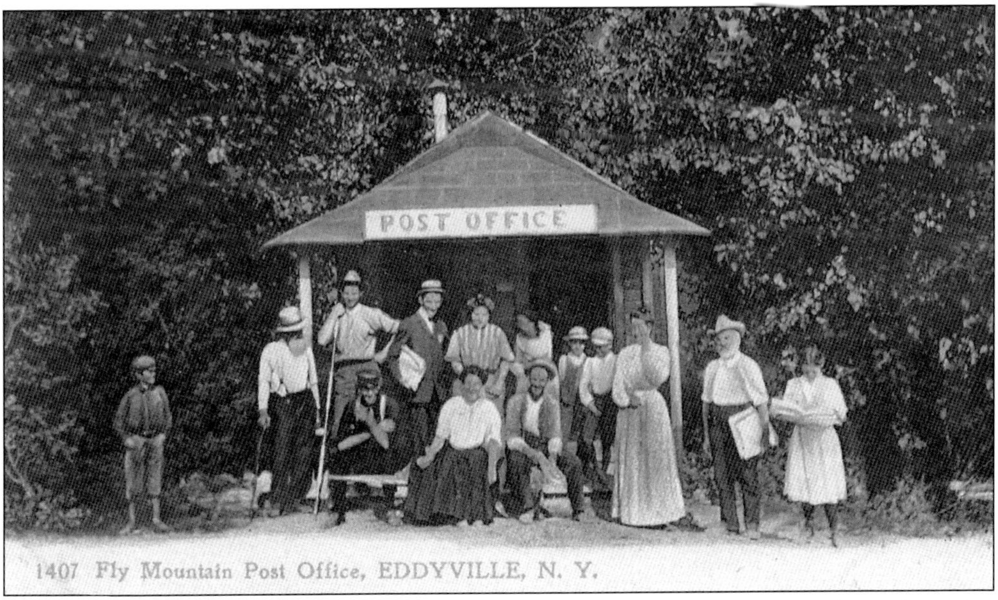

In 2004, the residents surrounding Fly Mountain stopped a mining company from disturbing their peace. Mining the earth, whether for gravel, cement, blue stone, or other valuable materials, has been taking place in Ulster County practically since it was settled. The Fly Mountain people pictured probably would have welcomed a new mining company, as that meant more jobs and competition for workers.

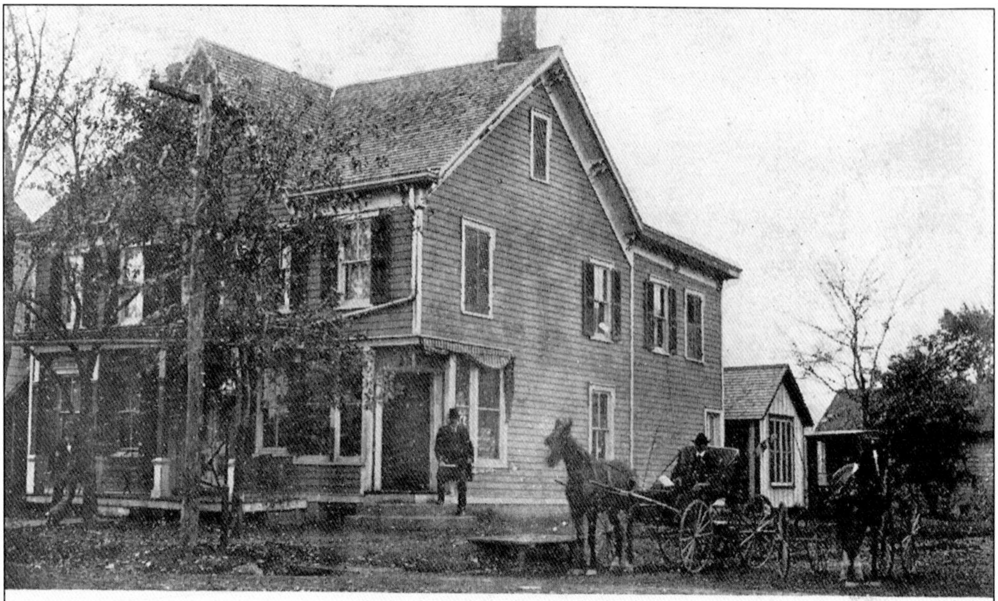

Post Office, Gardner, N. Y.

In his book *The Road to Gardiner*, Ed Thompson writes that the Town of Gardiner consists of parts taken from three townships: New Paltz, Shawangunk, and Rochester. It was officially formed in 1853 and named in honor of Lt. Gov. Adison Gardiner of the city of Rochester. The village, pictured here and in the next few pages, has fared well. Today, it is a sought-after second home market for New York City dwellers and has a lovely village center with shops, restaurants, and services. Views of the Shawangunk ridge and the Wallkill River add to its appeal. The Wallkill Valley Rail Trail runs through the village, connecting it to New Paltz, Rosendale, and Kingston. Thompson's book recounts the lineage of the many families who came together and formed Gardiner.

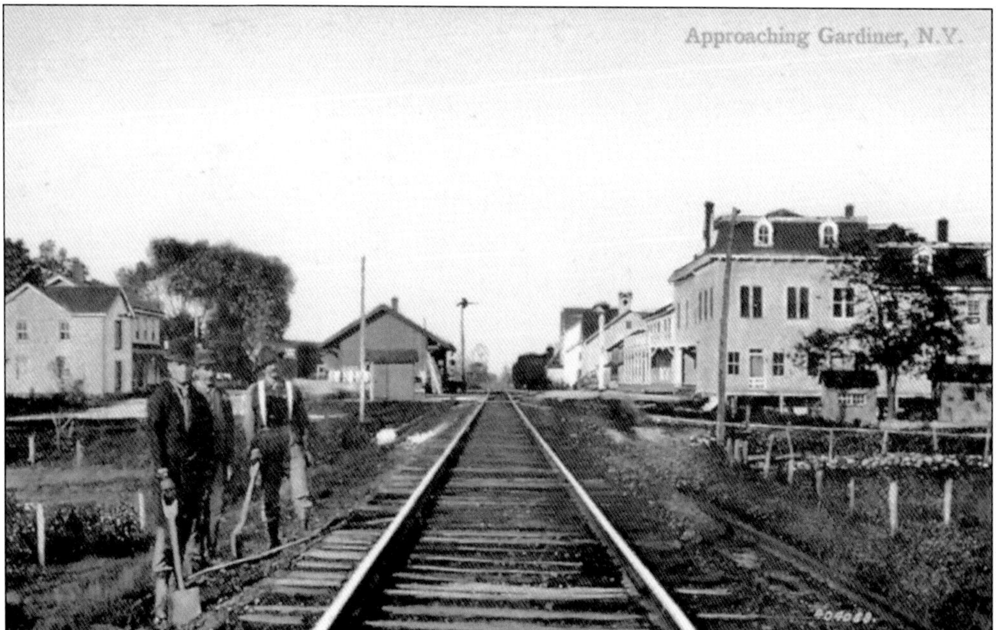

Approaching Gardiner, N.Y.

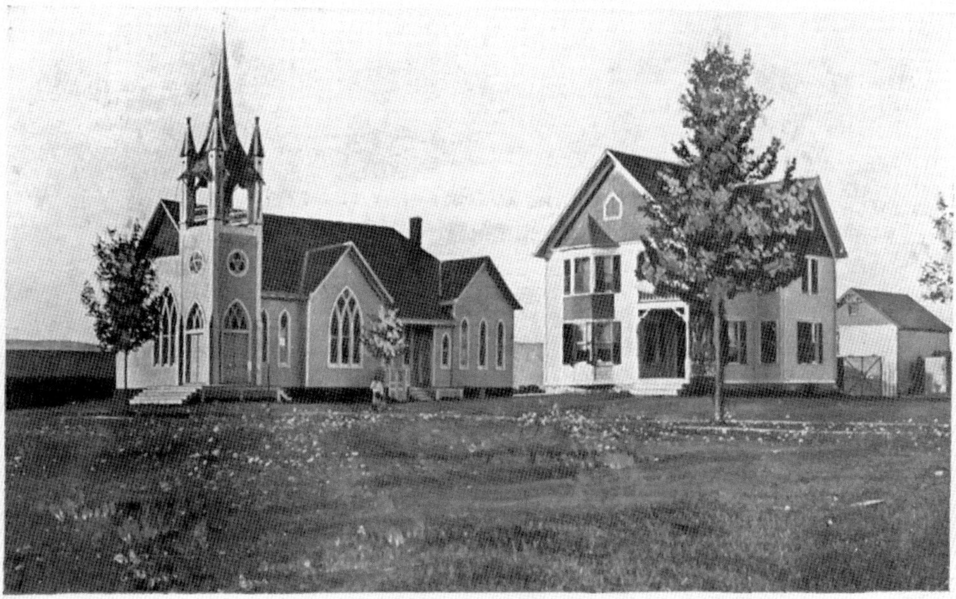

No. 4—R. D. Church and Parsonage, Gardiner, N Y.

Religion, schools, and railroads were all a help to a hamlet developing staying power as the world changed. Although the railroad ceased operation in the early 1970s, the rail bed it left behind has proven to be a draw on its own as the Wallkill Valley Rail Trail. Pictured above is one of the many lovely churches in Gardiner. On the left in the postcard below is the Callahan Hotel, which hosted travelers and vacationers. In the card on the bottom of preceding page, the view looks in the opposite direction. The Callahan Hotel is on the right. The Gardiner School District No. 2, not pictured, is now the town hall and is located on Route 44/55, just east of the main section of the village.

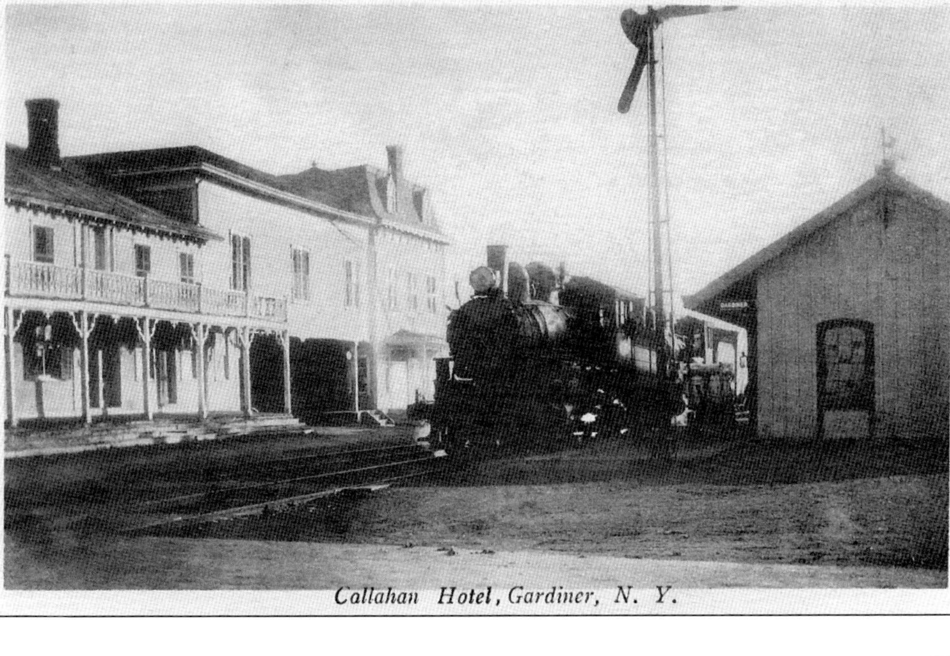

Callahan Hotel, Gardiner, N. Y.

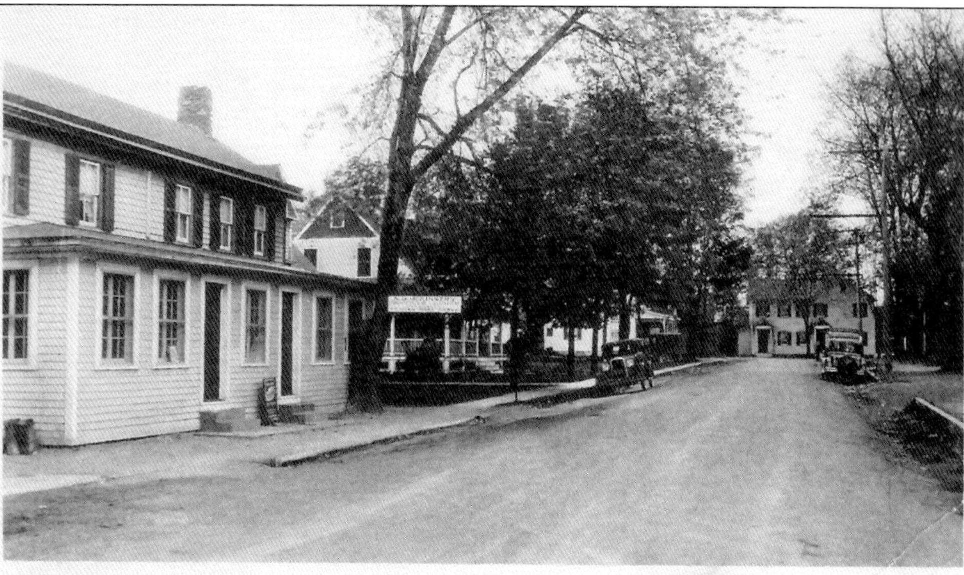

McKinstrys Store at Gardiner, N. Y.

The postcard above, postmarked in 1932, shows McKinstry's store on Main Street (Route 44/55), which today is HiHo Antiques and Interior Decor. Past it on the same side of the street is the post office. Past that, at the intersection with Dusenbarre Road, is the building below, J.M. Moran's General Merchandise store and gas station. The little boy on the steps is the owner's son John Moran. According to John's daughter Ann Moran Dippel, there was always a big block of cheddar cheese on the counter and any hardware tool you could imagine. Today, the building is Majestic's Hardware store. Of the three substantial remaining commercial centers of the early 1900s—Highland, Gardiner, and New Paltz—only New Paltz is actually an incorporated village. The other two are unincorporated villages, with no governmental bodies separate from the townships in which they are located.

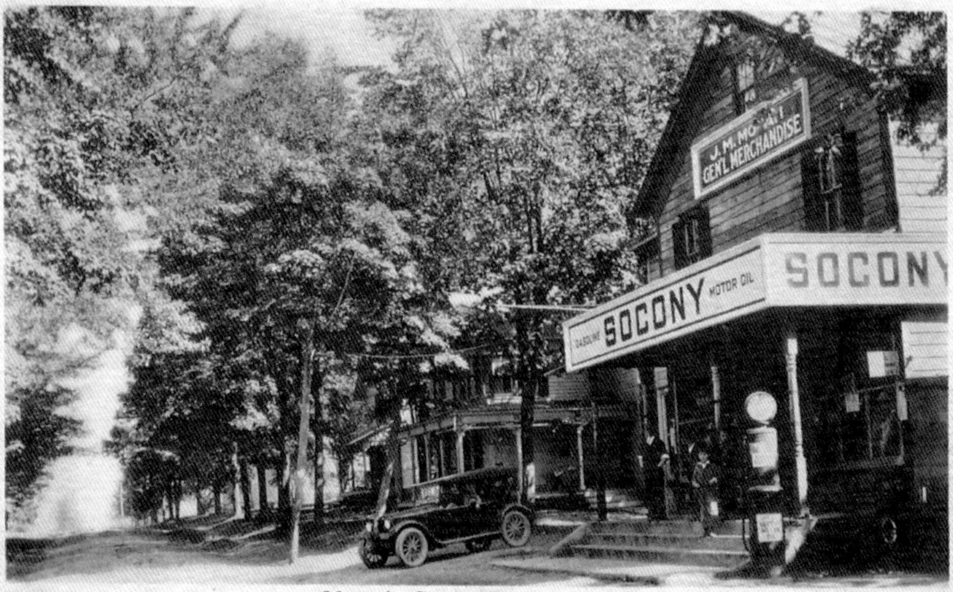

Moran's Store, Gardiner, N. Y.

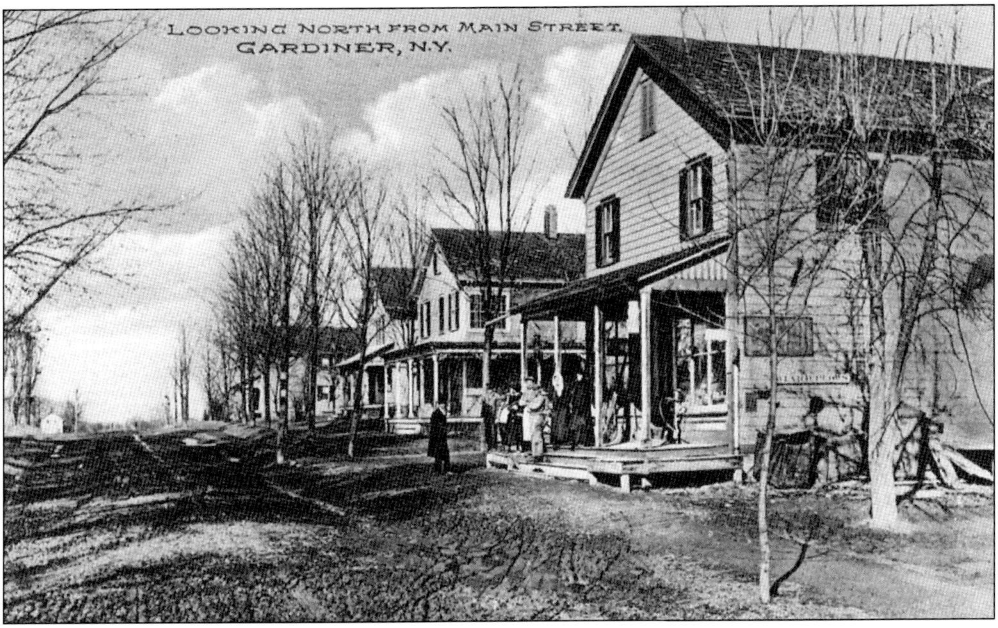

Another early view of Main Street in Gardiner is shown above. Note the dirt road. Today, Gardiner is a sports haven, offering rock climbing, skydiving, hiking, biking, and fishing, but it was not always such a place for play. Below is the steam-driven mill of J.S. Rosekrans. The card reads, "Hello Will, How are you. Got your card to day. This is the plant that makes me all the money that I spend now. It is right across the road from the one you learned to be a millwright in. Yours, JS Rosekrans." The card is postmarked January 26, 1912, in Gardiner, New York. At that time, mills powered by steam engines and internal combustion engines were rapidly replacing the less efficient, water-powered mills of the 19th century. Although today people may look back with nostalgia at the postcards of yesteryear, people of that earlier era were looking forward to a better standard of living made possible by new inventions.

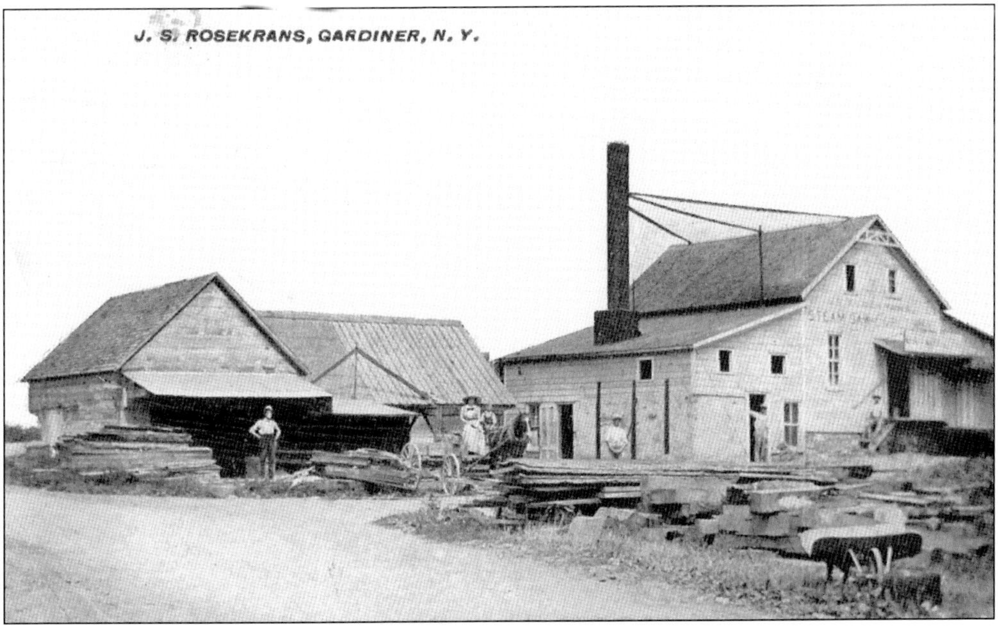